European Security and
the Atlantic System

INSTITUTE OF WAR AND PEACE STUDIES
of the School of International Affairs of
Columbia University

European Security and the Atlantic System is one of a series of studies sponsored by the Institute of War and Peace Studies of Columbia University. Among the Institute studies also dealing with war, peace, and national security are *Defense and Diplomacy* by Alfred Vagts; *Man, the State, and War* by Kenneth N. Waltz; *The Common Defense* by Samuel P. Huntington; *Changing Patterns of Military Politics* edited by Samuel P. Huntington; *Strategy, Politics, and Defense Budgets* by Warner R. Schilling, Paul Y. Hammond, and Glenn H. Snyder; *Stockpiling Strategic Materials* by Glenn H. Snyder; *The Politics of Military Unification* by Demetrios Caraley; *NATO and the Range of American Choice* by William T. R. Fox and Annette Baker Fox; *The Politics of Weapons Innovation: The Thor-Jupiter Controversy* by Michael H. Armacost; *The Politics of Policy Making in Defense and Foreign Affairs* by Roger Hilsman; *Inspection for Disarmament* edited by Seymour Melman; *To Move a Nation* by Roger Hilsman, jointly sponsored with the Washington Center of Foreign Policy Research, Johns Hopkins University; and *Planning, Prediction, and Policy-making in Foreign Affairs* by Robert L. Rothstein. Institute studies now in press include *The Origins of Peace* by Robert F. Randle; *German Nuclear Weapons Policy* by Catherine M. Kelleher; *American Arms and a Changing Europe: Dilemmas of Deterrence and Disarmament* by Warner R. Schilling, William T. R. Fox, Catherine M. Kelleher, and Donald J. Puchala; and *Technology, the Future, and American Policy* by Victor Basiuk.

European security
and the
atlantic system

Edited by William T. R. Fox
and Warner R. Schilling

COLUMBIA UNIVERSITY PRESS

New York and London / 1973

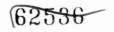

William T. R. Fox is Bryce Professor of the History of International Relations and Director of the Institute of War and Peace Studies.

Warner R. Schilling is Professor of Government and Associate Director of the Institute of War and Peace Studies.

Library of Congress Cataloging in Publication Data

Fox, William Thornton Rickert, 1912–
  European security and the Atlantic system.

  Includes bibliographical references.
    1. Europe—Defenses.   2. Europe—Politics—1945–
3. Europe—Foreign relations.   4. North Atlantic
Treaty Organization.   I. Schilling, Warner Roller,
1925–   joint editor.   II. Title.
D1053.F68   327.4   72-4248
ISBN 0-231-03640-X

pReface

SINCE THE EARLY 1950s the security of Western Europe has been assured by a combination of treaties, commitments, coalition military arrangements and credibly available American nuclear power. By the early 1970s Europe and the world were very different from two decades before. An inconclusive and potentially disastrous strategic arms race, a reassertion of domestic priorities in budget allocations everywhere in the NATO countries, and insistent Soviet calls for a European security conference were only three of the elements making for change in the Atlantic system as a device for promoting Western Europe's and North America's security against pressures from the East.

Thoughtful observers of the European scene had long known that some prescriptions for arms control and some for Western European security were on a collision course. Not until the late 1960s, however, did the quest for strategic arms control arrangements become so urgent and the prospect of Soviet-American agreement so promising as to require systematic reconciliation of policies of arms control and European security.

In 1968, accordingly, the Institute of War and Peace Studies, a research facility in the Faculty of International Affairs at Columbia University, agreed to undertake for the Arms Control and Disarmament Agency a study of implications of arms control for various existing and proposed European security arrangements. One of the editors of this volume, William T. R. Fox, developed plans for the study; the other, Warner R. Schilling, was project director. *European Security and the Atlantic System* contains essays which, as originally drafted, were seven of the background papers for the larger study. A companion volume, *American Arms and a Changing Europe: Dilemmas of Deterrence and Disarmament*, by Warner R. Schilling, together with William T. R. Fox, Catherine M. Kelleher and Donald J. Puchala, is a somewhat revised version of the final report submitted to ACDA.

During the academic year 1968–69 members of an Institute study group drafted, discussed with each other, and redrafted background papers for the more general analysis for which ACDA felt a need.[1] Research throughout was on an entirely unclassified basis, and the authors of the background papers and of the general analysis have sole responsibility for the form in which their studies were finally submitted to ACDA and the form in which some of them now appear. We gladly acknowledge, however, the usefulness of many detailed comments made by the ACDA staff on our draft manuscripts.

Not surprisingly we found that arms policies for Europe and the Atlantic alliance system and arms control policies for dealing with the Soviet Union had to be studied together. We also found that we were able to do least well what we may hope ACDA does best, to identify and evaluate the optimum technical means for achieving desired arms control goals.

The present volume therefore addresses itself to aspects of the emerging Western European and North Atlantic environment— economic, technological, strategic, and domestic political—in which the twin goals of Atlantic security and strategic arms control are to be sought. It contains in somewhat revised form all of the background papers prepared for ACDA except those which dealt with matters internal to the Soviet-dominated bloc.

It is a source of ironic satisfaction and frustration that in certain respects history has eaten its way into this collection of es-

---

[1] Background papers were written by Victor Basiuk, Annette Baker Fox, William E. Griffith, Catherine M. Kelleher, Klaus Knorr, Wilfrid L. Kohl, Andrew J. Pierre, Donald J. Puchala, and Marshall D. Shulman. All except Professors Knorr and Griffith were regular participants in the study group, which also included William T. R. Fox, Louis Henkin, Harold L. Hitchens, Philip Mosely, Nils Ørvik, and Warner R. Schilling.

says, satisfaction because the predictions of 1969 are many of the realities of 1972 and frustration because studies prepared by scholars now separated from their editors and from each other could not be again revised to take systematic account of such important developments as the Berlin accord, the expanded Common Market, SALT accomplishments, and President Nixon's summit diplomacy. (Some contributors to this volume *have* revised their essays to take account, in varying degrees, of events since 1969. Others have not, but the basic findings in either case seem as relevant in 1972 as in 1968 and 1969.)

As with previously published research sponsored by the Institute of War and Peace Studies, Jane Schilling's penetrating editorial queries have improved many murky or otherwise infelicitous passages. Myra Bergman Ramos, Gaynor Ellis, and Linda Wangsness Threlkeld have served the project and the authors of the essays in the present volume with fidelity and imagination.

William T. R. Fox
Warner R. Schilling

notes on contributors

Victor Basiuk is Advisor to the Chief of Naval Operations, Department of the Navy. He is the author of a number of articles on technology and international relations; a monograph, *Technology and World Power* (New York, Foreign Policy Association, 1970); and a forthcoming book, *Technology, the Future, and American Policy*.

Annette Baker Fox is Research Associate of the Institute of War and Peace Studies and Lecturer in Government at Barnard College. She is the author of *Freedom and Welfare in the Caribbean: A Colonial Dilemma* (New York, Harcourt, Brace, 1949); *The Power of Small States* (Chicago, University of Chicago Press, 1969); (with William T. R. Fox) *NATO and the Range of American Choice* (New York, Columbia University Press, 1967); and of a forthcoming book on Canadian-American and Mexican-American relations.

Catherine M. Kelleher is Assistant Professor of Political Science at the University of Illinois at Chicago Circle. She is the author of "The Issue of German Nuclear Armament" in *The "Atlantic Community" Reappraised, Proceedings of the Academy of Political Science* 29, no. 2, 1968; and of a forthcoming book, *German Nuclear Dilemmas 1955–1968*.

Klaus Knorr is William Stewart Tod Professor of Public Affairs at Princeton University. He is the author of *The War Potential of Nations*, 1956, *On the Uses of Military Power in the Nuclear Age*, 1966 (both published by Princeton University Press), and *Military Power and Potential* (Englewood, N.J., D.C. Heath, Co., 1970).

Wilfrid L. Kohl, formerly with the international division of the Ford Foundation, has recently completed an assignment on the staff of the National Security Council. The author of *French Nuclear Diplomacy* (Princeton, N.J., Princeton University Press, 1971) and, with William Taubman, of "Toward A New American Policy in Europe" (forthcoming), he is currently Associate Director of the Institute on Western Europe and Associate Professor of Political Science at Columbia University.

ANDREW J. PIERRE is Research Fellow at the Council on Foreign Relations. Formerly on the staff of the Brookings Institution and the Hudson Institute, he has also taught at Columbia University. From 1962 to 1964 he was with the Department of State, first in Washington and later at the American Embassy in London. He is the author of *Nuclear Politics: The British Experience with an Independent Strategic Force 1939–1970* (London, Oxford University Press, 1972); "Europe and America in a Pentagonal World" in *The European Community in the 1970s,* ed. S. Warnecke (New York, Praeger, 1972); and articles in *Foreign Affairs, Foreign Policy, Interplay,* and other publications.

DONALD J. PUCHALA is Associate Professor of Government at Columbia University. He is the author of *International Politics Today* (New York, Dodd, Mead, 1971); "Economic Partnerships in the North Atlantic Area," in *Quantitative Aspects of International Politics,* ed. David Singer (New York, Free Press, 1967); "Integration and Disintegration in Franco-German Relations 1954–65," *International Organization,* Spring, 1970; and "NATO and the Future of Europe," in *NATO: Prospects for the Seventies,* ed. Edwin Fedder (St. Louis, Center for International Studies, University of Missouri, 1970).

contents

ABBREVIATIONS AND SHORT TITLES

ABM	Antiballistic missile
ACDA	Arms Control and Disarmament Agency
ACE	Allied Command Europe
CDU	Christian Democratic Union
CERN	European Center for Nuclear Research
COMECON	Council for Mutual Economic Assistance
Comsat	Communications Satellite Corporation
CPSU	Communist Party of the Soviet Union
CSU	Christian Social Union
CTR	Controlled thermonuclear reaction
EEC	European Economic Community
EFTA	European Free Trade Area
ELDO	European Launcher Development Organization
ESRO	European Space Research Organization
Euratom	European Atomic Community
FDP	Free Democratic Party
GDR	German Democratic Republic
GNP	Gross national product
ICBM	Intercontinental ballistic missile
Intelsat	International Telecommunications Satellite
IRBM	Intermediate-range ballistic missile
MBFR	Mutual balanced force reductions
MHD	Magnetohydrodynamic energy
MIRV	Multiple independently targeted reentry vehicles
MLF	Multilateral Force
MP	Member of Parliament
MRBM	Medium-range ballistic missile
MRV	Multiple reentry vehicles
MSBS	Mer-Sol Balistique Stratégique
NADGE	NATO Air Defense Ground Environment
NAFTA	North Atlantic Free Trade Area
NASA	National Aeronautics and Space Administration
NORAD	North American Air Defense Command
NPG	Nuclear Planning Group
OECD	Organization for Economic Cooperation and Development
SACEUR	Supreme Allied Commander Europe
SALT	Strategic Arms Limitation Talks
SHAPE	Supreme Headquarters Allied Power Europe
SPD	Social Democratic Party

SSBS	Sol-Sol Balistique Stratégique
STANAVFORLANT	Standing Naval Force Atlantic
USAFE	United States Air Forces, Europe
VLF	Very low frequency
VTOL	Vertical takeoff and landing
WEU	Western European Union
WTO	Warsaw Treaty Organization

European Security and
the Atlantic System

/ *Klaus Knorr*

economic factors
in future arrangements
for european security

In the past, the security outcomes for every area and country have been determined by a rich concatenation of geographic, military, political, social, cultural and economic conditions. This paper raises the question of whether (and, if so, which) economic factors can be expected to play a significant and discernible role in the processes that will determine the structure of Europe and the nature of its security problems over the next decade.

Many elements of Europe's present and evolving economic realities have presumably little or no bearing on the future security situation. Other economic elements can be anticipated to have such an effect only in the presence of appropriate noneconomic realities. It would therefore be wasteful to begin with a comprehensive analysis of economic life in Europe, proceed to appropriate projections into the future, and then inquire into the significance of this contrived economic map for the course of external military security.

An alternative approach would begin with extensive identification of the conceivable future arrangements for Europe's security in order to ask whether, how, and to what extent economic developments might favor or obstruct the emergence of these arrangements. This approach, however, is also wasteful. Systematic description of a series of possible security arrangements for Europe is a task to be performed in the companion volume to this study, *American Arms and a Changing Europe: Dilemmas of Deterrence and Disarmament*. Moreover, one would probably find that some distinguishable security arrangements for Europe do not differ in their demands on European economic structure and life.

The best approach is to ask which kinds of security arrangements could be affected substantially in terms of their evolution and stability by possible developments over the next ten years in Europe's economic structure and life. Since the merit of this approach is obviously limited by the imagination and judgment, as well as the knowledge, of the author, this paper considers some possible developments mentioned by other observers, even though the author thinks them to be extremely improbable.

Because of the specific task of this study, most attention is paid to Western Europe—the Continent west of the countries now within the sphere of the Soviet Union. For most purposes of the following analysis, the focus is mainly on a core group of countries in this area: the countries of the European Economic Community (EEC) plus, in most cases, Britain. The narrower focus commends itself because the future of European moves toward unification rests primarily with these countries. This key grouping includes all the European "second-tier" powers and the large bulk of Western European population and resources. The future security arrangements for this group of nations will surely dominate the security situation of the entire area west of the Soviet sphere. Nevertheless, consideration of security arrangements that affect all of geographic Europe has not been precluded by the focus on Western Europe and its core countries.

Different European security arrangements mean possible Europes that have essentially different external security problems, especially in terms of security needs, and different opportunities for serving security needs, including means of arms control and disarmament. At this stage it need not matter that the security futures to be outlined do not seem equally likely. The past record of prediction suggests that such conjectures are not worth much. Indeed, the kind of Europe that will actually emerge might well be inconceivable today. One need only recall the unpredictability of Europe ten years before 1915, 1925, 1935, and even 1945 (only 1955 in this series would have turned out to be easy to guess).

One possibility is that ten years hence the security situation of Europe will be essentially what it is today. The North Atlantic and Warsaw alliances will continue; a fairly sharp military and political line will divide the Continent; and, to the extent that Western Europe requires protection from actual or latent military pressure or aggression emanating from the Soviet Union, the Western European nations will depend largely on the deterrent power of the United States. The various Western European countries will make roughly the same contribution to deterrence and defense that they make at the present time. (Under this assumption, the exact nature of the changing strategic-nuclear relationship between the United States and the USSR, including various kinds of nuclear arms control, would clearly make a difference to the security of Europe, but this range of variation is not germane to the purpose of the present paper.)

A question highly relevant to this security arrangement would seem to be whether there is any likelihood that future economic developments west or east of the dividing line will render the maintenance of this solution impossible or unnecessary. Whether the future economic integration of Western Europe or the development of East-West trade in Europe will undermine the conditions on which the present security arrangements for Western Europe rest are also relevant questions, but these will be raised in connection with other possible security arrangements.

A second possible security arrangement is one characterized by a Western Europe that is appreciably more unified than in 1969 and is essentially independent in terms of security or is strongly moving in this direction. "Essential independence" denotes a Western Europe far more independent in security terms than its member states are at the present time. Such a Western Europe would not be fully independent since, in general terms, such freedom is inconceivable in the contemporary world for any power or coalition and since, specifically, the security of the area would presumably continue to benefit—even if perhaps diminishingly, and to a substantially lesser extent than is the case now—from the United States' interest in the preservation of the area's integrity. A sharply lessened degree of Western European dependence on the United States could come from two sources: a large increase in the local capacity for deterrence and defense or an evolution of Soviet behavior that greatly and dependably reduced any security threat from the east. In the security arrangement discussed here it is assumed that reduced security dependence is primarily the result of increased local effort, although this assumption does not rule out a progressive détente contributing to the achievement of security in Western Europe. On the other hand, the possibility of a greatly *increased* security threat from the Soviet Union is disregarded. Although an enlarged threat might stimulate stronger local efforts of defense, it would increase the security needs of the area to an extent that could not possibly be met with local resources during the time period under consideration. With an assumption of an increased Soviet threat, the previous security arrangement, involving continued dependence on the United States, would be apposite.

A Western Europe composed of highly autonomous, even if loosely allied, states could achieve a high degree of security independence only if security needs were extremely low, that is to say, if the actual behavior of neither the Soviet Union nor any Western European state (e.g., Germany) caused any practical concern. This negligible-threat possibility is an aspect of another security arrangement, discussed below. It is a vital assumption of this security-independent arrangement that Western Europe be more highly integrated than at present along military and political as well as economic lines. For reasons explained in the following section, increased integration is a precondition of greater locally supplied security. A degree of integration amounting to a federal structure would obviously satisfy this condition, but achievement of a federal structure is unlikely within the next ten years. It is more realistic to define this arrangement in terms of the presence of a strong *movement* in a federal direction, expressing itself in the increased integration of national activities (especially in the areas of defense and defense support) rather than in terms of any particular, sharply or vaguely delineated, *state* of Western European integration.

The integrating group of nations need not, and would not, involve the entire area west of the Soviet sphere. But in order to possess the material basis for a more independent security arrangement, the group would have to include all or most of the large industrial states. As a minimum, this would mean the states of the EEC, which together comprise an imposing agglomerate of resources. For two reasons, however, it is reasonable to assume that the group would also include Britain. The fear of domination by West Germany (the Federal Republic) would probably prevent a strong movement toward increased and expanding integration among members of the EEC alone. Furthermore, only the involvement of Britain would give an integrating Western Europe enough of a nuclear potential to make possible the achievement of considerable independent deterrent power. Of the other states of Western Europe, Sweden, Switzerland, and Austria would certainly prefer their status of neutrality to inclusion in a militarily integrating Western European community. The accession of Spain and Portugal is precluded on political grounds. The inclusion of Norway, Denmark, and Ireland would have only marginal significance.

Three relevant economic questions (or questions with significant economic aspects) arise with reference to this possible arrangement. Does Western Europe possess, or can it develop over the next ten years, the economic and technological basis for producing the deterrent and defensive capabilities on which the area's greater security independence would rest? Does the progressive economic integration now under way in Western Europe exert a significant push in the direction of military (and political) unification? What is the time scale to be considered in speculating about Western Europe's ability to produce appreciably more security than it is now producing?

A third possible security arrangement for Europe is one in which external security requirements have fallen strikingly from recent and current levels because any dangerous military threat from the Soviet Union has decreased to the extent that Western European states need fear the USSR no more than the United States. Preconditions which make this arrangement interesting from the economic point of view are the following: (1) An all-European security community has been organized, involving a European nonagression pact.[1] (2) There are no American troops on the European continent. (3) There are no Soviet troops stationed outside the European boundaries of the USSR. (4) The Communist countries, including Russia, although retaining socialist economic systems, are engaged in economic experimentation toward permitting equilibrating prices to play a decisive role in steering resource allocation. They are engaged in political experimentation toward the political and cultural freedom of self-directed individuals. (5) Economic and especially political integration in the West has not progressed substantially beyond the present level. (6) The two Germanies cooperate economically and culturally and permit free migration but have agreed not to seek political and military integration. (7) As a result of all the foregoing circumstances, the dividing line has virtually disappeared, and there is a dense and ramifying network of economic, cultural, and political transactions between the states of Eastern and Western Europe.

In 1966–1968, people in both Western and Eastern Europe expressed the hope that the European nations could contract out of the Cold War, develop a network of cooperative relations throughout the entire continent, and set the foundations for its permanent pacification.

An interesting question here is whether there are powerful *economic* forces at work in both Western and Eastern Europe which could propel these societies in the direction of a cooperative and peaceful all-European community and, especially, whether the ex-

[1] There could be several other kinds of security arrangements characterized by an all-European nonaggression pact. Such a pact is conceivable while the North Atlantic and Warsaw alliances remain operative (producing a security arrangement close to the present one). Or a highly integrated and security-independent Western Europe could negotiate an agreement with the Warsaw Pact members (producing a security arrangement resembling the security-independent arrangement described). Or an unintegrated Western Europe could turn neutralist in order to placate the Soviet Union. Another possibility is an unintegrated Western Europe whose members no longer believe in any Soviet threat to their security, have withdrawn from NATO, and have reduced their security outlays from current levels. This possibility is uninteresting from an economic point of view.

pansion of foreign trade between the two spheres could act as a precipitating catalyst. (At the extreme limits of imaginability, one could also ask whether adverse economic factors could *compel* such a development. But this question will be dealt with essentially with reference to the first European security arrangement.)

I

The economic feasibility of the present security arrangement for Europe can be taken for granted. With respect to the Western European members of the North Atlantic alliance, Table 1 shows that in 1966 the nations of the EEC and Britain together spent on defense 4.6 percent of their GNP, compared with 8.5 percent on the part of the United States, and probably a still larger percentage by the Soviet Union. Similarly, these Western European countries as a group allocated 0.8 percent of their population to their armed forces, compared with 1.6 percent in the United States and 1.4 percent in the USSR. There is nothing in the economic situation of

Table 1   Military Expenditures as a Percentage of GNP and Armed Forces as a Percentage of Population, 1966

	Military Expenditures as Percentage of GNP	*Armed Forces as Percentage of Population*
USA	8.5	1.6
USSR	13.2 [a]	1.4
EEC and Britain	4.6	0.8
Eastern Europe	4.4	1.1

Source: U.S. Arms Control and Disarmament Agency, Economics Bureau, *World Military Expenditures and Related Data: Calendar Year 1966 and Summary Trends, 1962–1967* (Washington, D.C., 1968), pp. 9–10.

[a] "The relationships between GNP and other dollar amounts shown or implied here may not be valid due to use of differentiated conversion rates for particular sectors. If measured in national currencies and at factor cost rather than at market prices, Soviet military expenditures would be in the vicinity of 8 to 9 percent of GNP" (fn. 12).

these Western European countries that could jeopardize their present military effort. It is possible that their incomes will grow less rapidly in the future than in the post–World War II past (see below). But even a lesser rate of income growth will not per se render the current level of their military contributions unfeasible. In 1966, twenty-four poorer countries of the world, most of them appreciably poorer, spent a higher percentage of their GNPs on defense. Indeed, slower growth, and hence probably lesser inflationary pressure, could make it politically easier to maintain present real outlays on defense. And in the most unlikely event that Western European incomes should decline sharply, a cut in public expenditures would seem a perverse remedy in the Keynesian or post-Keynesian world.

If these nations and their governments should come to regard the present level of their defense expenditures as excessive, it will happen because they no longer perceive a commensurate Soviet threat to their security, or because they judge *their* contributions to their security (in contrast to the United States contribution) to be irrelevant, or because they prefer an increase in private or other kinds of public expenditures to a lessened risk to their security. In any of these cases, the diminution of Western European security contributions would result from essentially *noneconomic* considerations, i.e., particular strategic intelligence estimates or strategic capability analyses, or changes in subjective utility functions.

It has been posited that many contemporary societies, especially those that are affluent, are suffering from an increasing insufficiency of resources in relation to social demands made on them, and that this factor will put a growing pressure on military expenditures.[2] The main reason for progressive scarcity in the midst of unprecedented wealth is that nearly everywhere previously disadvantaged population groups are finding it possible to make politically effective demands for more income or costly public expenditures. It could also be argued that the economically most advanced societies, which have relied on private enterprise as the main

[2] See Harold and Margaret Sprout, *An Ecological Paradigm for the Study of International Politics*, Princeton University, Center of International Studies Research Monograph no. 30 (Princeton, N.J., 1968).

mechanism for creating wealth, have grossly neglected certain types of public efforts that would have prevented the unfettered pursuit of private enterprise from causing cumulative and accelerating ecological impoverishment. This long-standing neglect is now presenting urgent problems that can be solved, or at least mitigated, only by means of greatly enlarged public expenditures. Of course, insufficiency of resources has been a perennial human problem. But it is possible that the political competition for available resources is becoming keener (although there is no way to measure this). Scarcity is *the* economic problem. But how societies allocate available resources is ultimately a political problem, actual allocations reflecting the preference patterns and political influence of various groups. There is no economic necessity for military expenditures to decline even if in the wealthiest societies the total demand tends to exceed available resources and, perhaps, to exceed them by an increasing margin. In fact, as Tables 2 and 3 show, the tendency in recent years in developed countries as a group has been for the real military expenditures to mount in absolute volume, per capita, and as a proportion of GNP.

Regarding the ability of the United States to maintain its vital contribution to European security over the next decade, the answer is similar to that for the Western European countries. If there has been any, even latent, Soviet military threat to Western Europe to be deterred (which cannot be known), this threat has been contained, or prevented from materializing, chiefly by an American strategic retaliatory threat. The American economy has not found it difficult for virtually two decades, to bear defense expenditures amounting to 8 to 10 percent of GNP, and this level of outlay has certainly been sufficient to maintain the American deterrent posture vis-à-vis Russia. There is no economic reason why the American economy should not continue to bear this level of burden in the future.[3] At this level of expenditure, the United States can fail to maintain roughly its present strategic posture only by a gross blunder of military management (i.e., an extremely inefficient use

[3] Some non-Marxist observers have argued that security expenditures at this level have been indispensable to American economic growth and prosperity; this author does not share that view.

Table 2   Trends in Military Expenditures and GNP, 1964–1967:
Totals (in billions of constant 1967 dollars)

	1964	1965	1966	1967
Military				
expenditures				
Worldwide	147	148	164	182
Developed	128	128	145	162
Less developed	19	20	19	20
GNP				
Worldwide	2,159	2,264	2,403	2,500
Developed	1,761	1,847	1,966	2,040
Less developed	398	417	437	460
Percentage of GNP				
spent on military				
expenditures				
Worldwide	6.8	6.5	6.8	7.3
Developed	7.3	6.9	7.4	7.9
Less developed	4.8	4.8	4.3	4.3

Source: U.S. Arms Control and Disarmament Agency, Economics Bureau, *World Military Expenditures and Related Data: Calendar Year 1966 and Summary Trends, 1962–1967* (Washington, D.C., 1968), p. 8.

of resources allocated to defense) or by bad scientific-technological luck in competitive innovation in weapons. Regaining decisive strategic superiority over the Soviet Union would probably require, however, considerably increased outlays of resources, plus superb military management, and possibly also scientific-technological good luck. But such superiority is probably unnecessary for the kind of protection that the United States is prepared to give Western Europe. Even a small probability that the United States would retaliate, in a manner risking strategic nuclear war, against any deliberate Soviet attack on Western Europe seems enough to deter rational Soviet governments. In any case, whether the United States will continue to afford defense outlays at the accustomed level does not turn on the capacity of the economy (which is adequate), but on the opportunity-cost notions of American presidents, Congress, and the electorate. As noted above, this is not primarily an economic problem but rather a matter of political preferences for various patterns of expenditures.

It might be asked, however, whether pressures on the American balance of payments will permit the United States to retain as sizable military forces on the Continent as it has been maintaining in recent years. It is fairly clear that recent pressures on the United States balance of payments have occurred despite conditions operating in American financial transactions with the rest of the world that make the American position fundamentally strong.[4] Current balance-of-payments problems are caused as much, or more, by inadequacies in the world monetary order, which is badly in need of reform in the direction of increased international liquidity, as by excessive American expenditures abroad. The big items in expenditures abroad are investments, tourist outlays, and merchandise im-

Table 3   Trends in Military Expenditures and GNP, 1964–1967:
Per Capita (in constant 1967 dollars)

	1964	1965	1966	1967
Military *expenditures*				
Worldwide	46	45	49	53
Developed	138	135	153	170
Less developed	9	8	8	8
GNP				
Worldwide	671	688	715	729
Developed	1,901	1,958	2,073	2,141
Less developed	174	177	181	186
Percentage of GNP *spent on military* *expenditures*				
Worldwide	6.9	6.5	6.9	7.3
Developed	7.3	6.9	7.4	7.3
Less developed	5.2	4.5	4.4	4.3

Source: U.S. Arms Control and Disarmament Agency, Economics Bureau, *World Military Expenditures and Related Data: Calendar Year 1966 and Summary Trends, 1962–1967* (Washington, D.C., 1968), p. 8.

[4] See Francis M. Bator, "The Political Economics of International Money," *Foreign Affairs*, October, 1968, pp. 51–67; C. Fred Bergsten, "A New Monetary System?" *Atlantic Community Quarterly*, Summer, 1968, pp. 193–98; Harold Van B. Cleveland, "The International Monetary System Muddles Through," *Atlantic Community Quarterly*, Spring, 1969, pp. 105–113.

ports. To be sure, American expenditures on military accounts (especially for the war in Vietnam) add appreciably to the stream of expenditures. But foreign expenditures attributable to the American military protection of Western Europe are relatively modest. In recent years, West German offset transactions have covered the large bulk of United States foreign-exchange outlays incurred by the American military presence in Germany. It is virtually certain that West Germany will continue compensatory expenditures as long as the presence of American forces is deemed necessary for its security. There is a real question, however, whether the purpose of these forces (which is primarily to increase the credibility of an American strategic response to a massive Soviet attack) requires their maintenance at present levels. In any case, the United States enjoys considerable bargaining power vis-à-vis the Federal Republic if it is ready to reduce American forces in Germany. There should therefore be little difficulty in managing the United States foreign-exchange outlay that is occasioned by a continuation of the present security arrangement in Europe. If the United States desires to reduce American forces in Europe because political pressures on the defense budget have led to a substantial dimunition of overall nonstrategic capabilities, the problem arises not from compelling economic factors but from political preferences favoring a restructuring of public expenditures.

Finally, there is no economic reason why the Soviet Union cannot maintain its contribution to the present European security arrangement over the next ten years, that is to say, maintain military capabilities of a size and kind that inevitably cast a menacing shadow across Western Europe. Although the Soviet economy did not expand as rapidly in the 1960s as during the 1950s, its rate of growth for 1960–1965 exceeded appreciably that of the United States and Western Europe as a whole (Table 4). Even if the rate should fall somewhat below the 1960–1965 rate over the next ten years, the economic situation will not compel Soviet governments to cut the level of military outlays, especially since the growth rate will continue to permit a steady and perceptible expansion of private consumption. Soviet governments may desire to reduce the military budget sharply in conjunction with drastic and effective measures of international arms control and disarmament. But it is

Table 4   Average Annual Rates of Product Growth

	Real Gross Domestic Product at Factor Cost (%)	
	1950–1960	*1960–1966*
USA	3.3	5.0
EEC and Britain		
France	4.4[a]	5.2
West Germany	7.9	4.5
Italy	5.2[a]	4.9
Netherlands	n.a.[b]	n.a.
Belgium	2.9[c]	4.6
Luxembourg	n.a.	n.a.
Britain	2.5	2.8
	Real Net Material Product (%)	
	1950–1960	*1960–1966*
USSR	10.2	6.5[d]
Eastern Europe		
Bulgaria	9.1[e]	6.7
Czechoslovakia	7.6	3.3
East Germany	8.1[c]	3.6
Hungary	5.9	5.1
Poland	7.5[c]	6.6
Rumania	10.4	9.2
Yugoslavia	8.6[c]	7.7

Source: United Nations, Statistical Office, *Statistical Yearbook 1967* (New York, 1968), pp. 572–75.
[a] Period was 1951–1960.   [d] Period was 1960–1965.
[b] Data were not available.   [e] Period was 1952–1960.
[c] Period was 1953–1960.

hard to imagine their effecting such cuts because they prefer major increases in consumption or investment. And even if they do, the motivation will be political.

In conclusion, relevant economic factors are likely to be permissive as far as the continuation of present arrangements for Europe's security are concerned. If these arrangements become unacceptable over the next ten years, change will result from one or more of many possible noneconomic conditions.

II

With respect to the alternative that involves a security-independent Western Europe, a pertinent question is whether Western Europe possesses or can develop over the next ten years the economic and technological basis for producing a level of local deterrent and defensive forces that would make these countries largely independent in terms of military security. The countries of the EEC plus Britain would be the primary constituents of a military strong Western Europe. Their present military capabilities obviously fall far short of the level of deterrence and defense capabilities that would make Western Europe's security dependent only on the rationality of Soviet governments and not on their autonomously peaceful intentions. This shortfall is reflected in the fact that in 1966 these European countries spent $19.8 billion for defense, compared with $63.3 billion spent by the United States and an estimated $47 billion by Russia.[5] In addition, since the Western European amount is spent on six military establishments, the military-budget dollar is therefore spent much less efficiently than in the United States or the Soviet Union. If these nations had decided to spend on defense the same proportion of the GNP that the United States allocated, their aggregate defense budgets would have amounted to $34.6 billion, which is appreciably closer to the estimated Soviet level. Indeed, since both the United States and Russia maintain considerable military forces for deployment outside Europe, and since other Western European countries would make an additional contribution, such a budget level would over time permit on financial grounds, a defense effort adequate for the protection of Western Europe. This conclusion is not surprising, for Britain and the EEC countries have a combined GNP substantially exceeding that of the Soviet Union and amounting to almost 60 percent of the American GNP.

Table 5 presents some ten-year projections of GNPs for the EEC

[5] See U.S. Arms Control and Disarmament Agency, *World Economic Expenditures 1966–67* (Washington, D.C., 1968), p. 9.

Table 5   1966 GNP and Projected GNP for 1978 (GNP in millions of dollars at current prices and exchange rates)

Area	1966 GNP	Rate of Growth (%)[a]			Projected GNP in 1978[b]		
		Low	*Predicted*	*High*	*Low*	*Predicted*	*High*
USSR	357,000	6.0	7.0	8.0	718,320	804,000	898,962
Eastern Europe	131,220	6.0	7.0	8.0	264,029	295,521	330,425
USA	747,600	3.0	4.5	5.5	1,065,853	1,267,780	1,421,262
EEC and Britain	427,266	3.5	4.5	5.0	645,599	724,558	767,284

Source of 1966 GNP: U.S. Arms Control and Disarmament Agency, Economics Bureau, *World Military Expenditures and Related Data: Calendar Year 1966 and Summary Trends, 1962–1967* (Washington, D.C., 1968), pp. 9–10.

[a] These hypothetical growth rates are reasonable conjectures based on experience from 1950 to 1966.
[b] Projections are according to compound formula.

countries, Britain, the United States, the Soviet Union, and Eastern Europe. Selecting the correct future growth rate is a matter of judgment and (mostly) luck. The predicted rates are those that seem most reasonable to this author. They are recent rates (see Table 4) somewhat modified by an appreciation of various problems likely to affect future growth. The reason for expecting somewhat more moderate growth rates in Western Europe is that some of the major expansionary factors of the late 1950s and early 1960s have lost their vigor; i.e., the expansionary effect of the EEC (and EFTA) and other more universal moves liberalizing trade have been mostly spent; the market for durable consumers' goods has begun to lose its initial dynamism; the rate of growth of labor resources for manufacturing and service industries is falling; American investments will not likely return to the level of 1958–1964. New major stimuli to expansion may, of course, appear in the future. But they are not visible now and are unlikely to sustain an exceptional rate of output growth. On the other hand, a healthy potential for further expansion in West Germany, France, and especially Italy makes it unlikely that there will be much further decline in the growth rate.

Nevertheless, Table 5 also shows for comparison the results of growth rates that are lower and higher than the predicted ones, presenting three possible economic futures for Western Europe and, of course, many more patterns of possible GNP relationships with the other areas. At the predicted rates, the Western European grouping will lose some ground in total economic capacity vis-à-vis the USSR. But its combined GNP would be only 10 percent less than the Soviet GNP. Moreover, the worst possible combination of growth rates (i.e., the highest for the Soviet Union and the lowest for Western Europe) is probably irrelevant for this study, because a sharp increase in the Western European defense effort would provide a major new stimulus to economic growth in that area. And even on the worst possible set of assumptions, the Western European group would not be outclassed by the Soviet GNP if allowance is made for the Soviet need to maintain military forces for deployment outside Europe, especially in the Far East.

The conclusion arrived at on aggregate financial grounds is reinforced by a look at military economic potential in real terms. As

Table 6   Population and Population Growth

	Population 1966	Growth Rate 1963–66 (%)	Projected Population for 1978[a]	
			Direct Projection[b]	Compound Projection[c]
EEC and Britain	235,909,000	1.1	267,049,000	268,983,400
USA	196,920,000	1.3	227,639,500	229,923,800
USSR	233,105,000	1.2	266,672,100	268,979,800
Eastern Europe	121,154,000	0.7	131,330,900	131,718,600

Source of estimates of population and rates of growth: United Nations, Statistical Office, *Statistical Yearbook 1967* (New York, 1968), pp. 26, 80–86.

[a] Estimates are based closely on rates prevailing between 1963 and 1966.

[b] $N(r)P + P$, where N = number of years = 12; r = rate of growth; P = present (1966) population.

[c] $P(1 + r)N$.

Table 6 reveals, in 1966 the population of the Western European grouping slightly exceeded that of the Soviet Union and exceeded that of the United States by one-quarter. A ten-year projection of recent growth rates changes these relationships very little. Table 7 compares three types of production that are indicative of relative industrial capacity. In 1968 the EEC countries plus Britain pro-

Table 7   Selected Indices of Industrial Power for EEC, Britain, USSR, and USA in 1968

	Crude steel (thousand metric tons)	Electricity (million kwh)	Motor vehicles, including commercial (thousands)
West Germany	3,430	16,994	259.0
France	1,699	9,782	172.9
Belgium, Luxembourg	1,368	2,379	
Netherlands	309	2,802	4.7
Italy	1,413	8,497	138.5
Britain	2,190	18,429	185.4
EEC and Britain	10,415	58,883	760.5
USSR	8,878	53,200	81.5
USA	9,911	119,416	897.0

Source: United Nations, *Monthly Bulletin of Statistics*, May, 1969.

duced more crude steel than either the United States or the Soviet Union. Surprisingly, the Western European group's output of motor vehicles amounted to about 85 percent of American production and more than 900 percent of Soviet production. In the output of electricity—probably the best general index of a country's industrialization—the group's output was about half the American output and exceeded Soviet production by 10 percent.

If the structure of the resource base of the EEC countries and Britain is examined, it becomes clear that this group is less self-sufficient than either the Soviet Union or the United States. Probably the most critical dependence is in sources of energy, e.g., oil. Table 8 shows that in 1966 the group imported more than half of the energy it consumed and that the percentage has been rising rapidly since 1958. It is bound to rise further in the course of the next ten years. However, this kind of dependence is probably insignificant from the point of view of this study. For obvious reasons Western

Table 8   Energy Production, Trade, and Consumption in Western Europe (in million metric tons of coal equivalent)

	1958	1966
Production		
Total energy	582	553
Coal and lignite	531	452
Crude petroleum	17	27
Natural gas	10	32
Hydro and nuclear electricity	24	43
Net imports		
Total energy	240	596
Bunkers		
Total energy	30	54
Consumption		
Total energy	764	1,083
Solid fuels	540	486
Liquid fuels	190	520
Natural and imported gas	10	33
Hydro, nuclear, and imported electricity	24	43

Source: United Nations, Statistical Office, *Statistical Yearbook 1967* (New York, 1968), pp. 64–65.

Europeans prefer to deter aggression rather than to defend themselves against it. The production of sufficient strategic forces for deterrence would take place in time of peace, when foreign trade is normally uninterrupted. Defense against limited attacks would hardly pose a supply problem since the Atlantic approaches to Europe presumably would remain open.

The supply of basic resources indicates only the presence of sheer manpower and industrial economies easily able, or capable of adaptation, to provide troops with conventional supplies and weapons, e.g., food, clothing, fuel, road vehicles, ships, aircraft, guns. Since a security-independent Western Europe would require adequate means for strategic nuclear deterrence, the question arises whether these countries possess, or could develop, the sophisticated technological resources necessary for the production of appropriate forces. The relevant resources now on hand in the area, mostly in Britain and France, are inadequate for this purpose, although they constitute a sizable beginning.

For developing or expanding these resources of high technology, Western Europe certainly has most of the basic resources and top-flight scientists and engineers (the supply of talented management is more doubtful). What has held back the development of large nuclear-weapons, aerospace, and computer industries has been mainly low public demand (expressed as a lack of large and continuous funding), plus a far less than optimum scale of production (especially with respect to research and development), which results in part from the low level of funding and in part from the maintenance of separate national efforts. For developing adequate units for the production and maintenance of independent deterrent power, an act of will and finance and a Community-wide scale are the chief prerequisites. Of course, for achieving an adequate level of local production, time is a third prerequisite. The initial effort, involving a complex learning process, would be especially difficult, and with resource supply not very income-elastic over the short run, the development curve would be far from linear. On the other hand, the achievement curve would be made more nearly linear because Western Europe would at first rely (except for nuclear warheads) on advanced foreign technology by importing components. Such imports would be possible because the balance-of-payments position and the international liquidity reserves of the EEC-plus-Britain group are basically very strong. Weaknesses in Britain and less intractable ones in France are offset by great strength in Germany, Italy, and the Netherlands.

The *separate* national production of military capabilities for deterrence and defense within Western Europe is a grave handicap affecting the entire defense sector. Even though Western Europe undoubtedly has basic resources large enough to sustain an independent security effort vis-à-vis the Soviet Union (and the United States), as long as its component countries maintain separate military efforts, they cannot achieve independence even if they double the allocation to the military sector. Several kinds of tremendous waste inherent in the dispersal of effort would be eliminated by unification of efforts. First, a given resource input would yield far more output in the production of all sophisticated weaponry and other equipment (in terms of research and development and end products) if one market replaced the several markets now in existence. This gain would result from the benefits of specialization and scale, benefits which are potentially very large. Second, the effectiveness of Western European military forces would improve operationally from uniformities of training and material, i.e., uniformity would make for more efficiency per unit of military manpower. Third, the combination of different kinds of military forces would yield more effective military strength if their proportioning were set at an optimum level (for instance, these countries, taken together, maintain too much conventional naval strength in relation to land forces). Fourth, the military effectiveness of Western European forces for deterrence and defense would be greatly enhanced by unity of command. In other words, the rich resource base of Western Europe could provide independent security only if the use of these resources were subject to one center of decision-making.

Concerning institutional prerequisites, one important condition identified above could be met even if the EEC countries and Britain remained formally independent but entered a close defensive alliance and created one unitary market for defense products. On the basis of historical experience, however, one would not expect them to integrate more than partially, and probably not more than marginally. The rigidities and inertia of nationally separate military services and government ministries, political sensitivity to the preoccupation with the incidence of geographic production shifts, preoccupation with equality of burdens shared and rewards reaped, and other factors would strongly militate against such a move. Moreover, several of the conditions identified above could be met only if the military services and command structures of these nations became integrated. In turn, this integration would require the integration of all foreign policies which are sensitive to the presence of military power. In short, Western Europe could gain security independence only if it were far along the way to a federal political structure or had achieved it.

In conclusion, regarding the development of a Western Europe capable of producing independent military security, economic factors are permissive. Over a ten-year period, these countries could be well on the way to such independence. The crucial prerequisites are political—the will to achieve and pay for security independence and the will to federate.

Another question concerning a security-independent Western Europe is whether the progressive economic integration now under way in Western Europe exerts a significant, or perhaps compelling, pull in the direction of military and political unification. Such an effect has been asserted in terms of spillover effects, that is, essentially political by-products of economic integration.

Historically viewed, economic integration does not produce political integration automatically. During the third quarter of the nineteenth century, Western Europe achieved approximate free trade (i.e., a common market) and, beyond this, a great deal of economic and monetary integration as a result of adherence to the international gold standard and the absence of various fiscal, social service, and labor union practices that now differentiate these countries. Political integration between Britain, France, Germany, and Italy did not result. Political integration followed economic integration in the case of the German union. But in this case, the will to political unification *preceded* economic unification, which was regarded as a step toward political integration.

With respect to the past and present conditions and prospects of the EEC, it is useful to distinguish between a customs union, which is a free trade area surrounded by uniform restrictions on imports, and an economic union, which, although less clearly definable, presupposes ultimately (or ideally) common fiscal and monetary institutions and policies and uniform legal regulations of business and labor for all its members.

When the EEC was founded, many (but far from all) of its supporters hoped or expected that the envisaged economic integration would lead eventually to political and military integration as well. It is clear that the EEC has succeeded in establishing, although not necessarily irreversibly, a customs union. The EEC members are now poised on the threshold of economic union. On their agenda are a common trade policy toward the outside world, a more viable agricultural policy, a common fiscal system, a common transport policy, a uniform company law, which will facilitate intra-EEC business mergers, and a common monetary arrangement. These objectives are proving to be difficult to achieve because the relevant obligations of member countries are less clearly defined by the Treaty of Rome than were those pertaining to the formation of a customs union and because the solution of these problems must be found in more politically sensitive fields. An example may illustrate the inherent difficulties.

The present EEC agricultural system set up a unified structure of prices which are too high and hence lead to burdensome agricultural surpluses, especially of butter and beef. The costs of the system ran to $1.8 billion in 1968, with France receiving net payments amounting to $400 million. West Germany, the main loser, is becoming increasingly reluctant to pay huge amounts for French surpluses. The Mansholt plan, now under review, would revolutionize the EEC agricultural structure by retiring about 10 million agricultural acres and pensioning off a large number of marginal farmers. Opposition to the adoption of the plan is strong because of its high financial costs and because of the social upheaval that would be caused by a large-scale retirement of farmers, especially in West Germany.

As the EEC economies have become progressively interlocked by the consummation of a customs union, the need for more integrated monetary and economic policies has become more apparent and insistent. An economic union may be necessary if the customs union is to survive. But it is hard to see that an integration of monetary and fiscal policies—which really means a common policy in such crucial matters as inflation, employment, and redistributive finance—could be made effective by some simple mechanism like periodic meetings of government officials. Truly effective integration would require the supranationalization of these policies. Moreover, in order to close the technological gap between Europe and the United States in the development of some key technologies where large-scale effort is a sine qua non, these countries also need shared computer and nuclear industries and a common system of defense research and development. Indeed, in its attempts to gain entry into the Common Market, the British government has pointed in these directions, as have some veterans of the European integration movement.[6] But past experience suggests that such integration will not go very far without a common defense policy, which in turn would call for a high degree of foreign-policy integration.

As the EEC economies have become increasingly intermeshed, the policy areas within which intra-Community conflicts are apt to arise have inevitably become enlarged. For instance, if West Germany is to bury half of its agriculture, as the Mansholt plan implies, a wide range of German interests is affected adversely; and with the Christian Democratic party and the Social Democratic party competing electorally for government authority, it would be surprising if either party turned a deaf ear to complaints and fears voiced by a substantial part of the electorate. Nations might be willing to agree to what they regard as sacrifices if there were great and salient advantages to justify full compensation of adversely affected interest groups. But the great economic advantages

[6] See Altiero Spinelli, "European Unification Revisited," *Atlantic Community Quarterly*, Spring, 1969, p. 128.

to be derived from the creation of a large market have already been reaped. Strictly economic benefits obtainable by means of economic union are marginal unless the continued existence of the customs union is jeopardized by lack of progression to a full economic union. This means that at this stage the compensatory advantages would have to be political and military. The future shape of Western Europe will be determined by political, not economic, considerations.[7] (From a strictly economic point of view, the EEC countries do not need a local computer industry. They can be very prosperous without it.) Yet the present political climate does not seem to favor a big push in the direction of political and military integration.

As certain experts have observed,[8] the way toward political integration has been cleared of some roadblocks which impeded progress in the mid-1960s: the Soviet occupation of Czechoslovakia has dispelled the hope that a gradual disappearance of the dividing line between East and West would open up big prospects for all-European unity; Washington's attitude toward Europe has become more detached, and there is some apprehension in Western Europe that the United States might become isolationist; and, perhaps most importantly, General de Gaulle has ceased to be in charge of France. Yet even though the road ahead has been cleared of those particular obstacles, the eagerness to travel it has declined perceptibly since the 1950s. The leaders of Monnet's European movement are aging and have failed to imbue large sections of Western Europe's youth with their spirit. The most politically active part of this youth, the rebellious students, are uninterested in "building Europe" as long as a united Europe would mean only a consolidation of the political, economic, and social order they despise. Some of the early motivations behind the European movement have more or less decayed or disappeared, e.g., desires for furnishing a solid basis for economic prosperity, for uniting against the Communist menace, and for creating the means

---

[7] Jacques Freymond, "Whither Integration?" *Atlantic Community Quarterly,* Summer, 1968, p. 249.

[8] E.g., Theo. Sommer, "Worauf Noch Warten?" *Die Zeit,* June 17, 1949, p. 1.

of exercising a world role, and the acute disillusionment with national government, which the economic depression of the 1930s and the horrors of World War II had stimulated.

The basis for progressive prosperity exists now, without any further integration. The Communist threat is by now largely discounted. Even the Soviet action against Czechoslovakia is now generally understood to have been an essentially defensive move to protect the status quo. At this time, few Western Europeans hanker after a world role for their own countries or for Western Europe which requires military strength for its performance. And although the confidence of Western Europeans in their respective governments is not very high, there are now no widespread feelings against the very conception of national sovereignty.

Any decisive push toward political and military integration must be shared by the key states: France, West Germany, and Britain. The major initiative cannot come from the Federal Republic, which would be suspected by its neighbors of making another attempt at German hegemony. Britain can hardly act as the protagonist as long as it has not secured access to the Common Market. This means that in the shorter run France occupies the key role in any enterprise to build Europe. France, however, is probably not in the mood at this time to become the architect of a united Western Europe. The Gaullists and the French Communist party account for at least two-thirds of the French vote, and in the past both have opposed far-reaching integration. The fact is that not a single major political party in Western Europe is disposed to make the building of an integrated Europe its major (or even *a* major) objective.

Some European federalists attach considerable hope to British entry into the EEC; and some members of the British elite, perhaps unsatisfied with the identity of postwar Britain, have in fact expressed considerable interest in the making of a strong Western European system. However, even if Britain enters, the absorption of so large a trading country (and probably also of Norway and Denmark) into the EEC would engender protracted digestive problems. Whether, in the end, the British government would want to become the federator of Western Europe, whether it would be in a position to do so if it wanted to, and whether it could succeed if it were in such a position, are at this point certainly open questions.

For the time being and for some time to come, the prospects are that the countries of the EEC will make slow progress toward a partial economic union, that they will do so by harmonizing *national* policies to some degree, and that they will delegate only restricted administrative tasks to the Brussels Eurocrats. The chances are much less that they will move in a federal direction by greatly increasing the authority of the Commission and the powers of the European parliament as the instrument for exercising democratic control over the Commission. At this time, the prospect is one of slow and halting evolution, with some risks of setbacks and retrogression. It would probably take a profound shock—which could be administered only by the Soviet Union or the United States—to create a sudden and dramatic forward movement.

To sum up, it seems clear that the pace of Western European economic integration has been slowing down for reasons which are apt to persist in the years immediately ahead. Rather than the process of economic integration pushing strongly toward political (and military) unification, the achievement of more advanced economic integration now demands a strong political impetus which seems to be absent from the Western European scene, again for reasons that are not ephemeral. Even if the unexpected occurred and rapid progress toward political and military union took place, it would be the result of a political impetus rather than the push of economic forces.

The examination of the first two questions regarding the economic feasibility of a security-independent Western Europe has supplied the answer to the third. One conclusion has been that Western Europe could not attain a high degree of security independence without the EEC countries, preferably plus Britain, having achieved a degree of integration which represents a strong movement toward a federal structure. Another conclusion has been that this integration is unlikely to occur during the next few years. If it began to happen, the process would take years of negotiations, internal political testing, and administrative implementation. And after a sufficient institutional basis for a common defense effort had been provided, it would take more years to develop the armaments industries on which an independent security effort would have to rest in large and increasing part. In view of these time shapes, it is almost certain that Western Europe will not achieve virtual security independence during the next ten years. At best, the area might be on the way toward this achievement. But although this possibility cannot be ruled out, from the perspective of the present it is not a likely development.

III

The third European security arrangement described earlier generated the economic question whether an expansion of foreign trade and other economic cooperation could lead to the creation of an all-European security community in which all the members were dependably at peace with one another and in which national defense capabilities could or would be subjected to various controls and perhaps considerably reduced.

In market-oriented economies, international trade tends to grow with the volume of economic activities and hence with the level of economic development. In view of the stage of industrial development reached in Eastern Europe and the Soviet Union, on the one hand, and in Western Europe, on the other, the trade between these two areas is extremely low. Table 9 shows that although trade between the EEC countries and the Eastern European countries has been rising strongly over the past decade, the absolute amount is still small. In 1967, only 6.5 percent of total imports into the EEC came from Eastern countries and, correspondingly, only 6.6 percent of total EEC exports went to the East. That this is not a peculiar pattern is shown by Table 10. The Eastern countries accounted for only about 10 percent of aggregate world imports in 1968, compared with 36 percent for the EEC and Britain. Since more than two-thirds of the trade of the Eastern European coun-

Table 9   East-West Trade, 1958, 1965, 1967
(in millions of dollars)

	Imports from Eastern Europe and USSR	Total Imports	Exports to Eastern Europe and USSR	Total Exports
EEC[a]				
1958	56	1,346	52	1,326
1965	131	2,382	118	2,258
1967	167	2,564	175	2,636
Britain				
1958	24	874	18	773
1965	51	1,345	27	1,143
1967	58	1,773	40	1,198
USA				
1958	5	1,105	9	1,493
1965	11	1,476	12	2,250
1967	14	2,228	16	2,596

Source: European Communities, Statistical Office, Monthly Statistics of Foreign Trade, March, 1969, and Supplement to Monthly Statistics of Foreign Trade (Brussels, 1969).
[a] Excluding intra-EEC trade.

tries is among themselves, the East's share of extra-East world trade is much smaller and is roughly in keeping with the proportion of its trade with the EEC countries.

In view of the relatively high industrialization of both areas, one would expect manufactured articles, machinery, and vehicles to figure highly in the trade between them. The exports of EEC and EFTA countries to Eastern Europe are in fact relatively high in this category of goods, but foodstuffs and raw materials figure prominently in EEC and EFTA imports from the Eastern countries. The implication is that manufactures, machinery, and vehicles produced in the Eastern countries are not on the whole competitive in Western European markets. There is other evidence that this is indeed the case. This structural factor could impede a large expansion of EEC-Eastern European trade even if other obstructions did not exist.

Other obstacles do exist, however. Communist doctrine, as propounded in Moscow in the 1930s, 1940s, and 1950s, favored a high degree of national self-sufficiency and preferred trade between Communist countries to trade with the non-Communist world. Trade with the non-Communist world was based mainly on political considerations, and on economic considerations only to the extent that foreign goods were needed because there was no domestic equivalent. Notions of comparative advantage and the benefits of international specialization played no part. These notions did play some role in structuring trade among the European Communist countries (in COMECON), but only to the extent that planners could recognize conditions of comparative advantage and did not want to base intra-sphere specialization on contrary political desiderata.

There are significant developments in the European Communist national economies and economic systems which strengthen economic considerations favoring more trade along economic lines and make these systems institutionally somewhat more amenable to expansion of foreign trade. One major factor is a much greater emphasis than before on goods for private consumption—a change that is motivated by the growing importance of social welfare ideas characteristic of economies that have reached advanced stages of development. This emphasis has two relevant implica-

Table 10   Imports, 1961 and 1968 (amounts in millions of dollars)

	1961		1968	
	Amount [a]	Percentage of World Total	Amount [a]	Percentage of World Total
World	124,600	100.00	225,100	100.00
EEC and Britain	44,890	36.03	81,016	35.99
USA	15,942	12.79	36,012	16.00
USSR [b]	5,832	4.68	8,535[c]	3.79
Eastern Europe [d]	9,344	7.49	15,204	6.75

Source: International Monetary Fund, Statistics Bureau, *International Financial Statistics,* May, 1969, p. 33.

[a] Valued c.i.f. unless otherwise noted.

[b] Valued f.o.b.

[c] Amount is for the year 1967, but percentage is of the world total for 1968.

[d] Bulgaria, Czechoslovakia, East Germany, Poland, and Rumania valued f.o.b.; Hungary and Yugoslavia valued c.i.f.

tions. One is that increased imports to Eastern Europe would create immediately an enlarged supply of consumer goods. The other is that such imports would exert pressure on domestic consumer-goods industries to become more responsive to local consumers' tastes.

Another major factor is the interest of the Communist authorities in boosting the efficiency of resource allocation. This interest has led to various economic reforms, most advanced in Hungary and Czechoslovakia, designed to stimulate a more rational employment of resources by rewarding management and labor more directly than in the past for top performance. However, the greater use of prices and decentralized decision-making has stopped far short of permitting market forces to serve as important an equilibrating function as is customary in the Western economies. In the Soviet Union, for example, prices now reflect total output costs more accurately, but the new prices are set arbitrarily by the authorities and reflect changes in supply and demand, especially shorter-run changes, little more than before.[9] A complete break with centralized economic planning is unlikely in the Soviet Union in the foreseeable future, even though it is likely to make more progress in the other Eastern economies.

Nevertheless, the increasing concern with a more efficient use of productive factors should push the governments of Eastern Europe toward considering the productivity-increasing effects that a greatly expanded foreign trade, *based on comparative production advantages,* would confer on their economies.

A vast increase in East-West commerce depends at this stage primarily on governmental decisions in the Eastern countries. But such an increase would require more than a willingness to expand trade on the basis of present practices. It would call for institutional adaptation of the economies of these countries to permit much more flexibility in resource allocation than prevails at present, and it would also need special efforts at making Eastern manufactured goods more competitive in quality with Western goods. The governments of Eastern countries do display increasing inter-

[9] See Gertrude E. Schroeder, "The 1966–67 Soviet Industrial Price Reform: A Study in Complications," *Soviet Studies,* April, 1969, pp. 462–77.

est in expanding economic transactions with the developed Western countries. This interest is notably exhibited in the fostering of
East-West industrial cooperation [10] (e.g., the FIAT deal with
Russia) and in commercial investments made by Eastern countries in
the Western economies.[11] But there is at this time no indication of a
push which would open up dramatically all channels of economic
transactions between Europe's East and West. A disposition to move
in this direction has been substantial in Czechoslovakia and
Hungary and is probably stronger in all the countries of Eastern
Europe than in the Soviet Union, but the governments of these
countries have not been completely free to make bold decisions of
the kind under consideration. They have been reluctant to undertake moves that would risk serious Soviet displeasure. The imposi-
tion of the Brezhnev Doctrine will reinforce this caution. Over the
longer run it is possible, indeed probable, that the forces which
provoked the Czech Communist party in 1967–1968 to reform the
political and economic system of the country—namely, a rebirth
of nationalism, a determined drive toward greater economic efficiency, and a search for a new political identity—will reassert
themselves in Eastern Europe.[12] But for the time being, the expression of these forces has received a severe setback by Russian intervention.

The conclusion is that, regarding the next ten years, East-West
trade and economic cooperation in Europe are likely to grow. But
it will probably be a gradual rather than a revolutionary process.
Since the present volume of trade is extremely low, it may triple or
quadruple and yet remain relatively small.

There is, of course, the future question whether any sizable expansion of trade between the Eastern and Western countries of
Europe could have a substantial effect on the continent's security
arrangements. History indicates that expanding trade is compatible
with peaceful relations but that the former does not cause the lat-

[10] See United Nations, *Economic Survey of Europe, 1967* (New York, 1968),
pp. 79–86.
[11] Marshall I. Goldman, "The East Reaches for Markets," *Foreign Affairs*,
July, 1969, pp. 721–34.
[12] James H. Billington, "Force and Counterforce in Eastern Europe," *Foreign Affairs*, October, 1968, pp. 30.

ter. Most European expectations, voiced in the mid-1960s, of a rapprochement of Eastern and Western Europe that would culminate
in an all-European security community did not assume that a dramatic expansion of trade per se would bring about such a development. Rather, increasing trade was viewed as part of a growing
stream of transactions that would do away with any dividing line
and that would be generated ultimately by essentially political
changes in the Communist countries, namely, a liberalization of
political, cultural, and economic life, a dissolution of the Warsaw
Pact alliance, and a gradual return of the Communist societies to a
free European civilization. Forces conducive to such a striking
transformation are indeed operating in the Communist societies of
Eastern Europe, though more so in some than in others. But it is
clear now that these forces must make converts of the decision-
making authorities in Moscow before they can reshape the organization of Europe. That is not likely to happen during the next ten
years, even if the possibility of such an event cannot be completely
excluded. In fact, as the example of Czechoslovakia demonstrated,
Soviet authorities are exceedingly sensitive to any liberating
changes in Eastern Europe that threaten perceived Soviet security
interests. Sharply increasing ties between Eastern and Western European countries are at present anathema from this point of view.
Advanced polycentrism will not happen if the Soviet Union can
prevent it.

IV

The general conclusion of this chapter is that, in their effects on
possible European security arrangements of the next decade, economic factors are permissive. They are not compelling in the sense
of pushing developments in one direction rather than another.
Only if a politically effective unwillingness of the various societies
—in Western Europe, Eastern Europe, the Soviet Union, the
United States—to pay for the high costs of national security were
probable (which it is not) would there be a possibility that economic considerations could substantially affect the future security

of Europe. To put the conclusion differently, the future organization of European security will be determined by a combination of the political factors analyzed subsequently in this volume and in the companion volume, *American Arms and a Changing Europe.*

/ Victor Basiuk *

futuRe technoloGy and
westeRn euRopean secuRity

THIS CHAPTER EXPLORES how Western Europe's secu-
rity and viability as a region of major political significance will be
affected by future technology. It describes three alternative "technologically influenced" future Western Europes and discusses the
variables that can bring them about. These alternative future
Western Europes are then analyzed in the context of the American
national interest, and various possible policies for the United
States are considered.

It should be pointed out that in this paper technology is viewed
mainly as an independent variable. Quite apart from what Western
European countries may do, certain technological developments
will take place—in the United States, the Soviet Union, or
elsewhere—and they will produce an impact on Western Europe.
Thus, to an extent, technological developments are a "given" for
Western Europe, to which Western European nations will have to
adjust by either adopting the new technology or, for better or
worse, bearing its outside impact without adopting it. Even if a
certain technology is developed and utilized by Western Europe

* This chapter was written before the author's present affiliation with the
Department of the Navy as Advisor to the Chief of Naval Operations. The
views expressed in it are the author's own and do not necessarily reflect those
of the Department of the Navy or any other agency of the United States government.

(or any other society) first, it tends to produce an impact as an independent variable by, among other things, modifying human values. Modification of values in turn may require other social adjustments. In short, to a degree, technological change sets up requirements of its own, which one can disregard only at a price —if at all.

TECHNOLOGICAL TRENDS AND IMPACT

Before the impact of technology on Western Europe can be discussed, a brief outline of certain present and future technological trends and developments must be provided.[1]

One such trend is the decline of the deterministic effect of resource location on economic development and the resulting rise of new power centers. In the past, power centers were built around and their vitality depended upon the important resources of the period: coal and iron ore, rivers for hydroelectric energy, and foodstuffs. The impact of chemistry (which undertook to make "resources" of the most ubiquitous materials and made substitution commonplace), progress in transportation (which substantially reduced shipping costs and thus greatly increased the mobility of raw materials), and other technological innovations have made the availability of superior technology and the organization and will to use it—rather than the location of raw materials and energy sources—of primary importance. This has been well demonstrated by Japan, which has managed to develop the third largest steel industry in the world with the use of raw materials which for the most part (88 percent of the iron ore and 64 percent of the coking coal) are imported at an average distance of 5,500 miles.[2] The development of nuclear and controlled thermonuclear energy will further undermine the deterministic effect of the location of resources.

---

[1] For a more extended treatment, see Victor Basiuk, "The Impact of Technology in the Next Decades," *Orbis*, Spring, 1970, pp. 17–39.

[2] "Steel is Where You Make It—in Japan," *Resources*, January, 1967, p. 18. The figures are for 1965.

This trend towards the loosening of traditional constraints imposed on industrial development by the location of resources has several implications. The vistas for organized human will backed by advanced technology have broadened immensely. On the other hand, the technological superstructure of advanced societies creates rigidity and a deterministic effect of its own. Thus, what will increasingly produce differential benefits from science and technology among the advanced nations will be not so much their present positions as differences with respect to farsightedness in planning, determination in the pursuit of selected goals, and willingness to reshape and modify existing social institutions and technological superstructures to meet the requirements of future technology.

Another technological trend is the integration of human activity and spatial units into one global geotechnical system. The only areas that have not yet been fully integrated into the global system (or not integrated at all) are the inhabited but underdeveloped regions, the uninhabited or scarcely inhabited regions, and the ocean floor. Major strides will be made in this and the next decade in incorporating these remaining regions through such advanced technology as international television networks based on satellites, inexpensive global telephone communications, marine-resource development, and weather and climate modification. The integrative process continuously increases the degree of global and regional interdependence. At the same time, it gives a differential advantage in the form of international influence, power, and vitality to those nations and regions that are capable of developing and controlling the instruments of the integrative process.

A closely related trend is the growing and increasingly versatile global projection of national influence and power through technology. From such relatively rudimentary instruments of the nineteenth century as British sea power and transoceanic-cable communications, technology enabling global projection of influence and power has advanced to voice and picture broadcasting, ICBM's, and the lunar landing (politically, if not physically, aimed at the earth). The means for projecting a state's power and influence will grow. These means will take the form of highly sophisticated technology for the development of the less-developed countries (e.g., satellites capable of surveying and exploring a country's resources, satellite-based community television networks for educational purposes, agro-industrial complexes based on nuclear energy and capable of providing water and fertilizer for arid regions), technology for the modification of weather and climate over other states' territory, for direct beaming of television programs into receivers in foreign countries, and of various other technologies projected abroad through multinational corporations. Since World War II the United States and the Soviet Union have been the principal powers projecting their influence globally through science and technology; Western Europe is considerably behind in this respect and tends to be an object of technological influence projected from the outside, as are the less-developed countries.

Other trends of technology are its growing scale and increasing economies of scale, requiring enormous resources for development and utilization. The cost and scale of the present advanced technology, such as the technology of outer space exploration, particle accelerators for advanced nuclear research, supersonic transport, and nuclear weapons development, are very large, and they are imposing a heavy burden even on a country of the United States' wealth and resources. Future technologies will be even more demanding in this respect, and they are proliferating. The benefits from the nuclear agro-industrial complexes are expected to be important, but an economic scale of operation requires an investment of half a billion to a billion dollars for each complex. Significant progress has recently been made in controlled thermonuclear reaction (CTR); commercial fusion reactors may have a capacity as large as 10,000 megawatts, and reactors of 20,000 megawatts are conceivable and would be even more economical. (For comparison, the total generating capacity of Poland in 1967 was less than 10,000 megawatts.) The production of magnetohydrodynamic (MHD) energy is especially subject to the economies of scale, and huge MHD plants are likely to be operational in about fifteen years.[3] Al-

---

[3] The magnetohydrodynamic process utilizes superheated gases passing through a magnetic field to generate electricity directly and the resulting exhaust gases to produce steam for conventional generators; in this process a given input of fossil-fuel thermal energy yields about 25 percent more electri-

though large surface-effect ships such as hovercraft, which may have the capability of operating on land as well as at sea, would be commercially attractive (no roads or docking facilities needed), they would require major financial outlays for research and development and construction. Technologies for the development of marine resources and for climate modification will require the expenditure of billions of dollars in large increments.

The new technology promises to be so costly initially that even the superpowers will not be individually able to take full advantage of its potential. High costs will increasingly create pressure for international cooperation in technological development among the second-rank powers, between the superpowers and the second-rank powers, and perhaps between the superpowers themselves. The countries that will not be able to pool resources on a large scale to utilize, if not develop, modern technology will fall behind decisively, with concomitant economic and political consequences.

Technological change is rapid, and its tempo is accelerating. Over half of the products manufactured by American industry today did not exist twenty years ago. Major progress is expected in the next decade in the areas of CTR, MHD, and superconductivity,[4] resulting in substantial reductions in the cost of energy. Biology, especially in its application to medical science, is on the threshold of multiple and significant breakthroughs.[5] Quite apart

---

cal energy than in conventional processes. For a state-of-the-art discussion of MHD and projections into the future, see William D. Jackson, Michael Petrick, and James E. Klepeis, "Critique of MHD Power Generation" (Paper presented at the Winter Meeting of the American Society of Mechanical Engineers, November 16–20, 1969) (ASME, 69-WA/Pwr-12).

[4] Superconductivity involves the use of superconducting metals (pure unstrained lead, tin, and others), refrigerated to extremely low temperatures, to transmit electric current over distances with complete or almost complete elimination of resistance and therefore almost no loss of energy. The cost of refrigerating the lines is as yet too high to make application of superconductivity to transmission of electricity an economical proposition, but the principle has been utilized, with significant economies, in electric motors and generators. For an account of commercial application of superconductivity, see "Tapping a Cool Idea for Power," *Business Week*, September 7, 1968, pp. 53–54; for a more fundamental discussion of the subject, see Richard McFee, "Application of Superconductivity to the Generation and Distribution of Electric Power," *Electrical Engineering*, February, 1962, pp. 122–29.

[5] See Gordon R. Taylor, *The Biological Time Bomb* (London, Thames and Hudson, 1968), pp. 13–21, 202–31.

from any major technological innovation that may take place in a particular field or subfield, synergistic effects involving innovations from various fields that reinforce each other provide a major dynamic force in modern technological change.

Rapid and accelerating technological change has two effects. First, countries in the forefront of technological development reap disproportionally large benefits from it, economically and politically. The countries that are only a little behind frequently find themselves beginning to manufacture products already on the threshold of obsolescence. Unless they have a commercial advantage in another respect (e.g., cheap labor or unusually effective marketing techniques) these nations are thus significantly handicapped in the world market. Second, while the social impact of modern nonmilitary technology has been relatively limited so far, rapid technological change will significantly increase this impact; the result may be important discontinuities in social and political trends. The changing values of American youth and the resultant turmoil can be traced to the direct and indirect effects of technology,[6] thus suggesting that a discontinuity in social trends in response to technological impact is now taking place in the United States.

The late 1970s and the early 1980s can be expected to be a particularly crucial period in terms of the effect of technology on institutions and the daily lives of individuals. At that time the impacts of a number of technologies will converge and may produce major, perhaps radical, changes in society. Producing the impacts will be such things as the extensive use of computers, truly global mass communications and travel, extensive development of ocean resources, and the imponderable effects of advances in biomedicine. Moreover, during this period countries will have to begin adjusting their technological superstructure and institutions for the even larger scale of the technologies of the later 1980s and the early 1990s, i.e., for MHD energy, thermonuclear plants, large surface-effect vehicles moving at a speed of more than 100 knots, and large-scale climate modification.

[6] For details see Daniel Seligman, "A Special Kind of Rebellion," *Fortune*, January, 1969, p. 67; Basiuk, "Impact of Technology," pp. 32–35.

The nature and extent of the social discontinuities that might develop would depend inevitably on a timely appreciation of the emerging problems and on effective policies to cope with them, on the recognition of the degree to which the change being introduced by new technologies is inevitable and legitimate, and on the adjustment of institutions and the creation of new ones to meet the requirements of the change. For a variety of reasons, not all societies will be equally successful in coping with the impact of technology. The price for failure, however, may be large: it may involve extensive social dislocation, widespread personal insecurity, severe social instability, and a serious weakening, if not collapse, of governmental authority and capability for defense.

A final trend to be noted is the increasing importance of nonmilitary technology as an area of direct relevance to national security. The possibility of changing the distribution of world and regional power through nonmilitary technology is increasingly greater than the possibility of changing the distribution through military technology.

Historically, through wars and conquests the qualitative and quantitative gains in weapons have been able to change the distribution of power much more swiftly and more dramatically than nonmilitary technology; hence, it has been the military sector on which states' concern for security has been focused. In the long run, however, nonmilitary technology has accounted for at least as much change in the distribution of world power as has military technology. The military sector still monopolizes attention in concerns with national security, but its ability to affect distribution of power in real terms has decreased. A stalemate prevails on the level of strategic nuclear weapons: any input of resources into the nuclear umbrella by either the United States or the Soviet Union is soon neutralized by the opposite side, the destructiveness of nuclear weapons having discouraged either protagonist from taking advantage of a temporary superiority.

There are signs that for political, technological, and military reasons the stalemate that characterizes the nuclear balance is being paralleled in the conventional-warfare sector. The fear of escalation, which induces the superpowers to impose constraints on local wars, the growing global projection of Soviet military power, which tends to stalemate potential American military action at various points of the globe (e.g., given the Soviet presence in the Mediterranean, the United States would think twice before undertaking another landing in Lebanon), and the tendency of certain conventional-warfare technologies to stalemate each other (e.g., the aircraft versus surface-to-air missiles and antiaircraft batteries in Vietnam; perhaps lasers in the future) account for the growing stalemate. Although for a variety of reasons the conventional-warfare sector can never be fully stalemated, the fact remains that, unlike the situation in prenuclear times, only a part of the total military sector can contribute to an effective change in the distribution of world power.[7]

There is no sign of a stalemate—either now or in the future—in the ability of nonmilitary technology to effect change in the distribution of world power. To mention but a few examples: Computers provide a major impetus to the growth of other areas of technology in a country and facilitate economic planning, investment, and the marketing strategy of corporations, providing a differential advantage for the countries and regions leading in this area of technology. Technological capability for the development of marine resources opens up new vistas in a virtually unexplored, unexploited, and unsettled three-quarters of the globe, with concomitant geopolitical implications. Countries that succeed in reducing the costs of energy sooner than others will be able to enjoy major advantages in world markets and strengthen their industrial capability and leverage of influence in the less-developed world. Global television capabilities and weather modification are also important instruments in this connection. The possibly negative social impact of technology—especially that producing social instability—has major implications for national power and security as well. Therefore, during this and the next decade non-military technology will

---

[7] A meaningful change in the distribution of power could take place if nuclear weapons were acquired by minor states for regional purposes (e.g., Israel or Egypt). Unless the weapons were used, the initial change in the regional balance of power would be nullified when the opposite side acquired nuclear weapons, thus creating a regional nuclear stalemate.

rise in importance in American security policy in general and with regard to Western Europe in particular.

RESURGENCE OF EUROPE'S VITALITY

In comparison with the interwar period, in the years since World War II Europe has established an impressive record of progress in bolstering its growth and vitality by utilizing the available technological potential, although Western Europe has been and is now facing some major problems in science and technology. Western Europe's achievements and assets since the war have been largely a product of the voluntaristic factors, i.e., the organized will and energy of its people, although there has been an important contribution from certain favorable conditions and external factors.

The Marshall Plan belongs mainly to this latter category. From the point of view of Western Europe, it was a given; whatever credit Western Europe can claim for its success—and this credit is not negligible—lies in the successful organization of institutions and manpower for the plan's implementation.[8] The destruction of plants and equipment and the low level of capital formation during the war years facilitated the introduction of technological advances into Western European economies.[9] The long-postponed demand for consumer goods provided a stimulus for investment in new productive facilities.

A combination of other miscellaneous developments tended to fuel the economic-technological vitality of Western Europe in the post–World War II years. The rearmament program, especially after Korea, was important in this respect. Historically strong in

[8] For a comprehensive discussion of the impact of the Marshall Plan on Western Europe, see *Sixth Report of the Organization for European Economic Cooperation: From Recovery Towards Economic Strength* (Paris, 1955), passim; for the organizational efforts to implement the plan, see Harry B. Price, *The Marshall Plan and Its Meaning* (Ithaca, Cornell University Press, 1955), pp. 71–86.

[9] Cf. Angus Maddison, *Economic Growth in the West* (New York, Twentieth Century Fund, 1964), pp. 58–59.

chemistry and aided by worldwide demand for chemical products, Western Europe was able to restore its chemical industry to a position second to none. The full-scale emergence of new technologies (in particular, television) and the sudden blooming of some that were not so new (the automobile and the passenger airplane) [10] contributed directly to Western Europe's growth and also acted as catalysts with respect to other sectors of the economy. The postwar discoveries of petroleum in the Middle East did not solve Western Europe's energy problem, but they certainly alleviated it. The later discovery of gas and oil in the North Sea strengthened Western Europe's energy position and stimulated its growth, although this discovery also was not significant enough to solve the Continent's energy problem.

Favorable as these factors were, they would not have been effective in producing the postwar resurgence of Western Europe without deliberate policies and planning on the part of the Western European governments. Management of the economy has become not merely an acceptable but actually an essential feature of governmental activity in postwar Europe. In this respect Western Europe has gone beyond the United States, and the development as a whole represents an important deviation from the past.[11] Economic integration of the EEC countries, although stimulated by the outside influence of the Marshall Plan, properly belongs to the new

[10] For a discussion of the transport revolution in Western Europe, see J. Frederic Dewhurst, John O. Coppock, and P. Lamartine Yates, *Europe's Needs and Resources* (New York, Twentieth Century Fund, 1961), pp. 279–311. The spectacular expansion of the means of transportation in Western Europe after World War II amounted to more than just the rise of another major sector of the economy. Aside from the demand for many products which the expansion has created, the new mobility is helping to erase national boundaries, multiplying trade and tourism, widening markets, shifting the location of industry and population, and creating a vast new complex of supporting activities. An interesting innovation in the European transportation picture—one that became an established feature of American transportation years ago—is the spread of a pipeline network for transmission of petroleum and gas, a network which cuts across the frontiers of European countries.

[11] See Andrew Shonfield, *Modern Capitalism* (New York, Oxford University Press, 1965), especially pp. 62–67, 121 ff. The extent of governmental management of the economy varies. Germany is perhaps the most capitalistic (in the traditional sense of the word) in her adherence to some of the basic tenets of market ideologies. However, even Germany is devoted to market ideologies much less than is the United States.

rational voluntarism; the integration was important in facilitating the technological modernization and economic vitality of Western Europe. Perhaps the most radical single innovation was the introduction of scientific and technological policies by Western European governments, the most remarkable example of which is France. From being a country that was conspicuous in neglecting the potential of science and technology in the pre–World War II decades, France succeeded in developing the most energetic and purposeful (if controversial in the context of the European political environment) policy in science and technology in Western Europe.[12]

PRESENT TECHNOLOGICAL AILMENTS

Considering that Western Europe has successfully recovered from the effects of World War II, has attained a GNP which is about two-thirds that of the United States and is growing at a rate as rapid as, if not more rapid than, the United States' GNP, and considering that Western European governments have developed policies in science and technology, it may be surprising that Western Europe has problems in effectively utilizing its scientific and technological potential. But it does, and the reason is fairly simple. Western Europe's policies in science and technology are a vast improvement over those of the prewar period, but, in the light of present technological trends and requirements, an effort that would have been more than adequate in the past is inadequate for the present and will become increasingly inadequate for the future.

It may be helpful to appraise the situation in Western Europe in the context of one important technological trend discussed previously. Western Europe is potentially a major beneficiary of disappearing determinism of the location of raw materials and energy sources and of the rise in the importance of scientific and techno-

---

[12] For an excellent analysis of the development of French policy in science and technology after World War II, see Robert Gilpin, *France in the Age of the Scientific State* (Princeton, N.J., Princeton University Press, 1968), pp. 151–238, 326–31.

logical capability as the critical factor in the viability and power of countries and regions. Western European countries are seriously deficient in a number of resources, but they do possess an impressive technological potential. However, both the form and the extent of voluntaristic effort which these countries have been displaying in recent years have been inadequate to fulfill that potential. The lack of coordination and unified purpose among the policies of the various Western European countries has been a very important handicap.

Although France's science and technology policy has been dynamic, it has failed to generate enthusiasm and unequivocal support from her Continental neighbors, since it is aimed primarily at bolstering France's power position and prestige and using European regional scientific and technological programs for that end. Moreover, in her striving for power through the development of a broad spectrum of advanced technology, France badly overcommitted her resources; the resultant crisis has led to a thorough review of policy by the Pompidou government.[13] The West German effort in science and technology is not as centralized as that of France but, strengthened as it is by a buoyant economy, is flourishing. Originally timid in any activities that might imply political aggrandizement, the Germans are now looking to fields that are increasingly important for international trade, politics, and prestige: outer space, computers, and oceanography. The budget of the Federal Ministry for Education and Science is growing at a substantial rate: from 4.7 percent of the total Federal budget in 1969, it is projected to increase to 9.6 percent or $3.05 billion in 1974. The Germans have shown themselves to be the best Europeans in their support of Western European regional cooperation in science and technology, but lack of progress in that sector is inducing Germany in the direction of bilateral cooperation, including that with the United States.[14] In contrast to her Continental neighbors, Italy has

[13] See Robert Gilpin, "Technological Strategies and National Purpose," Science, July 31, 1970, pp. 442–443.

[14] For details of West Germany's policy in science and technology, see Christopher Layton, European Advanced Technology (London, George Allen and Unwin, 1969), pp. 74–82; D.S. Greenberg, "Germany: Booming Research

been slow in developing a comprehensive national policy for science and technology and her present institutions in this field are relatively weak, although she has been doing remarkably well in certain areas of technology such as outer space and, especially, consumer products.

Having emerged from World War II as the only major Western European power that had not suffered defeat, Britain tried to maintain the versatile military capability of a near-superpower for some twenty years. This gave her the leading position in military technology in Western Europe, but was a major factor in straining her resources. The British have evolved a fairly effective governmental machinery for science and technology; it has the disadvantage of lacking a central steering wheel, but it is not beset by excessive pluralism as is the case in the United States. Public disillusionment with science, financial constraints, and a not-so-spectacular performance in producing marketable technologies have lately created a ferment in science-technology policy in Britain somewhat similar to (but certainly not as strong as) that in the United States.[15] These qualifying factors notwithstanding, Britain still has, by a considerable margin, the strongest general capability in science and technology of any Western European state. Britain's much delayed entry into the European Economic Community, however, has prevented the potentially major impact which the British scientific and technological capability could have made on the continental European scene.

Thus, in an era characterized by integration of technologies and of space through technology and requiring large-scale, rational, and concerted efforts for an effective utilization of technological potential, Western European governments are incapable of produc-

---

Effort Turning to Space and Computers," *Science*, April 18, 1969, pp. 281–83; D. S. Greenberg, "Dr. Leussink's New Ministry," *Nature*, June 13, 1970, pp. 1019–20; "Budget and Planned Expenditure up to 1974," *Science Policy News*, November, 1970, p. 35.

[15] For details, see Alan G. Mencher, "Management by Government: Science and Technology in Britain," *Bulletin of the Atomic Scientists*, May, 1968, pp. 22–27; Layton, *European Advanced Technology*, pp. 61–63; and John Walsh, "British Science Policy: A Crisis of Confidence," *Science*, November 5, 1971, pp. 572–574.

ing significant results through their compartmentalized policies.[16] Western Europeans have been attempting to remedy the situation by establishing institutions of regional cooperation in science and technology which not only cut across the EFTA-EEC division (and thus include Britain), but reach across the oceans to include such countries as Australia. The success in regional cooperation has been mixed at best. Euratom suffered from the initial self-exclusion of Great Britain and later from the highly nationalistic policy of de Gaulle's France, which was echoed by other members and seriously undermined the functioning of the organization. Britain and Australia were charter members of the European Launcher Development Organization (ELDO), but ELDO has had a number of crises since its inception in 1962, and the British are debating whether they should stay in the organization. The most successful so far of all the European scientific and technological organizations is the European Organization for Nuclear Research (CERN), followed by the European Space Research Organization (ESRO), both of which are engaged primarily in scientific research. The problem of adequate funding by member states, however, has plagued all of the organizations at various times and in various degrees.[17]

Aside from governmental policies, Western Europe has a number of other handicaps which in their sum total are perhaps even more important. In some respects the existing technological superstructure of Western Europe is not suitable for ready absorption of modern technology and would require a major change to meet the requirements of the future. Britain, France, and Italy have national grids for distribution of electric power which can absorb, in varied degrees, the moderately large capacity of present-day nuclear reac-

[16] The governments of the major Western European countries are facing double problems because of the compartmentalized policies. Individually they do not have adequate resources to establish an effective capability across the board in the principal areas of science and technology. On the other hand, in certain selected areas of high priority they are wasting resources by duplicating each other's efforts in research and development. Thus, Britain, France, and Germany are individually engaged in research and development on fast-breeder reactors, at a total cost of $1.5 billion.

[17] For details of the functioning and problems of these organizations, see Layton, *European Advanced Technology*, pp. 91–100, 107–114, 162–71, and Gilpin, *France in the Age of the Scientific State*, pp. 392–400, 403–413.

tors. However, the huge reactors of the future would require power grids cutting across national frontiers. Other countries, such as Germany, with highly fragmented systems, find it difficult to utilize present nuclear reactors,[18] not to mention the potentially very large scale of generating stations of the late 1970s and the 1980s. Another case in point is the relatively undeveloped telephone network of Western Europe, which will require considerable investment of capital, modernization, and standardization of systems if it is to cope with the increased volume and speed of telecommunications that will become necessary as computerized data transmission is added to the rapidly growing traffic of international telecommunications.

In a number of Western European nations, and to a varying extent, there are distinct gaps between the development of science and its application. The enterprising spirit so characteristic of the American business scene and the venture capital are generally lacking. By and large, European companies are relatively small, and the existing legal structure, frequently aided by obstructionist governmental policies, creates serious obstacles to mergers across national frontiers.[19] There are no suitable institutions to provide the large-scale financing necessary for modern companies' scope of operations. Western Europe has several patent systems; this multiplicity impedes technological innovation. In a number of European countries the educational and scientific institutions lack the flexibility needed to supply the skilled manpower and research and development essential to keep abreast of technological advances.[20]

[18] Cf. Mason Willrich, "Politics of Civil Nuclear Power in the 1970's: Economic Background" (unpublished paper, University of Virginia Center for the Study of Science, Technology and Public Policy, 1969), pp. 15–17.

[19] See "Towards the European Company," *Economist,* June 15, 1968, pp. 60–61; "Obstacles to Mergers," *Economist,* March 1, 1969, p. 67. One of the principal obstacles to multinational enterprise in Europe is a provision in the laws of all countries that in order to merge across borders or establish a subsidiary in another country, the original company or companies must be dissolved. This means that the shareholders become liable for capital gains tax, which makes them highly reluctant to approve such mergers or the establishment of foreign subsidiaries.

[20] For a more detailed discussion of the various factors impeding technological progress in Europe, see Gilpin, *France in the Age of the Scientific State,* pp. 17–33 and passim; John Diebold, "Is the Gap Technological?" *Foreign Affairs,* January, 1968, pp. 276–91.

THE DOUBLE CHALLENGE: RAPID
TECHNOLOGICAL CHANGE AND THE
LARGE SCALE OF TECHNOLOGY

As a result of the factors mentioned above, Western European countries are facing two serious problems that are separate although distinctly interrelated. One is the making of timely technological innovations, so important in a period of accelerating technological change and rapid obsolescence. The other is utilization of technology on a sufficiently large scale. To be sure, the development of technology in itself requires an increasingly large scale; thus the problem of scale plagues Western Europe on more than one level. However, even if future technology were developed elsewhere and freely offered to Western Europe, this would not assure that Europeans could use it. In this respect, the implications of technology in the next ten or twenty years are very different from what they were in the pre–World War II decades.

Because of transferability of technology, timely technological innovation is ultimately less critical than inability to utilize technology on a sufficiently large scale,[21] especially because the importance of the latter will increase in the future. As things stand, however, Western European nations suffer on both counts and are thus facing the prospect of falling behind in the competition for world markets, potential military power, and political influence.

One vivid illustration of the relative weakness of Western Europe is provided by the activities of American companies there.

---

[21] This is not to suggest that obtaining technology from abroad does not create problems or that its cost is negligible. From 1963 through 1966, West Germany alone had a deficit of $452 million with the United States because of purchases of licenses and expertise. It has been estimated that purchases of communications licenses and payment of other fees to the United States will cost Europe some $200–300 million by 1980. Because of rapid changes in technology, profits are largest for those whose products come first into the market; firms that buy technology come into the market as competition begins to cut profit margins severely and often not long before a new product displaces the one they have bought. Layton, *European Advanced Technology*, pp. 19, 190, 274.

Possessing large-scale capital, superior technology, and dynamic management, American companies have been actively establishing subsidiaries in Western Europe and securing greater benefits than have the European companies from the advantages of disappearing tariff barriers between the Common Market countries. In several cases, American companies have transformed European scientific innovations into profitable products—something Europeans themselves had failed to do. American-owned firms dominate the European scene in computers, are strong in telecommunications and various other electronic products, and now are trying to break into the European stronghold—the chemical market.

What, then, is the outlook for Western Europe in the next decades? One can distinguish three possible outcomes, three alternative technologically influenced Western Europes; their shapes are determined by differences in the way Western Europeans meet the challenges of new technological developments. One outcome assumes that the existing inertia to change will dominate and that Western European governments will pursue basically nationalistic policies with respect to science and technology. Another outcome assumes that both the potential advantages from science and technology and the outside pressure of scientific and technological advance will induce Western European governments to undertake more cooperative policies in scientific and technological matters and will result in changes in European attitudes and institutions without, however, leading to the establishment of a federal Western Europe. The third outcome assumes that, motivated to a significant degree by factors related to technological impact, Western Europeans decide to establish common political institutions and solve their technological problems within the framework of a common government.

These outcomes are not equally probable. Furthermore, none is likely to materialize in the exact form described here; it is likely that an approximation of one outcome will develop but that it will incorporate elements of the others.

Outcome 1: Development Counter to Technological Trends. If Western European governments pursue narrow nationalistic policies with respect to scientific and technological matters, and if inertia and apathy prevail with respect to changes required by advanced technology, Western Europe's capability in science and technology will be weakened, and its power position will decline. The course of events could run along the following lines:

In the immediate future, the United States and perhaps the Soviet Union effectively develop lasers for industrial application and make major progress in superconductivity. The United States continues to dominate the field of computers and makes further strides in telecommunications and other electronics. The margin between the technological superiority and efficiency of American and European companies broadens. American products increasingly penetrate the European market, and American subsidiaries in Western Europe continue to grow.

American investment in Europe results in some transfer of technology, which is beneficial to European enterprise. Pressed by budgetary considerations and motivated in part by the desire to stop the erosion of Western Europe's power position, the United States makes attempts to establish joint programs in selected areas of advanced science and technology with Western European countries. European governments, however, cannot successfully agree among themselves on joint programs with the United States. Accordingly, the United States undertakes only a few minor bilateral programs with selected nations, such as France, West Germany, and Britain. Thus, whatever transfer of technology from the United States to Western Europe takes place merely slows down the relative decline of Western Europe; it does not stop the decline. Western European nations are losing their influence on the world markets to American and Japanese products, eventually joined by those of the Soviet Union. This causes increasing unemployment and a partial shift of employment towards services (e.g., hotels and other facilities to serve the needs of tourists); the gap between the standard of living in the United States and in Western European countries widens. Personal insecurity and social ferment increase.

The trend is gradual and grows throughout the 1970s, but it does not reach serious proportions until the very late 1970s or, even more likely, the early 1980s. By that time third-generation computers are solidly established in the United States, further strengthening the efficiency of the American economy and its worldwide enterprises. Mainly through American companies, computers as public utilities are introduced into Western Europe. Their early impact is unsettling, inasmuch as they introduce actual or potential infringements on privacy, changes in employment patterns, abolition of money, and accelerated impersonalization in urban environments. Either the Soviet Union or the United States or both have a partial capability for modification and control of Western European weather. First the Soviet Union and later the United States begin to beam television programs through satellites directly into the receivers of the Western European population, vying for influence in a more intensive and effective way than is currently pursued through radio broadcasting. The United States and the Soviet Union also compete through television for influence in the less-developed world. Western Europe has no unified capability for beaming television programs into the less-developed countries; at best only some individual European states have a partial capability in this respect, which is sustained through cooperation with the technical facilities of one of the superpowers. Political and economic influence of Western European states in the less-developed countries declines rapidly.

The United States and the Soviet Union develop operational MHD energy stations and achieve further progress in superconductivity and nuclear reactors, developments that result in a reduction in the cost of energy. This reduction is not drastic as yet —thermonuclear reactors are merely in the prototype stage—but it does give the superpowers an important marginal advantage in manufacturing new products and producing old products at lower costs. Some European countries are more successful than others in utilizing advanced technology. Possessing a national electricity-distribution grid and advanced nuclear technology, Britain assimilates medium and even large conventional nuclear reactors, but MHD energy plants of 10,000–20,000 megawatts are beyond Britain's capability. European countries cannot individually develop thermonuclear reactors, and the outlook is also bleak for their being able to utilize on a national basis the more economical large thermonuclear reactors of about 10,000 megawatts. While the superpowers are moving rapidly into the development of deep ocean areas for minerals and oil, European countries have but a limited capability in marine exploitation, and only a handful of their oil companies operate globally, mainly on the continental shelves and slopes of the less-developed countries.

Except for certain highly specialized items (Swiss watches, German optical equipment), Western European countries are now badly behind in the competition for world markets, and they are losing domestic markets to cheaper and better products manufactured outside Western Europe or by foreign subsidiaries in Europe. The extent to which Western Europe becomes an object of the projection of influence by the superpowers considerably increases. Although some European countries (Britain, Germany) are doing better than others, by 1985 all are hopelessly behind in most areas of advanced technology. Most of their influence in the less-developed nations is lost. A high level of unemployment is a chronic phenomenon in Western Europe. The feeling of insecurity in the Western European population is now acute, and unrest in a number of countries results in street riots and frequent governmental crises. Western European governments are preoccupied with domestic affairs; they attempt to alleviate personal insecurity by improvements in social legislation, which helps the situation in some countries, but not significantly.

The state of Western European science and technology is incapable of supporting advanced military weapons; even aside from this, budgetary pressures compel Western European governments to cut their armed forces significantly. NATO is still in existence on paper but is completely ineffective. The Soviet Union is fairly successful in extending its influence in Western Europe. In some states the Soviets have gained allegiance of large social groups, and coalition governments with the Communists have been established. Other Western European states actively cooperate with the Soviet Union in science and technology in an effort to improve their weak positions. Still other Western European states seek active cooperation with the United States for the same purpose. Germany is still divided, but the demarcation between the East and the West in Europe is blurred.

Outcome 2: A Functionally Oriented Western Europe. The outcome just described does not take account of the fact that there are at present two main forces in Western Europe: one is the force of inertia, traditionalism, and nationalistic attitudes of governments and individuals, and the other is the force of change, of willingness and desire to adapt to the requirements of modern technology and to use the benefits which it offers.

One sign of potential change is that Europeans raised the cry of "the technology gap" as early as 1962—at a time when it was quite insignificant—although the gap's full impact will not be strongly felt until the late 1970s. Except for some individual proposals, the direction of European response has not fully crystallized, although there is a strong feeling in responsible European circles that Europeans "have to do something about it." There are, however, a number of specific developments that carry promise of considerably strengthening Western Europe's capability for taking advantage of future technology.

As a result of initiatives by the EEC Commission, two draft conventions are under consideration. One would provide a uniform patent system for the member countries. The other, prepared in 1968, proposes the creation of a new type of company which would be subject to the laws of the convention rather than to the individual states, thus stimulating cross-national mergers. While the approval of these conventions has been delayed for quite some time, it is generally expected that they will eventually be ratified.[22] In June, 1970, five of continental Europe's largest aircraft manufacturers agreed to cooperate so that they could compete with American companies. Although the American aviation industry still clearly dominates the multibillion-dollar international commercial market, by the spring of 1971 voices had been raised in the United States expressing concern about "Europe's commercial challenge"

[22] See "Common Company Law," *Economist,* February 6, 1971, pp. 72–73. Although Western Europe is thus adjusting itself to the pressure of technology for enterprises of a huge size, there will be room for smallness as well, as shown by the following news item: "A Norwegian dwarf is taking up competition with international giants in the computer field and plans to fill most of the requirements of the Norwegian market during the years to come. With a staff of twelve and a production capacity of one computer a month, the company [Norsk Data-Elektronikk] even expects a small surplus for exports." "Norway Enters Computer Field," *News of Norway*, March 31, 1969, p. 21.

in aviation.[23] Lately European companies have become more active in direct investment in the United States, thus seeking expansion in the huge American market.[24] Companies providing venture capital are beginning to be established in Europe. Observers also expect that within the next few years financial institutions (probably backed by governments) will be established for the purpose of providing large-scale capital for European corporations. In the past couple of years, business concerns have become much more merger-minded than previously. Steady progress is being made toward achieving industrial standardization throughout Western Europe. Plans are under way to combine ELDO and ESRO into a single European space agency which, as one European journal put it, "could begin to look NASA in the face." [25]

Probably a greater immediate impact on the European scene will be provided by the activity of American companies and by the entry of Britain into the Common Market. American companies introduce an element of dynamism and competitive spirit, which is making inroads into European business practice. It has been noted that although the top posts in the European business hierarchy are held by the traditionalists, the younger executives of a number of European countries have been educated largely in the United States and share American business attitudes. The entry of Britain into the Common Market would provide a very substantial addition of advanced technology to the know-how of continental Europe and would remove a number of obstacles to regional cooperation in science and technology. It is noteworthy that the three principal technological powers of Western Europe—Britain, France, and Germany—are basically complementary in their strong and weak points pertaining to scientific and technological development. Provided that Britain joins the Common Market and

[23] Robert Hotz, "Europe's Commercial Challenge," *Aviation Week and Space Technology*, May 31, 1971, p. 21.

[24] In 1969, Western European firms directly invested $550 million in the United States, more than twice the amount invested in 1967. This, however, was still substantially below the $1.2 billion of direct American investment in Europe in 1969 (including funds raised abroad). See Richard Howe, "The European Challenge," *The Atlantic Community Quarterly*, Fall 1971, pp. 344–352.

[25] "Is It Goodbye to ESRO and ELDO?" *Nature*, June 13, 1970, p. 1011.

an active cooperation in science and technology follows, each could exert a beneficial catalytic effect on the others.[26] In some five to ten years this could produce a truly major takeoff in scientific and technological development, eventually resulting in an impressive capability.

The United States is showing interest in expanding its cooperation in science and technology with Western Europe. Depending on the extent and form of this cooperation, it could exert important beneficial effects on Western Europe. Although European regional organizations in science and technology have not displayed unqualified success, their existence provides an institutional framework and a fund of experience for future cooperation, as the impact of technology increases. There are also hopeful signs in the changes of governmental attitudes towards cooperation, in new programs established to bypass existing hindrances (like that among Britain, Germany, and the Netherlands to develop gas centrifuge technology for enriching uranium), and in the relative success of some bilateral undertakings.[27]

Assuming, then, that these trends prevail and pick up momentum under the impact of the sciences and technologies of the 1970s

[26] France has at the top the most purposeful and dynamic science and technology policy, but its arrangements lack the intimate association between universities and industry found in Germany, an association which bridges the gap between science and its application and creates a strong foundation for technological capability. On the other hand, the exalted status of the professor in both France and Germany introduces an element of rigidity into scientific research and inhibits the teamwork so important for advance in modern science and so successfully utilized by the British. France could learn something from both Britain and Germany about the advantages of greater decentralization in science and technology—in particular, the greater degree of freedom of university scientists from a somewhat stifling dependence on the government. The German experience on the university-industry level and the French setup on the policy-formulation level could help the British to bridge the dichotomy between science and technology which still persists in Britain.

[27] The Concorde as a case of cross-Channel cooperation has had difficulties and it may never be a commercial success, but the somewhat surprising aspect of the undertaking is that the joint project has progressed so far in spite of very serious questions about the Concorde's technological future and commercial viability. On the agreement (concluded in March 1969) between Britain, West Germany and the Netherlands, see D. S. Greenberg, "Uranium: Three European Nations to Build Centrifuge Plants," *Science*, April 4, 1969, pp. 53–55. It provides an interesting example of regional cooperation intended to bypass the hindrance of de Gaulle's France.

and 1980s, how far can Western Europe proceed in augmenting its technological capability and power, short of creating a unified political structure? What is a likely outcome under these conditions? The scope for progress is considerable, but it is important in this context to differentiate between military and civilian technology and between the development of technology and its use.

The scope for joint development in the absence of agreement on how military technology will be used—which is necessarily a political question—is much more restricted than in the case of nonmilitary technology. A decision by Western European states to pool resources and to develop jointly a military nuclear capability is practically inseparable from some hard decisions on the use of the end product, e.g., who is going to have a finger on the trigger? Thus the political issue of the use of the product in itself imposes a restriction on joint development. This restriction is not as significant with more conventional weapons like tanks, machine guns, and aircraft, and here resources can be more readily pooled to achieve savings in costs. But even in this category of weapons political purposes must always exist, and considerations related to such purposes—e.g., concern about a resurgence of Germany; the need, or lack thereof, to maintain a strong NATO against possible Soviet aggression—are likely to provide an everpresent hurdle for joint development and procurement of technological hardware.

Although nonmilitary technology is closely related to power considerations, it does not require an agreed-upon political purpose for its joint development. Indeed, as functionalists are fond of pointing out, technology tends to erode political barriers. Thus, if Europeans want to maintain their economic viability, keep the standard of living of Western Europe's populations among the highest in the world, avoid being objects of the growing projection of influence by the superpowers, and minimize the potentially injurious impact of the postindustrial society, they can go rather far in joint utilization of technology without political federation. A noteworthy hindrance might be created by intra-European commercial competition: each government might continue to support companies of its own nationality, impeding technological cooperation on a European scale. This problem, however, is not as restrictive as that of political considerations, and it is likely to decrease in importance as the technological pressure from the outside increases (from the United States and the Soviet Union) and as existing trends toward functional integration evolve further.

It is thus entirely reasonable to conceive of the Western Europeans creating an all-European patent system, institutions providing venture capital, and banking facilities making available large-scale fixed-return capital, each of which stimulates the growth of all-European companies. Western Europe also creates a European Space Authority by merging ELDO and ESRO. It revitalizes its nuclear energy sector by strengthening both Euratom and CERN and by reversing priorities so as to make regional institutions the focal points for national programs, thus avoiding waste and duplication. The three technologically strong powers—Britain, Germany, and France—exert a catalytic influence on each other, creating a dynamism in science and technology which post–World War II Europe has never experienced. The three, joined by others, eventually evolve a Western European body that determines priorities in the development of science and technology. Western Europeans develop their own capability in weather and climate modification and join the United States and possibly the Soviet Union in some large-scale intercontinental programs for improving the environment.

Under these conditions, greater intercourse and homogeneity evolve in Western Europe. To accommodate nuclear energy, electric grids cutting across national frontiers are developed. An efficient European telephone system evolves, linked with computer utilities and the global communications system. Western Europe is crisscrossed by a network of gas and oil pipelines. The value system of European business becomes more like that of American business, although the influence of American companies in Western Europe declines with the development of large European companies which assimilate American techniques and management practices. Self-confidence and a feeling of security on the part of Western European populations grow. Unless Western Europe has witnessed some saber-rattling by the Soviet Union, there is great temptation to reduce armaments and to utilize the saved resources for coping with the problems of the postindustrial society and for further development of nonmilitary technology.

As this outcome develops, however, a point is reached when Western Europeans begin to feel the anomaly of having power without political purpose. The availability of a large economic and technological capability increasingly requires political decisions on how it should be used. Western Europe has the capability of beaming television programs into the less-developed world, but what should be their message? Economic and political influence frequently go hand in hand and, unless a government follows through with a political strategy, economic influence can decline. Furthermore, mobilization and development of scientific and technological capability inevitably reach a point when its further growth requires decisions that will be increasingly political. If Western Europe evolves an institutional mechanism to determine priorities in allocation of resources for science and technology, this in itself is a quasi-political body. Eventually, questions of major magnitude arise. Should Western Europe compete or cooperate with the Soviet Union in weather-modification technology or in major climate-modification programs? Such problems require decisions by the political authorities of Western European nations and, to be timely and effective, such decisions require changes in Western European political institutions.

To repeat: in order to develop and utilize future technology in all its ramifications—of which large-scale enterprises and global projection of power are but two of the more important ones—Western European states will eventually have to evolve joint political purposes. Short of this, Europeans will be handicapped in utilization of the full potential of science and technology. In particular, Western Europe will not be able to develop technology as an instrument of power comparable to that of the United States and the Soviet Union. In the last analysis, a central political will is essential for a truly effective utilization of technology as an instrument of policy, and that applies to nonmilitary as well as military technology.

Outcome 3: A Unified Europe. The last outcome to be considered involves the establishment of central political institutions that pool resources and technologies to strengthen Western Europe's scientific-technological capability. Viewing technological factors as independent variables and taking them as the point of departure, one can envisage three sets of circumstances under which the establishment of federal European institutions might be possible.

One set of circumstances assumes a considerable degree of rationality on the part of Western Europeans. By 1975 both the requirements of technology and the advantages of unity are fairly clear. The pressure of technology is increasing, and Western Europeans are absorbing part of the pressure through regional scientific-technological institutions, but they can see much more of that pressure in future years, and they see more clearly the advantages of unity. The influence of technology is reinforced by the political sentiment of the Europe-oriented Western Europeans. Western Europe spends the next several years in restructuring its political institutions, and by 1980 a supranational government is formed.

Such a development cannot be completely ruled out, but it is the least likely of the three ways in which a unified Europe might come into being. It assumes too much rationality on the part of Europeans and underestimates the forces of nationalism and inertia, which are still strongly entrenched in Western Europe. It also overestimates the influence of Europe-oriented circles.

A second route to a unified Europe takes off from Outcome 1, a Europe developing counter to technological trends. Western Europe is basically incapable of taking advantage of advanced technology. The weakening of the European position and the unrest and political instability which continuously plague Europe produce a reaction. By the early 1980s Western Europeans feel they have had enough turmoil and establish a supranational government to remedy the situation. The next five to ten years are devoted to remedying the relative backwardness—as compared with the superpowers—of Western Europe in advanced science and technology. Cooperative programs with the United States help to accelerate the improvement. In a pessimistic view of the effect of

Western Europe's failure to take advantage of advanced technology, unification occurs under the aegis of a totalitarian or dictatorial regime.

A third route to a united Europe takes the second outcome, a functionally oriented Europe, as a point of departure. Western Europe uses regional scientific and technological institutions as the principal lightning rods for withstanding the shocks of modern technology. But by the early 1980s Western Europe, without central political institutions, increasingly feels restricted in large-scale development and global projection of technology. In addition, the availability of technological and economic capability creates the temptation to capitalize on it for political purposes, which in turn require a further strengthening of the technological potential—a situation somewhat similar to the one in which Japan and West Germany find themselves at present.[28] Europe-oriented groups gain in influence in Western Europe. Their activity is facilitated by the habits of mutual exchange and contact established by European officials and industrialists, who for the past fifteen years or so have frequently been in touch across national frontiers and have worked side by side in regional institutions. As a result of these various factors, Western Europe establishes a supranational structure in the mid-1980s.

If these developments were to take place, there would be a distinct possibility that by the mid-1990s Western Europe could catch up with and perhaps even exceed the United States as the foremost technological power. The success of Western Europe in this respect would depend largely on its ability to capitalize on nonmilitary technology, to forego the option of diverting resources into strategic nulcear capability (at least for the next ten to fifteen years), and perhaps to curtail its expenditures in the conventional-warfare sector.

[28] Both West Germany and Japan, of course, have central political institutions, but for the past ten years they have been timid in using their considerable technological and economic capability for political purposes. The picture appears to be changing.

A MODIFIED FUNCTIONALLY
ORIENTED WESTERN EUROPE:
THE MOST LIKELY OUTCOME?

The impact of technology on Western Europe in the next ten to twenty years will most likely result in a functionally oriented Western Europe with some elements of counter-technological-trends Western Europe, because of the strength of nationalism, inertia, and resistance to change. The reasons for choosing this outcome are derived from the previously noted signs of change discernible in Western Europe at present and in the compelling technological trends. Unlike the situation during the past twenty years, when Western Europe could afford to procrastinate and proceed by half-measures in the development or utilization of advanced technology, the alternatives for the future are becoming so divergent that the old policies simply will not do. Room for half-measures and procrastination in coping with the problems of advanced technology is progressively smaller, and Western Europe will have to make some difficult choices in the near future. Since the alternative to a functionally oriented Western Europe is a counter-technological-trends Western Europe, with its grim consequences, a belief that people act rationally when alternatives are clear-cut and divergent leads to the choice of an approximation of functionally oriented Western Europe as the most likely outcome. However, the second choice, and a close runner-up, is an approximation of counter-technological-trends Western Europe. It is entirely possible that this second choice will turn out to be the reality.

A FUNCTIONALLY ORIENTED
WESTERN EUROPE:
DIRECTIONS OF EVOLUTION

Another question that deserves to be considered concerns the directions which the evolution of a functionally oriented Western

Europe might take. A number of influential voices have recently called for functional cooperation of European nations in response to the American challenge in science and technology, for a unilateral European effort, not a transatlantic cooperation.[29] Viewed in the context of the 1970s, this approach might be a viable one and even has certain concrete advantages.

In the light of diminishing concern about the Soviet threat on the part of Western Europeans, "the American challenge" in non-military technology provides a convenient rationale and rallying symbol for action; at the same time, it directs the attention of the Western European public to an area of technology highly important to Western Europe's vitality and security. Because Western Europe is behind in certain areas of advanced technology and because lead times are required for catching up, for restructuring of institutions (including educational systems), modification of attitudes and values, and development of the necessary manpower, Western Europe may need the 1970s to accomplish most of these objectives and may be able to make significant strides along these lines with its own resources, especially since savings will be achieved through the pooling of resources and reduction of an existing duplication of effort. However, if one looks beyond the 1970s, a policy of reaction against American superiority in advanced science and technology is definitely short-sighted and might prove self-defeating. The simple fact is that no matter how good the intentions and how well they are carried out, Western Europe does not have adequate resources to take advantage of the technology of the future. For that matter, neither does the United States.[30]

[29] See, for example, Jean-Jacques Servan-Schreiber, *The American Challenge* (New York, Atheneum, 1968); Layton, *European Advanced Technology*; and Laurance Reed, *Ocean-Space—Europe's New Frontier* (London, Bow Group, 1969). This last monograph was written under the auspices of the Bow Group, the influential political research society of younger members of the British Conservative Party. Among other things, the monograph calls for appropriation by Western Europe of the Atlantic seabed up to the 4,000-meter (13,500-foot) isobath, to be owned and developed by a truly supranational European body, the Oceanic Development Commission. This acquisition would give Western Europe an additional 5 million square miles of territory.

[30] For an excellent analysis of the changing demands on available resources in a historical perspective, with particular reference to Britain and the United

A number of questions arise in this connection. If Western Europe chooses an approximation of the functionally oriented outcome as a reaction to America's technological superiority, could Western European countries later (e.g., in the late 1970s) successfully readjust their policies to large-scale cooperation with the United States in non-military technology in order to avoid the cul-de-sac of resource limitations? The response to the question would depend on the specific nature of the European action. If, as proposed by Laurance Reed,[31] Western Europe does lay claim to a vast chunk of the Atlantic seabed, begins to exploit it, and thus triggers an American-European rivalry for the resources of the Atlantic Ocean, it might not only be difficult to change the course of events to eventual cooperation in marine and other technologies, but the rivalry might also spill over into the political sphere, with concomitant repercussions for Western Europe's security. Accordingly, the eventual technological success of Western Europe would seem to depend on its ability to keep the options open for cooperation with the United States in science and technology while initially pursuing an anti-American policy. This is a thin line that might be difficult to tread.

A different question can be asked: Why should Western Europe not immediately begin to pursue a course of action involving much more extensive cooperation with the United States in science and technology? This, certainly, would be a rational approach advantageous to both Western Europe and the United States, since the latter is already feeling the pinch of resource limitations for advanced science and technology. However, a rational approach may not necessarily be the most realistic and hence the best approach. Suspicions of American technological superiority are likely to persist; commercially and politically motivated obstacles are likely to keep

---

States, see Harold and Margaret Sprout, "The Dilemma of Rising Demands and Insufficient Resources," *World Politics,* July, 1968, pp. 660–93. The Sprouts' discussion focuses on internal social needs versus external requirements for maintaining states' positions in the world and does not address itself to the trends in and demands of nonmilitary technology in particular; however, the requirements of nonmilitary technology strengthen the Sprouts' analysis.

[31] See the proposal by Laurance Reed in fn. 29.

arising on both sides of the Atlantic and may prevent a truly effective cooperation. In the face of these various obstacles, Western European countries might fall back on a policy of inadequate intra-European programs, procrastination, and such palliatives as compartmentalized bilateral cooperation by European nations with the United States. In an age of polarizing alternatives, this policy would result in Western Europe's relapsing into an approximation of the counter-technological-trends outcome, with associated political perils.

The choice of early and considerably more extensive cooperation between the United States and Western Europe in science and technology does not, however, have to result in the relapse of Western Europe into the counter-technological-trends outcome. It is important to keep the potential perils and difficulties in mind, but the outcome would ultimately depend on the policies and the perception of enlightened self-interest on both sides of the Atlantic. If such perception develops and finds its way into concrete policies, it will provide the shortest road to a viable and secure Western Europe in a future pervaded by the influence of technology.

If Western Europe succeeds in adjusting its legal and fiscal structure, its scientific and technological institutions, and its values to the requirements of modern technology and if it considerably enhances its technological capability and weathers or avoids the potentially disruptive effects of the technological impact that are likely to affect Europe about 1980, political changes in the European picture are likely to follow. Although later than suggested in the third route to a politically united Europe, an aggregate of factors—the temptation to translate technological and economic capability into political power, the impact of the quasi-political authority of regional scientific and technological institutions, greater cohesiveness of Western Europe, habits of mutual exchange and contact among its officials and industrial leaders, and ideas of European unification—is likely to exert its influence for a federal Europe. Its timing? Perhaps 1990. In any event, around that time Western Europe may have to make a choice between unifying politically or relegating itself permanently to second-rate status in the face of the overshadowing strength of the superpowers as they develop and utilize technology on an immense scale.

WESTERN EUROPE'S ALTERNATIVE
FUTURES AND AMERICAN POLICY

Which of Western Europe's alternative futures will become a reality depends to a considerable degree on what the United States chooses to do. Because of its resources, technological capability, and important stake in European security, America has both the potential for and a vital interest in steering Western Europe into one of the alternative futures—or at the very least in steering it away from the least desirable alternative. In considering the implications of the various alternatives for American policy, it is important to keep in mind the two principal components of the American national interest involved: European security, and America's security and vitality to the extent that they depend on an effective development and utilization of science and technology by the United States.

A Europe that moves counter to technological trends is obviously an undesirable alternative from the point of view of the American national interest. It would create instability in Western Europe, weaken its defenses, and provide a temptation for the Soviet Union to apply political pressure and resort to other means in order to capitalize on the new opportunities available. This alternative is thus likely to rekindle the American-Soviet conflict. The United States would have to compensate for the declining Western European capability for defense by strengthening American military power, with a consequent curtailment of the resources available for the nonmilitary technology so important to America's national security and vitality. Whatever chance for regional disarmament in Europe had existed would disappear. It is conceivable that an intensified rivalry between the United States and the Soviet Union over a weakened Europe would result in an arms race in conventional forces, which then would spill over into strategic nuclear weapons. If at the time that Western European power declined (about 1980) an arms control agreement on strategic weapons were in force, it is possible that its effect could be significantly weakened by resort to any escape clauses that might have been provided.

While the need for preventing a counter-technological-trends Western Europe is clear, the questions which of the other alternatives is the more desirable and whether it could be realistically implemented with the assistance of an appropriate American policy are more complex. In general and as a simplification, it can be said that both a functionally oriented Western Europe and a unified Western Europe would be desirable alternatives; an exception would be the Western Europe which had been unified by a dictatorial or totalitarian regime as a result of a period of instability generated by movement counter to technological trends. In the next decade or two, however, the likelihood of a unified Western Europe is small, except perhaps for the dictatorial variant just mentioned. Therefore, an American policy which opts for a unified Western Europe as a *direct* goal is not likely to be productive and would involve a waste of effort.[32] The range of American choice thus narrows down to the support of a functionally oriented Western Europe.

In deciding on such a policy, it will be necessary to consider which of the two functionally oriented outcomes to promote: a functionally oriented Western Europe engaged in extensive cooperation in science and technology with the United States or a Western Europe devoted to countering the American challenge. The latter outcome has a certain appeal in that the American policy designed to bring it about might be relatively simple—a narrowly nationalistic policy for science and technology (involving, among other things, strong support of subsidiaries of American companies in Western Europe) which would trigger a strong European reaction. While such a policy might be effective in achieving a functionally oriented, anti-American Western Europe, strengthened technologically and successful in avoiding internal instability in the 1970s, it would carry a number of disadvantages: undesirable political repercussions on American-European relations, no sharing of the costs of technological development and utilization with Western Europe, no guarantee of Western European success in meeting the requirements of technology beyond the 1970s.

[32] This is not to say that American support of a functionally oriented Europe might not eventually lead to political unification. To the extent that these two objectives overlap, an American policy aimed at European unification would be justifiable.

It thus appears that the most desirable alternative is an American policy designed to support a functionally oriented Western Europe through the establishment of cooperative scientific and technological programs. This policy has the disadvantage of being difficult to implement. If it is not carefully thought out, not purposeful and energetic, or does not enjoy an adequate allocation of resources by the United States, it may result in a watered-down mix of the two outcomes—a functionally oriented Europe engaged in some cooperation with the United States and a partially anti-American Europe. Unless given emphasis in one direction or the other, such a mix would not differ greatly from the present situation and, as noted previously, would eventually degenerate into an approximation of the Europe moving counter to technological trends.

On the other hand, if this policy is successfully implemented, it would meet both the medium- and long-range objectives of European security. A dynamic, functionally oriented Western Europe might attract Eastern European countries (and perhaps even the Soviet Union) in their own search for growth. A suitable climate might thus be created for cooperative programs in science and technology with Eastern Europe in which the United States would have an opportunity to participate. Such cooperation could help break down divisions between East and West and prove helpful in eventually solving some internal European problems that hinge on East-West relationships.

The Soviet-German treaty, agreed upon in August, 1970, accentuates the importance of a strong, functionally oriented Western Europe. The treaty has dimmed the outlook for further steps toward political unification of Western Europe in the near future by weakening Franco-German relations, on which European unification largely depends. It established a bridge between Western and Eastern Europe, but in itself it did not determine to whose advantage the bridge will work. If Western Europe develops dynamism and vitality by strengthening its scientific and technological capability, the treaty could serve as an important medium for exerting influence on Eastern Europe and the Soviet Union. If, however, the preponderance of scientific and technological vitality emanates from the East, the opposite would be true.

In view of the stakes involved, an early crystallization of American policy with regard to the future impact of technology on Western Europe is important. Present American scientific and technological policy towards Western Europe does not appear to have a strong sense of direction; it mainly pursues targets of opportunity. As a result, the United States has been drifting in the direction of bilateral cooperation with European nations, the most notable example of which is with France. This course of action will not provide a solution. To meet the requirements of the large-scale technology of the future and the high costs associated with it, Western Europe must develop a large market and internal institutions capable of coping with technology on a sufficiently large scale. Compartmentalized bilateral relationships between the United States and individual Western European nations will not permit the attainment of this objective.

Thus the task of American policy in this decade—a task not adequately appreciated in Washington—is to be persistent in trying to induce Europeans to cooperate among themselves as well as to cooperate with the United States. There is no single and sure way to achieve this goal, but the formulation of mutually attractive, large-scale programs is one means towards it. The American proposal for post-Apollo cooperation with Western Europe in outer space, involving perhaps as much as $15 billion over the next ten years, is an example. Cooperation in the enrichment of uranium, proposed by Commissioner Wilfrid E. Johnson of the U.S. Atomic Energy Commission, might be another.[33] A third major undertaking might be a United States–European exploration and research and development program leading to the exploitation of marine resources. A unilateral American endeavor to exploit the oceans has been delayed for the lack of funds, and a joint program with Western Europeans would be mutually advantageous.[34]

If, however, the United States does not develop and articulate

[33] Wilfred E. Johnson, "Uranium Enrichment—U.S. Policy, Requirements and Capabilities," Remarks before 1970 Annual Conference, Atomic Industrial Forum, Washington, D.C., November 16, 1970, *AEC* (Atomic Energy Commission newsletter), Nov. 18, 1970, pp. 4–7.

[34] See Victor Basiuk, "Marine Resources Development, Foreign Policy, and the Spectrum of Choice," *Orbis*, Spring 1968, pp. 67–69.

the thrust of its policy and, instead of pursuing the policy with foresight and persistence, relapses into small-scale bilateral programs, it will be only postponing, and not averting, the peril which the impact of advanced technology is likely to bring to the security of Western Europe.

/ *Andrew J. Pierre*

BRItAIN ANd EURopEAN SECURITY: ISSUES ANd ChOICES FOR the 1970S°

Not long after the close of the Second World War, Winston Churchill depicted his vision of Britain's postwar foreign policy in terms of three overlapping circles. Britain was to be at the center of a world commonwealth of English-speaking nations, to be a major European power, and to maintain a special relationship with the United States. This vision has in large measure failed, and the attempts to implement its inherent contradictions account for many of the travails which have beset Britain in the past quarter-century.

In reaching this judgment one need not accuse British statesmen of myopia, for each circle had a historical and emotional logic of its own, and where the circles overlapped each other they did not always conflict. In the hazy light of the first postwar decade it was not evident that Britain would be under strong pressure to make a choice. Only in retrospect is it clear that the three circles left Britain overextended, with her commitments outrunning her capabilities. In seeking to satsify three international constituencies, Britain has fully satisfied none, and consequently her own expectations

° Written in 1969. A postscript brings this paper up to date as of March, 1971.

have not been fulfilled. There is almost universal acceptance in Britain today that the nation will not achieve economic well-being and psychological contentment until she has settled on her post-imperial role.

There are also numerous indications that as Britain faces the 1970s she has at least tentatively made her choice—entry into Europe. All three political parties supported the second application (1967) for entry into the European Economic Community, in contrast to the first application (1961–1963), which the Labour Party, including its leader, Hugh Gaitskell, generally opposed. Public acceptance of the necessity of entry into the Common Market is broader than it was nine years ago, and the alternatives to the EEC have diminished in their appeal. Britain has undertaken a major reorientation of her defense policy in deciding to concentrate her military efforts on European defense and winding up most of her responsibilities East of Suez. The defense decisions of the last three years have, in the words of Minister of Defence Denis Healey, "set the seal on the transformation of Britain from a world power into a European power."[1] Within the councils of NATO Healey has taken the lead in promoting an intra-European dialogue that would enable the European members to present a collective view to Washington.[2] For Harold Wilson, a reluctant European at best, the great adventure of entry into Europe is increasingly attractive as a way of shifting the spotlight from his and the Labour government's economic and social difficulties to a new cause and hopefully a brighter political future.

But even if Britain has chosen the path of European engagement, there is no certainty that she will be permitted to join her prospective family on the Continent in wedlock. Nor is it assured that a continuous recalculation of interests will keep Britain steadfast in her matrimonial pursuit. With the departure of grandpère de Gaulle, a personal veto has been eliminated. French opposition to British entry into the EEC appears to have softened under the

[1] From his speech introducing the 1969 Defence White Paper to the House of Commons, *British Record*, February 21, 1969.
[2] Denis Healey, "Britain's Role in NATO," *NATO Letter*, January, 1969, pp. 26–28.

government of Georges Pompidou, whose cabinet includes a number of persons, including Foreign Minister Maurice Schumann, who have in the past been sympathetic to European integration. Some of the previous political and psychological obstacles to the enlargement of the Common Market seem to be gradually fading, and there is a perceptible change in atmosphere.

This change was most evident after the Common Market summit meeting at The Hague in December, 1969. At that time it was agreed that the EEC should be prepared by June 30, 1970, for negotiations on the admission of Britain and the other applicants. Only a few months after coming into office, Willy Brandt took the lead in developing a new momentum and cohesion in the Common Market and has supported progress toward British entry.

Thus there has been a psychological revival in attitudes toward the British application, and London has responded with a fresh indication of earnestness and interest. Echoes of grandpère's skepticism can be heard, however, throughout the European family, and there are those who doubt the depth of Britain's commitment to a European way of life. They ask if Britain is really willing to undergo the "profound economic and political transformation" once requested by de Gaulle. They point to a reluctance to reorder British agriculture, to make the necessary industrial and fiscal reforms, to loosen the close ties with the United States, and to adopt eventually the political ideals of a federal Europe.

Britain's entry into Europe will therefore continue to raise many complex and difficult questions involving economic, political, and military considerations. There can be little assurance that 1980 will find Britain in Europe, whatever may be the merits or the logic of the case for it, and the alternatives must therefore be examined. A look into the 1970s suggests four principal alternatives, which will be considered in turn. One must bear in mind that "alternatives" are artificial delineations designed to facilitate analysis. The chosen course, in reality, will contain ingredients from more than one recipe. Section I of this paper examines Britain's alternatives as a member of the European family, in a new partnership in a North Atlantic free trade area, as a Commonwealth or "world" power, and "muddling through" alone. Section II discusses the implications of Britain's choice for her strategic contribution to European security and for the special relationship with the United States on nuclear matters, for her potential contribution to Europe in advanced technology, and for future British perspectives on European security. But first to entry into Europe, the most enticing course.

I

The European Option. What is perhaps most striking is how recently the British nation has come around to seeking entry into Europe. When Macmillan launched the first application to the EEC in 1961, he was dragging behind him a badly divided cabinet, a reluctant party, and the opposition of the majority of the Labour Party. The constraints which these conditions imposed upon the British negotiators in Brussels helped to account for the final results. In the first three years of the Labour government, Wilson looked not to Europe but to East of Suez and a "world role" for Britain's destiny. It was during this time that Wilson remarked that Britain would not be "corralled" into Europe and that her "frontiers" were on the Himalayas. Although she obviously did not possess the same economic and military resources as the superpowers, many in Britain thought that through her unique global interests and responsibilities she acquired the right to a special place in international councils. The worldwide role was welcomed as placing Britain in a different class from the European powers. Of course, in the first postwar years Britain allowed the leadership for building a United Europe to go begging and subsequently failed to support or join the European institutions launched on the Continent—the European Coal and Steel Community, the European Defense Community, and ultimately the European Economic Community, in which Britain could probably have obtained charter membership for the asking.

Why then did Britain decide in the 1960s to seek to "join" Europe, at first somewhat reluctantly under Macmillan in 1961–1963 and then more determinedly with Wilson from 1967 to the present? As with most major international realignments, the reasons were complex and shifted with events and time. The basic case for joining the Common Market has, however, remained remarkably stable and can be summarized briefly as follows:

1. The EEC is a political reality that must be recognized by Britain. Accordingly, Britain simply cannot afford to stand idly by while a major European bloc develops and prospers. Whatever the costs of going in, the long-term costs of staying out, though admittedly unpredictable, are likely to be higher. If Britain wishes to retain or increase her position in Europe, she is in a far better position to do so from within the Common Market than from outside.

2. As a full European partner, Britain would be in a position of leadership that would allow her to help shape the future course of Europe, including steps toward political integration. Britain's participation would provide assurance against a potential conflict between an independent Europe and the United States. Her inclusion would also provide a balance against West Germany's possible domination of the Continent, or against any West German tendencies toward extreme nationalism, neutralism, or an alliance with the East. If there should ever be a politically integrated Europe, its superpower role in international affairs would be greatly strengthened if Britain were included. Britain's initiative and leadership might spark a renascence of the "European idea."

3. Exposure to competition within the Common Market would force British industry to become more efficient and productive. British labor and management practices and traditions are severely outdated and must undergo major reforms if the economy is to have an acceptable rate of growth and if productivity is not to continue to decline in relation to the Continental nations. The "cold shower" of competition would invigorate industry, change outmoded but prevalent attitudes, and force Britain to cope with her fundamental economic and fiscal problems.

4. Industry would be stimulated also by the availability of a wider market. Modern technology, in which Britain is capable of making an important contribution to Europe, requires large-scale

markets because of massive research and development expenses and high unit costs. The larger British industries would profit from the opportunities offered in the European market.

Undoubtedly the intrinsic merits of the case for joining the Common Market were not lost upon Macmillan, nor were the urgings of some in the Kennedy administration, but his personal conversion appears to have been equally influenced by the need to give his tarnished political image a fresh, "Supermac" look. Nevertheless, at the time of the first application, Macmillan presented the EEC to his domestic audience as essentially an economic undertaking, playing down its broader political significance. As the negotiations progressed, Mr. Heath acknowledged in Brussels that Britain would have to accept the political implications of the Treaty of Rome. But at the same time the prime minister, in insisting upon the need for the American Skybolt missile for the next generation of the British "independent deterrent," was confirming the continuation of the transatlantic ties that had been the bedrock of his foreign policy. Whitehall was pursuing a schizophrenic policy of actively seeking entry into Europe while simultaneously attempting to continue the close bonds with the United States. In retrospect, it is clear that this was possible because the full significance of the 1961 decision to seek entry into the EEC dawned only gradually in Britain, perhaps only after de Gaulle's veto.

Upon achieving office in 1964, Labour was only too pleased that the issue of entry into Europe was dormant. The General Election had been fought on domestic themes and on the continuation of the independent deterrent. Wilson's first cabinet had a strong anti–Common Market bias, which reflected the views of a prime minister who was temperamentally insular rather than cosmopolitan, preferring the Scilly Isles to the Continent for his holidays. The rank and file of the Labour Party mistrusted Catholic Europe and Germany, feeling better disposed toward the more Protestant and socialist Scandinavian members of EFTA and the Association's neutral countries, which were less identified with the Cold War.

Moreover, the Wilson government preferred the Commonwealth, which an earlier Labour government had founded, to Europe. The former would offer opportunities for British influence and participation in peacekeeping in the areas where the real action was to be located. The main problems of international security in the coming decades were thought to be in Africa, Asia, and the Middle East, where Britain could make an effective contribution through limited intervention. Denis Healey had been favorably impressed by Britain's assistance in quelling the East African mutinies of 1964 and her performance in maintaining order in Cyprus, and he thought that in the future the country's armed forces should have an important role in peacekeeping activities. The military bases East of Suez would permit Britain to engage in peacekeeping operations that were no longer possible for the continental European countries, which had retrenched their forces from abroad. Shortly before becoming Minister of Defence, Healey had set forth his philosophy on Britain's world role:

Britain is a world power, whether we like it or not. History has saddled her with interests and responsibilities in every continent. The structure of her economy prohibits a regional approach to international affairs. . . . We should count ourselves fortunate that we have the power to exert some influence in every continent.[3]

Labour's espousal of Europe was therefore a gradual one, not a response to the first impulse. The lag between the veto of January, 1963, and the second application, in May, 1967, for entry into the EEC was not due to tactics of waiting for the propitious moment. Rather, the Wilson government was hauled by economic and political realities through an educational process that turned its attention toward Europe. In the process of reappraisal, a major review of defense policy provided the vehicle.[4]

On coming into office in 1964 the Labour government initiated a broad review of Britain's defense policy that was designed to bring the nation's military capabilities into balance with its economic resources and foreign-policy objectives. Many observers felt that Britain had been trying to do too much with too little, with the re-

[3] Denis Healey, *A Labour Britain and the World* (London, Fabian Society, 1964), p. 16.
[4] See Andrew J. Pierre, "Britain's Defense Dilemmas," *Proceedings of the Academy of Political Science*, November, 1968, pp. 64–79, for a more extensive treatment.

sult that the armed forces were seriously overstretched and to some extent underequipped. It was also assumed that unless defense expenditures were reduced, especially that portion that took place abroad, Britain could not eliminate recurrent balance-of-payment crises and advance toward long-term economic health. The severe sterling crisis in the fall of 1964 appeared to confirm this view. With approximately half of Britain's armed forces stationed overseas, the cost in foreign exchange was equivalent to 40 percent of the large 1964 trade gap.

In subsequent years the Labour government announced successive cutbacks in its overseas military capabilities. There was a conflict between the proclaimed desire to be a world power, that is, to remain East of Suez, and the perceived economic necessity to reduce overseas expenditures. This was most evident in the 1966 Defence White Paper, which retained British troops in Singapore and Malaysia (though not in Aden) but also announced a drastic curtailment of future weapons development and a much-debated decision not to purchase a proposed new aircraft carrier for service in the Far East. The latter decision led to the resignation of Minister of Defence for the Navy Christopher Mayhew, on the grounds that the range of British commitments was still too large and that, if the government wanted to remain East of Suez, it was obliged to provide the Royal Navy with the means—in this case, the aircraft carrier. There was something totally incongruous, he observed, about a nation "performing a proud world role of peacekeeping on borrowed money, with the sound of gunfire drowned by the rattling of collection boxes." The implication was clear: Britain must concentrate its energies on Europe.[5]

Mayhew's resignation added fuel to the growing debate about the political premises underlying the government's East-of-Suez policy. Many questioned whether in the nationalistic, highly volatile political atmosphere of the Third World any European nation should or could assume responsibilities for the maintenance of peace in the 1970s. Support for autonomous local balances of power not dependent upon a Western presence might be more de-

[5] See Christopher Mayhew, *Britain's Role Tomorrow* (London, Hutchinson, 1967).

sirable and realistic. The successful termination of the conflict between Indonesia and Malaysia eroded the rationale behind one
major argument for retaining troops in the area. The left wing of
the Labour Party became increasingly restive with the Wilson government's posture in the Far East, in part because it appeared to
provide moral support to the American position in Vietnam.

Meanwhile, the Conservative Party, under the new leadership of
Edward Heath, hoisted once again the banner of Europe. The
party presented itself in the 1966 General Election as being firmly
committed to making a new effort to join the EEC; at this time the
Labour leadership was still divided on the issue. Whitehall's senior
civil servants, moreover, were urging Wilson to make a new application. Their studies revealed that the Commonwealth, however pres-
tigious, was not a sensible alternative to the EEC and had become
an economic and financial liability. The Foreign Office establishment favored a second application.[6] The assumption that British
influence in Washington would be increased by "sharing the burden"
in the Far East was dissipated as Wilson's advice was less and
less sought or appreciated in Johnson's White House and as British
efforts to bring the Vietnam conflict to the negotiating table came to
naught. America was increasingly concentrating on Asia rather
than Europe. Public opinion and attitudes in Britain were increasingly focused on Europe. Hostility within the Labour Party to the
Common Market declined, in part as a consequence of the Community's own enfeeblement because of its internal differences. The
old bogey of losing British sovereignty to European supranationality was turning out to be mythical. Technical studies revealed
that the disadvantages of entering the EEC in terms of agricultural
policy and Commonwealth trade were not as great as before. In
sum, the old obstacles to a renewed application were being succes-
sively eroded.

Thus within two months, in mid-1967, the Wilson government
announced the second application to join the Common Market and
also that military forces in Singapore and Malaysia would be cut

[6] Nora Beloff, "What Happened in Britain after the General Said No," in
From Commonwealth to Common Market, ed. Pierre Uri (London, Penguin
Books, 1968), pp. 51–88.

in half by 1971 and withdrawn completely by the mid-1970s. Unrelenting monetary pressures, however, forced an even more rapid withdrawal of forces. After the devaluation of sterling in November, 1967, the government decided in early 1968 to accelerate the timetable by giving up Britain's bases (except Hong Kong) and traditional role East of Suez at the end of 1971.

It is clear that Britain in its second turn toward Europe avoided one of the major mistakes of the first, and this augurs well for eventual success. Unlike the schizophrenic policy of the Macmillan government, Wilson's policy, whether by necessity or by choice, assured that Britain's defense policy synchronized with her foreign-policy objectives in Europe. The Labour government evidently came to understand that to many continental Europeans the concept of Britain's being a world power was incompatible with her being a European power. Accordingly, Britain could best continue her world role from inside rather than outside the community of European states.

The beginning of the 1970s will find British defense policy concentrated on Europe. This change will have come about because of conditions of economic stringency, retrenchment from most military commitments beyond Europe, and a political interest in playing a greater role on the Continent. The Defence White Papers of 1968 and 1969 clearly point in this direction, as have the initiatives of Britain within NATO.[7] Unlike most members of the alliance, Britain is increasing its contribution to European defense, with troops and resources that have been made available by withdrawal from East of Suez. London has indicated its willingness to assign to NATO an additional infantry battalion, subject to the definition of a proper role for it. New Marine forces and naval vessels are being assigned to the Mediterranean, signifying a strength-

[7] Probably somewhat prematurely, the 1969 Defence White Paper concluded: "The basic aim of our defence policy is now fully established. It is to ensure the security of Britain by concentrating our major effort on the western Alliance. This aim is sensible, stable and vital. It is sensible because it recognizes the basic realities of our economic and political interests in the world today. It is stable because the task is irreducible; we can withdraw from East of Suez but not from our situation in Europe, on which our national security depends." *Statement on the Defence Estimate: 1969*, Command 3927 (London, HMSO, 1969), p. 9.

ening of British interest in that area. An additional squadron of VTOL Harrier strike aircraft has recently been stationed in Germany, and at home 20,000 men of the Strategic Reserve have been designated for NATO service.

It is unlikely, however, that there will be a massive increase in British forces on the Continent, barring a major crisis. There are now 51,000 men in the British Army on the Rhine, with approximately another 1,000 in West Berlin. In order to have a large continental standing army, on the order of the French or German forces, Britain would have to reintroduce conscription, a step which would be politically unacceptable except under extremely threatening circumstances. Nor is it likely that such a foreign-exchange drain would be entered into since balance-of-payments considerations helped to force the retrenchment from East of Suez in the first place. Because of her tradition of voluntary service, the structure of her armed forces, and her insular position, Britain would find it extremely difficult to make a large manpower contribution to the defense of Europe. It would make more sense if the primary burden were assigned to her naval and air forces, including their nuclear mission.

It is likely that Britain's defense policy will be used in courting Europe. Leaving aside for the moment the important question of nuclear forces, Britain will use her defense resources and political acumen to increase the range of her associations with Europe and to claim a position of leadership. Britain is the only European power that has accepted military responsibility by land, air, and sea on all three permanent NATO fronts. Britain has fully supported the work of the Nuclear Planning Group and sees it as an important instrument for coordination and education in nuclear and strategic matters. Accordingly, Healey and West German Defense Minister Gerhard Schroeder undertook detailed studies within the NPG to work out a doctrine on tactical nuclear war. The British will also contribute to various multilateral weapons projects, such as that involving an advanced combat aircraft, to expand their ties with the Continent.

In addition, Britain appears ready to take the initiative in establishing a "European identity" within the Atlantic alliance. In the past, London has been reluctant to engage in any alliance consultation or activity from which the United States was excluded, because of its self-image as the link between America and Europe and, in part, out of fear of encouraging a reduction in the American commitment to NATO. But lately British statesmen have been suggesting that Europe must express a collective will to Washington if it wishes to have an impact on the American-Soviet dialogue. Accordingly, Healey has been pressing for a "European caucus" and for greater military cooperation among the European members of NATO. It is interesting to note that in pleading for such a caucus Healey has suggested that movement toward a reconciliation between Western Europe and Eastern Europe might be made easier to the extent that the former becomes less dependent upon the United States for its security.[8]

Of course, one can with justification look somewhat skeptically at the recent turn of British policy toward Europe. The new emphasis of defense policy toward Europe is, thus far, more declaratory than actual. Defence White Papers and House of Commons speeches are declarations of intention; relatively little has been accomplished that would increase the political or material nature of the European commitment. It is not too difficult to talk about a European concentration of British defense policy when plans call for a withdrawal of forces from almost everywhere else. Somewhat unfortunately, from the viewpoint of British policy, Denis Healey's campaign for a European caucus has become a bit too strongly identified as a British initiative. Although some of the principal defense ministers have been meeting for "Euro-dinners" after recent NATO meetings, real intra-European consultations have yet to begin and will be difficult to implement.

Moreover, as Wilson indicated, to the displeasure of many in Brussels, Britain has no intention at this point of working toward the creation of a federal Europe. Wilson has rejected suggestions that Britain's entry be used, as many Eurocrats would desire, to provide a stimulus toward supranationality. In so doing he may well be in tune with the prevailing mood in both Europe and Brit-

[8] In a speech on European defense in Munich, February 1, 1969, printed in *Survival*, April, 1969, pp. 110–19.

ain. Certainly this position does Britain's application no harm in Paris, where similar views are held. The Wilson government has also raised doubts among the better "Europeans" whether Britain is really interested in joining the EEC and whether she fully understands what joining the Community implies in terms of its future development. Thus far the Labour government has been able to declare itself for entry while secure in the knowledge that Britain's admission was blocked. Now that the door may be opening, Britain may have second thoughts; already there have been signs of wariness and hesitancy.

These doubts are reinforced by Britain's failure to take the harsh steps necessary to prepare herself for adherence to market regulations. British agricultural policy, her tax system and monetary policies, and other aspects of the economy would have to undergo important transformations. It can be argued that Britain is not a suitable candidate for entry into the Community in its present condition. On the other hand, when—if ever—Britain is given and seizes the opportunity to enter Europe, she is likely to reverse the tactics of 1961–1963. Rather than listing the conditions that must be met and getting bogged down in details, a British government is likely to want to settle quickly on the principle of entry, trusting that the details can be progressively worked out in complex negotiations thereafter.

The second British application to the Community remains on the negotiating table and appears on the verge of making some new progress. Prior to de Gaulle's departure, London attempted to outflank his veto by using the Western European Union as a back door to closer associations with the Continent. For a time it appeared as if Whitehall hoped to isolate de Gaulle, but this was never possible, since the Germans would not remain steadfast and were unwilling to break with France. With new governments not only in France but also in West Germany, the entire situation has acquired new flexibility. Although one should not expect an early or complete change of French policy, the Pompidou government seems to lack de Gaulle's doctrinaire opposition to British entry. Perhaps of still greater importance, the Socialist–Free Democrat government in Bonn appears to be willing to take the lead in supporting the British application. There has always been a special affinity between the Socialists in Germany and the Labourites in Britain, reinforced by close contacts between leading members of the parties when both were in the political wilderness. At the Common Market meeting in December, 1969, at The Hague, Willy Brandt took a much stronger line in dealing with France on this matter than had any previous West German chancellor.

British entry into Europe sometime in the next decade is more likely than not. What may the consequence be for Europe? Extrapolation from current European trends suggests that the net impact in political terms may be quite different from what had once been expected. When the European Economic Community was formed, it was considered by its founders and supporters to be primarily a political enterprise, even though the goal of eventual political union was subordinated to the more readily obtainable aim of economic integration. But the commitment to the European idea has so weakened in the past decade—and not only in France—that it is highly questionable whether supranationality is not unrealistic in the perspective of the present international system. If the assumption is correct that the European nations are indeed unwilling to move toward a European federation, Britain may find itself joining nothing more than a customs union.[9] Under such circumstances, although Britain's political influence on the Continent would be increased in absolute terms, she still would not necessarily have the opportunity to help mold a new Europe.

The Atlantic Alternative. For some in Britain the preferred alternative for the 1970s would be the continuation of a special relationship with the United States. It has always been difficult to assess the true nature and significance of the special relationship, but never more so than today. The most tangible element in the relationship since the Second World War has been cooperation in nuclear affairs. Although this cooperation will continue into the 1970s, the question of renewal of nuclear-collaboration arrange-

[9] A recent pessimistic appraisal of the chances for further political and economic integration in the EEC is to be found in Harold van B. Cleveland, "The Common Market after De Gaulle," *Foreign Affairs*, July, 1969, pp. 697–710.

ments will arise, with no certainty concerning the eventual outcome.

It is probably still true that American officials, military and civil, consult more intimately and on a wider range of issues with their British counterparts than with officials of any other nation except perhaps Canada. But the significance of the consultations has diminished steadily in the past twenty-five years as Britain has gradually retrenched from its global activities and interests. The central issues of war and peace have increasingly become dependent upon the growing Soviet-American dialogue, as was made clear during the Cuban missile crisis and the 1967 Arab-Israeli war; the British have found themselves virtually unable to be of particular assistance to Washington at such times.

The Vietnam war has brought a new awareness of what separates the United States from Britain. Added to the frustration of official London in being unable to use its diplomacy to bring greater flexibility to the political stalemate has been the widespread public bewilderment about America's aims and intentions in the war. The British, it should be noted, have consistently differed with the United States since the Korean War on the nature of the Chinese Communist threat in Asia. In the ABM controversy the British made no contribution to American policy or to the public debate, even though it is precisely in the strategic field that Britain can still claim a special insight.

Consequently, those who support a strengthened American association in the 1970s as an alternative to Europe have been thinking primarily of economic relations. A proposal for a North Atlantic Free Trade Area—or NAFTA—has received considerable attention in recent years. NAFTA would initially include Britain, Canada, and the United States, but Australia and New Zealand would be expected to join at an early stage. In time, it is thought, NAFTA (under a changed name, presumably) would provide free trade in industrial products within a grouping that would also embrace the EFTA nations and possibly Japan.[10]

[10] For two complete and favorably inclined expositions of NAFTA, see Maxwell Stamp Associates, *The Free Trade Area Option: Opportunity for Britain* (London, Atlantic Trade Study, Moor House, 1967); and Thomas M. Franck and Edward Wiesband, *A Free Trade Association* (New York, New York Uni-

Some of those who have been drawn to NAFTA have been moved by distaste for or discouragement with the possibility of entry into Europe. But some of Britain's best economists have found the arguments in favor of NAFTA impressive, preferring it to the EEC on purely economic grounds.[11] In the EEC Britain would have to accommodate herself to the Common Market's agricultural policy, an adjustment that would be extremely costly to her balance of payments. NAFTA, on the other hand, would include at least two suppliers of inexpensive food, Canada and the United States, and would not disrupt the traditional Commonwealth supply of food. Moreover, NAFTA would be similar to the EEC in that it would provide a larger market for British industrial goods, but it would do so without binding the nation to various federalist commitments in Europe. Many professional observers agree that, if viewed solely on the basis of economics, the alternative of NAFTA has much merit.[12]

It seems doubtful, however, that NAFTA will ever go much beyond the stage of a proposal. There is not much to suggest that it would be a salable proposition in the United States. The acceptance of NAFTA would be harmful to America's relations on the Continent, since the association would look like an English-speaking club, affirming European suspicions of an Anglo-Saxon alliance. Moreover, protectionists in Congress are not likely to permit adhesion to a free-trade association, especially one that might eventually include Japan. Also, from the American point of view there remains much to be said for the advantages of Britain in Europe, bringing the benefits of her political stability and maturity to the Continent.

For the British, NAFTA would create grave risks. American wealth and technological development are so great that they might submerge Britain, making her an American economic dependency.

versity Press, 1968). See also Harry G. Johnson, ed., *New Trade Strategy for the World Economy* (London, George Allen and Unwin, 1969).

[11] Among those economists are Sir Roy Harrod at Oxford and Professor J. E. Meade at Cambridge. See Arthur Schlesinger, Jr., "Britain's Atlantic Option," *Interplay*, January, 1969, pp. 33–36.

[12] David Robertson, "EFTA and the NAFTA: An Economic Appraisal," *The World Today*, April, 1969.

Britain might be able to withstand, and perhaps even need, the cold shower of competition from the Continent, but she could well drown in an ensuing American downpour. The net result of competition with the United States might be to discourage the growth of an independent British technology. Thus Britain might end up as a very subordinate economic and political partner to the United States.

But the principal consideration that should be borne in mind is the future condition of European and European-American relations. NAFTA runs the danger of cutting Britain off from Europe and dividing the West into two economic and therefore political blocs. If Britain's principal military and political concerns are to be increasingly centered on Europe in the 1970s and beyond, it would be working at cross-purposes to create new bonds outside Europe. Of course, this consideration is dependent upon the expectation of an eventual break in the stalemate on Britain's entry into Europe. Thus NAFTA should not be dismissed for all time. If Britain is to remain outside Europe, an Atlantic alternative may still be preferable to "splendid isolation."

The Commonwealth: A Dubious Alternative. There are some who are still attracted to the vision of the Commonwealth as an alternative grouping to the EEC or an Atlantic association. The Commonwealth, consisting of twenty-nine nations, remains statistically impressive in terms of manpower and resources. Its 755 million people form one-quarter of the world's population, and its 14 million square miles of territory one-quarter of the globe's land surface.[13] A network of loyalties, interests, and traditions continues to connect the Commonwealth members with Britain. The leadership of such a large and far-flung group of nations would certainly give Britain a significant and worthy world role.

It is unlikely, however, that the Commonwealth will even offer Britain a real alternative role. The idea was widely held after the Second World War that by means of the Commonwealth Britain could continue to play a superpower role after the dissolution of

[13] David P. Calleo, *Britain's Future* (London, Hodder and Stoughton, 1968), p. 152.

the colonial empire; the idea has not proved tenable. The basic reason is that the Commonwealth consists of far too heterogeneous an assemblage of nations, with members of unequal power and conflicting interests spread out from North America to Africa and the Far East. Britain in the 1970s will not be powerful enough militarily to protect the Commonwealth nor rich enough to service its economic needs.

Indeed, it has been apparent for some time that it is quite unrealistic to think in terms of Commonwealth unity in politics, economics, or defense, and the trends appear to point toward even greater separation and diversity. The voting pattern at the United Nations suggests that Commonwealth members vote against each other no less often than they vote against nations outside the Commonwealth and that there is little group loyalty. The African members of the Commonwealth have been unable to reach agreement with other members on the proper course of action to end white minority rule in Rhodesia and, even if such an agreement were reached, one can doubt that the Commonwealth would have the means for successful implementation. The multiracial Commonwealth has been marred by racial turmoil, not only in the most obvious places but in Africa against Asians and also in Britain.

Intra-Commonwealth trade as a percentage of world trade has been steadily declining. The former Commonwealth trade pattern has been disrupted, as countries such as Australia and New Zealand sell more to Asian countries and the African Commonwealth members sell more to the EEC states. Consequently, the Commonwealth preference system has become less important and valuable, and the proportion of British exports going to the Commonwealth has dropped. In 1948 over 50 percent of British exports went to Commonwealth and colonial countries, and only 13 percent to Europe. By 1966–1968, exports going to the Commonwealth had fallen to 29 percent and those to Europe had risen to 20 percent.[14]

Britain has been, until recently, in an unusually good position to establish her military presence in Commonwealth nations. But presence does not necessarily offer security, and the principal

[14] John P. Mackintosh, "Britain in Europe," *International Affairs*, April, 1969, p. 251.

Commonwealth members have looked elsewhere for assistance in assuring security. Thus Australia and New Zealand have turned to the United States, India to the Soviet Union and the United States, Pakistan to China, and the black African nations to the United Nations or to regional cooperation. The decision to withdraw from East of Suez has been reluctantly accepted by Singapore, which now hopes to convert its large British base to a naval facility open to all nations.

Britain's current intention for the area East of Suez would not seem to offer much support for a significant Commonwealth defense role, and there is little reason to believe that Britain will ever again have as sizable military forces abroad as in the past. It would be a mistake to assume, however, that Britain will be totally out of Asia in the 1970s. The base at Hong Kong will be retained, and there are no plans to reduce the force of 10,000 men stationed there. The leader of the Opposition, Mr. Heath, has been saying for some time that if the Conservatives return to office by 1971 they will cancel the Labour government's plans to withdraw forces by the end of that year. Although the forces Heath plans to retain in Asia may not be large, they will be located in the Persian Gulf as well as in Malaysia and Singapore. Finally, Britain will continue to play an active role in Southeast Asia through defense cooperation with Australia, New Zealand, Singapore, and Malaysia. Even if British forces are totally withdrawn from their present postings, they will be returned for joint exercises, as will British aircraft and naval vessels. However, although the links with the Commonwealth will remain, they are not likely to be sufficiently strong or broadly based to offer a real alternative in Britain's search for a future connection.

"Muddling Through" Alone. Might Britain simply muddle through by herself in the 1970s, not entering the Common Market or joining a new Atlantic grouping or having a new mission at the center of a reinvigorated Commonwealth? Certainly this is a real possibility.

Joining the EEC may require economic adjustments so costly as to make entry not worthwhile for Britain. Or after a long period of

difficult negotiations the Continental nations may come to the conclusion that Britain is not a suitable partner and that they do not
wish to expand the Common Market. NAFTA and the Commonwealth may never be genuine solutions to the search for a new
role. In such circumstances Britain may wish to come to as complete an understanding as possible with France and the other EEC
members while reaffirming her greater loyalty to the Atlantic alliance. There is no a priori reason why Britain cannot continue to
straddle Churchill's three circles of Europe, the United States, and
the Commonwealth, if necessary.

It is important to remember that there is a formidable economic
case against joining the Common Market and that those who are
opposed to entry or who have voiced strong reservations on economic grounds include a number of eminent British economists.
Moreover, since the departure of de Gaulle, many who previously
supported entry into the Common Market have been forced to
think a second time and have lost some of their earlier enthusiasm.
Indeed, there has been a discernible rise in anti–Common Market
sentiment, with opinion polls showing public support for British
entry declining from the previous high. Now that the former
French veto has been at least partially lifted (or so one can assume, given Pompidou's statements disclaiming any doctrinaire opposition to British admission), the British are being made to face
more concretely the problems that would accompany entry into the
EEC.

The principal fear is that the cost of joining the Common Market
would be so adverse to the balance of payments that it would have
a disastrous effect on the economy and that, even after a period of
adjustment, the consequences of the damage done to the economy
would not make the long-term gains equal to the large short-term
losses. The main problems are agriculture and the almost totally
different food policies of Britain and the EEC nations. In Britain
the government gives direct subsidies to the farmers, who constitute only 5 percent of the working population. Half of the food
supply comes from abroad and enters duty-free; the agricultural
sector is relatively prosperous, and food prices are quite low. The

Common Market countries, on the other hand, have relatively more farmers and amass food surpluses. Food prices are maintained at a high level through a Common Market tariff designed to protect the European farmer by assuring him a reasonable profit. If Britain were to join the EEC under its current regulations, she would have to conform to the Continental system by raising her food prices and possibly by paying a disproportionate amount of the Common Market's joint agricultural fund. Recent unofficial British estimates indicate that the cost in agricultural subsidies for joining the EEC might amount to £400–500 million per year, much of it payable in foreign exchange.

Although there would be important economic benefits from entry into the EEC, these benefits may not compensate for the costs which some foresee and which they fear will be so great as to prevent the long-term advantages from coming into play. Therefore, there is room for the argument that the price of entry may be too high and that Britain should go it alone. Those taking this view tend to feel that Britain can rectify her own economic problems by more astute management of the national economy. Some believe that Britain should delay seeking entry until after the economy has been modernized and financial equilibrium has been restored, so that she can negotiate from strength.

Ultimately the balance of pros and cons as to Britain's choice will be decided by broad political considerations; so will the question whether Britain will be permitted to join the European Community. But whether by necessity or choice, Britain may find that she will remain alone in the 1970s. In such an eventuality, she will still be faced with the need to choose among alternatives. Britain could stake out an audacious new role as an Atlantic Japan, a European offshore island making its own way in the West much as Japan does in Asia. On the other hand, Britain could turn inward and go the way of Sweden. Although this might be economically attractive, it would not be in keeping with Britain's political character or traditions. Still another alternative would be for Britain to remain the suppliant applicant, waiting at the doors of Europe until the 1980s.

II

Section I has shown that the pattern of Britain's association with Europe in the coming decade cannot be predicted with much certainty. From the perspective of assuring European security, the model that Britain chooses or accepts will be an important factor in the evolution of the defense arrangements in the Europe of the 1970s. Whether Britain is to be in or to remain out, her influence will be felt on the Continent in a number of ways. Among the ways in which Britain will contribute to European security, three are now to be examined: the strategic nuclear contribution to European security, the range of technological association with the European nations, and the British contribution in ideas and diplomacy toward the possible construction of a new system of European security. It is of course obvious that the nature and form of these contributions will depend highly upon the broader role that Britain adopts for her primary political relationships, so that any discussion must retain a somewhat tenuous quality.

The Strategic Nuclear Contribution to European Security. Britain will be a military nuclear power in the 1970s and quite possibly for some time beyond. This fact needs to be underlined because of the lingering hopes, to be found mainly among some observers in Washington and on the British Left, that Britain will voluntarily cease to be a military nuclear power.[15] After an extensive ten-year debate on Britain's independent possession of nuclear weapons, it is clear in retrospect that the watershed was reached with the Labour government's failure to cancel the agreement with the United States to buy Polaris missiles. The result is that Britain will enter the 1970s with a small, Polaris-equipped submarine fleet capable of inflicting not insignificant damage—damage greater than, for example, that which the Chinese are likely to become capable of in the next five years.

[15] See, for example, the admonitions of George Ball, *The Discipline of Power* (Boston, Little, Brown, 1968), pp. 217–19.

Whatever may have been the merits of past arguments for getting out of the military nuclear business, Britain will not through an act of self-abnegation leave France as the only nuclear power in Europe. On the contrary, the development of the *force de dissuasion* has been watched in London with great interest and considerable envy. After an initial period of skepticism concerning the ability of France to marshal its resources to build on its own a nuclear force (with some unofficial delight whenever financial or technical difficulties or delays were reported in the program), the British will now have to face a new fact: although the French may not achieve their very ambitious goals, and their timetable may incur considerable slippage, they nevertheless will have an independently constructed strategic nuclear force equipped with sea- and land-based IRBMs, and perhaps in time ICBMs. The British have not been developing strategic missiles since the cancellation of the liquid-fueled Blue Streak in 1960, having decided then to purchase Skybolt for their bombers and later to buy Polaris missiles. In the coming decade, therefore, French missiles will carry the *tricolore*, and Britain's, the stars and stripes. For reasons of national pride as well as technological advancement and political aims, pressures will grow for more British activity in the technology of strategic missilery.

Another reason that Britain is not likely to give up nuclear weapons is that there has been a change in attitude toward the problem of nuclear proliferation. The once widespread argument that Britain, by voluntarily renouncing her nuclear arms, could strongly influence other countries to desist from acquiring them has lost much of its strength. Today the nuclear proliferation treaty is the center of the antiproliferation strategy, and the countries to be influenced are less those of Western Europe than those of Asia and the Middle East. These states, being primarily concerned with regional security and prestige, are not going to be much influenced by an exemplary action by Britain.

Finally, and of great importance, it is likely that Britain's nuclear capability will play some role, perhaps a big one, in the evolution of her future relationship with Europe. Anglo-French nuclear collaboration or some type of European nuclear arrangement is a plausible candidate for the European agenda in the next decade, as will be discussed. It is difficult to see how collaboration with Britain on nuclear matters could proceed very far without considerable simultaneous progress toward British entry into the EEC. Conversely, nuclear collaboration with France may well be part of the admission price that Britain will have to pay for entry into the Common Market. Neither Westminster politicians nor Whitehall planners are likely to forget that in their nuclear force they have an important bargaining asset and instrument of diplomacy.

The British Polaris flotilla of four submarines will be fully operational by 1970, when the last of the submarines is scheduled to undergo final trials and the test-firing of its Polaris missiles off Cape Kennedy. These submarines are equipped with sixteen A-3 Polaris missiles, each with a range of more than 2,500 nautical miles. It is planned that the missiles will be capped with multiple reentry vehicles (MRVs), which, unlike the American MIRVs, will *not* be independently targeted. Because of the extensive refitting required after each 60-day patrol, only one submarine is certain to be on station at all times, although normally there should be two. A fifth Polaris submarine that had once been scheduled was canceled for reasons of economy but, as total strategic nuclear expenditures are reduced, the Royal Navy may renew its pressure. It would not be surprising if the total British flotilla consisted of five submarines by the mid-1970s.[16] In addition to the submarines, a limited number of Vulcan bombers of the Royal Air Force—the last of Bomber Command's once great fleet of 180 V-bombers—still have a strategic mission, but they are expected to be transferred to a tactical one quite soon.[17]

In the 1970s British policy-makers will face some crucial decisions concerning the long-term future of the British deterrent. As with all strategic weapons systems, the Polaris force will even-

[16] The British submarines contain many American components in addition to the Polaris missiles. These include the nuclear fuel, high-stress steel for the structure, the navigation system, the fire-control system, and some of the communications equipment.

[17] In addition, a range of nuclear weapons is available for tactical use by the British military service.

tually wear out or become obsolete. The submarines will become subject to detection, or effective defenses will be built against their missiles (this is already on the way with the deployment of Soviet ABMs). Because of the long lead time necessary to develop strategic delivery systems (often seven to ten years), planning should already be under way for the next generation of the nuclear force and important decisions will undoubtedly have to be made in the early 1970s if Britain is to be assured of maintaining a relatively viable nuclear force.

In reaching their decisions, the policy-makers will have to grapple with some fundamental questions. Does Britain wish to remain dependent upon the United States for its strategic delivery systems? If not, should Britain seek self-sufficiency by embarking on a strategic missile program of its own? Or should Britain attempt to develop a collaborative arrangement with another nation or group of nations for the joint development and production of nuclear weapons? Should Britain seek a collaborative arrangement with France, or with other European nations, or with the United States? Will the United States agree to continue some sort of special nuclear relationship with the United Kingdom if this is Britain's choice? If Britain is to continue to seek to enter Europe, should the primary consideration in deciding on the future of the nuclear force be her attempt to become a good European? Therefore, should London take the intiative in proposing a European nuclear force or, at a more modest level, Anglo-French nuclear collaboration? Would London be willing to incur the displeasure of Washington, if this seemed necessary in order to forge nuclear links on the Continent? Finally, what type of deterrence should Britain, or Europe-cum-Britain, seek to achieve in the coming strategic environment with its emphasis on defense (ABM) as well as offense? Such questions are not open to simple answers.

A number of broad considerations will form the parameters of British thinking on the strategic force and its contribution to European security. These will include the nature of East-West relations and the prospects for reconciliation, the Soviet military threat to Western Europe and an appraisal of Soviet intentions, other potential nuclear threats to Western Europe, the steadfastness of the

American commitment to the defense of Western Europe and the credibility of the American nuclear guarantee, and the possible risks for Western Europe in a bilateral Soviet-American arrangement on nuclear matters. In addition, however, British planning will be strongly affected by three sets of issues that will present questions of operational significance.

The first will be the future of the special relationship on nuclear matters between the United States and Britain, a relationship which began during the Second World War with the Manhattan Project and which, despite many ups and downs, continues to this day. During a period stretching over a quarter of a century and covering the entire nuclear age, both nations have benefited from this association, although in recent years Britain has undoubtedly gained more than the United States. In 1958 the United States atomic energy legislation was amended so as to give the British a privileged access to American nuclear technology. The amendments permit exchange of information about the design and production of nuclear warheads and transfer of fissionable materials between the United States and nations that have already made substantial progress in the development of atomic weapons. Under these amendments Britain was given assistance on Blue Streak, was promised Skybolt if it was produced, was sold the Polaris missiles, and was given information in a number of areas, including warhead design. Although France in recent years could undoubtedly qualify under the terms of the legislation, it has not been American policy to assist the growth of the *force de dissuasion,* so that the British have in fact been treated *sui generis.*

In the middle 1970s the Anglo-American nuclear-exchange agreement, signed after the 1958 amendments were adopted, will become subject to termination.[18] Assuming that Britain will seek its extension, the question will then arise whether the exchange agreement should be renewed in a relatively routine manner or

[18] The agreement consists of two separate accords. The first provides for the exchange of nuclear information and, after an initial ten-year period, was automatically extended to 1974 when no notice of intention to terminate was given by December, 1968. The second accord provides for the exchange of nuclear materials and expires at the end of 1969 unless renewed. The *Times* (London), February 21, 1969.

whether a decision on renewal should only be undertaken in the context of a careful study of its broader implications. In case of the latter, the United States will want to take into consideration its policies on nuclear sharing, on nonproliferation, and on European unity. To renew Britain's privileged access to nuclear information and fissionable materials without extending it to France would be to continue the discriminatory treatment that has undoubtedly been an irritant in Franco-American relations. Now that both France and Britain are operational nuclear powers, and given the American desire to have friendly associations on all sides of this extremely important triangular relationship, there are good reasons for having Washington give both nations roughly equal treatment.

As to nonproliferation, it is of course true that Britain became a nuclear power very early in the nuclear age, before the proliferation phenomenon was widely recognized as a potentially destabilizing factor in international relations, and that she did so independently of American assistance. Moreover, a refusal to renew the 1958 agreements would not force Britain out of the nuclear club, since she has sufficient knowledge and resources to manage on her own. Nevertheless, nonnuclear nations may look at an extension of the Anglo-American accords as affirming the importance of nuclear weapons. Washington will therefore have to balance its historically close ties with Britain and the value of the British nuclear force in Western defense against its interest in diminishing the psychological value of nuclear weapons to would-be nuclear powers and its desire to discourage the creation of additional nuclear forces.

A further consideration arises out of the United States' interest in European unity and its encouragement of Britain's inclusion in the European Economic Community. If Britain is to be accepted by the Continental countries as a European state, she will have to strengthen her European identity by loosening her ties with the United States. In the past, the special nuclear arrangements have been a cause of uneasiness in Western Europe, particularly in France. De Gaulle's failure in his 1958 bid for equal treatment through a three-power directorate and Britain's choice, at the Nassau Conference, of the United States as her future nuclear partner undoubtedly contributed to keeping Britain out of the Common

Market. Moreover, and of perhaps still greater significance, the availability of a special political and military relationship with the United States in the past two decades has induced the British to look first across the Atlantic rather than across the Channel and consequently discouraged British participation in European affairs. Thus American policy-makers will want to weigh the risks of any action that may strengthen the opposition on the Continent to Britain's adhesion to Europe or may deflect her own attention from what is thought to be her European calling.

On the other hand, Americans should bear in mind that Britain's nuclear capability is one of her most valuable assets in her search for a European role. If American policy-makers wish to see Britain in Europe, they should take care not to weaken one of her strongest bargaining chips just when it is needed. Nuclear issues may quite possibly become part of the discussions concerning a package arrangement that would lift the French veto and allow Britain to enter the EEC. In such circumstances Washington may be faced with a request from Whitehall to permit nuclear collaboration with France, either on a solely bilateral basis or as the formative step in a European nuclear force. Because of the past pattern of nuclear exchange, Britain is under a moral and probably a legal obligation to receive Washington's concurrence before it collaborates with another country in a manner that would involve passing on any information derived from the United States. (It would probably be impossible for the British to disentangle what they learned on their own from the information and advice they received from the United States.) However, time has been gradually diminishing the number and value of American secrets in Britain's possession, and even if the United States should retain a negative attitude on British-French collaboration, London may be tempted to proceed with it. In sum, the question of future Anglo-American nuclear collaboration may raise complex issues for Washington policy-makers, issues which could inject the United States into considerations involving a European nuclear force and the entire future of the European-American defense relationship.

A second set of issues for Whitehall planners will arise from the deployment of ballistic missile defenses by the two superpowers.

The changes in the strategic environment which will occur through ABM deployment and the rise in the plateau of offensive forces which would be the result of mutual MIRV deployment raise major questions concerning the future of smaller nuclear forces. These matters are too complex to be examined more than briefly here and must await separate discussion. For example, it is impossible to deal here with the fundamental question of the effect of ballistic missile defense upon the credibility of the American nuclear guarantee to Western Europe or with the desirability and feasibility of a European ABM system.

For Britain, as for France, the new strategic systems serve as a stark reminder of the technological dominance of the superpowers. If the credibility of the British and French nuclear forces is to be preserved, there must be some assurance of their ability to penetrate Soviet defenses. The currently limited Soviet ABM deployment in combination with air defense is unlikely to be totally effective against the British and French forces, but a thicker Soviet ABM defense would pose real penetration difficulties. A growing Soviet defensive capability will therefore present earlier and far greater obstacles to European nuclear forces than to American forces.

This situation points to the possible need for Britain to acquire new missiles with greater penetration capabilities.[19] The Polaris submarines will be fitted with British-made MRV warheads as well as new penetration aids. But the British have decided that it would be too costly to follow the American example of converting the submarines from Polaris to Poseidon missiles, which would make possible the use of MIRV warheads. This decision conveniently permitted both governments to sidestep the question of whether the United States would be willing to sell Poseidon, should Britain

---

[19] Laurence Martin has pointed out, in his *Ballistic Missile Defense and the Alliance* (Paris, Atlantic Institute, 1969), p. 38, that an alternative to more and improved strategic missiles would be for the Europeans to concentrate their efforts on getting through Soviet air defenses rather than on overcoming Soviet ABMs. This would involve emphasizing the acquisition of aircraft, cruise missiles, and shorter-range ballistic missiles. The Europeans would thus be exploiting their greater geographical proximity to the Soviet Union, and they would also reap the collateral benefit of adding to their stockpile for local European defense.

want it. (Wilson, it is interesting to note, used the occasion of the announcement that Britain would not purchase Poseidon to imply that she was thus breaking the chain of technological dependency upon the United States and moving closer to Europe.)

Contrary to the assumptions of some analysts, the deployment of missile defenses by the Soviet Union and the United States would not spell the end of smaller, independent nuclear forces. In neither the British nor the French case was their creation or continuation ever totally dependent upon the calculus of nuclear deterrence. Numerous other incentives—political and psychological—and other interests—military, scientific, and bureaucratic—have always been at play and will continue to influence the domestic debate in both countries on the utility of their nuclear forces. Moreover, superpower ABM deployment would only marginally affect the political or strategic use of the nuclear forces outside the Soviet-American context, such as in dealings with China or in the Middle East.

Nevertheless, a new strategic environment that includes ballistic missile defenses will create added requirements for the existing European nuclear forces. In addition, the strategic and political rationale for the forces will be altered, and the perceived need for such forces may be strengthened. It is far too early to estimate what, if anything, will result from the Soviet-American discussions on the limitation of strategic forces. But is it not unlikely that the Western Europeans will feel, even if their governments are consulted at every stage, that American interests will coincide less with their own interest in the future than in the past and that they must therefore acquire a greater measure of strategic independence. Such perceptions may be strengthened by fear that an America partially secure behind its missile defenses but still somewhat vulnerable, and in tacit agreement with the Soviet Union on a rough parity in their mutual strategic postures, may be less than resolute in coming to the assistance of Western Europe. In such circumstances the Europeans may be driven to collaboration with each other on their future strategic forces. The combination of the need for larger, more complex, and more costly offensive (and probably defensive) forces in an ABM world, plus the strategic and political anxieties which superpower ABMs could foster, may well create the conditions for an entirely new European nuclear defense arrangement.

The third set of issues, it then follows, will be those pertaining to British policies and attitudes toward nuclear collaboration with France and toward the creation of a European nuclear force. As was suggested earlier, a nuclear marriage between London and Paris may provide the key to Britain's entry into Europe. As far back as Macmillan's meetings with de Gaulle in 1962, Anglo-French nuclear collaboration has been an unofficial side issue in discussions on Britain's application. Recent events in France may have increased French desires for nuclear collaboration with Britain. Pompidou is under less personal compulsion than his predecessor to maintain unbridled French independence and under greater public pressure to strengthen the economy by reducing the budget, including military expenditures. Since nuclear collaboration could provide considerable budgetary savings, its prospect must appear attractive. Taken together with other reasons for a change in French policy, nuclear sharing might reduce French resistance to Britain's entry. In any case, it is difficult to conceive of a real *entente nucléaire* between Paris and London while Britain continues to remain outside the Common Market.

By fortunate coincidence, the British and French nuclear programs have complementary strengths and weaknesses, so that each could benefit from the other's more advanced technology. Britain has considerably more knowledge of sophisticated warhead design and the production of thermonuclear weapons. She is also working on a new gas centrifuge technique for producing enriched uranium. France, on the other hand, has moved ahead of the United Kingdom in the field of solid-fuel missile propulsion, as Britain has had no strategic missile program of its own since the cancellation of Blue Streak in 1960. On the whole, Britain is still considerably ahead of France across the spectrum of nuclear-weapon technology. This is not surprising, given the far earlier start on nuclear weapons in Britain and the large amount of assistance received from the United States. The French program, however, is currently better balanced than the British one and has made impressive progress in a relatively short period of time. Altogether, it would appear that in terms of scientific and technological assistance France could gain more than Britain from an agreement leading to exchanges in information and materials. However, as noted, because of past agreements with the United States, there may be limits to the level of assistance Britain can render to France.

Thus far the Labour government has shown openly only a limited interest in nuclear collaboration with France and has been decisively opposed to any form of a European nuclear deterrent. The Conservatives, on the other hand, have been far more interested in a deal with France and in taking measures that would make the European members of the Atlantic alliance less dependent upon the United States for their security. Edward Heath has been on record since early 1967 as favoring a merger of the British and French nuclear forces and has suggested that they should be held "in trust" for the rest of Western Europe. Although Heath himself is not a member, the Tories have in recent years had a "Gaullist" wing that favored doing business with the General and developing a less American-oriented foreign and defense policy. Wilson has fairly consistently opposed any new European strategic arrangement that he believed might reduce America's interest in or commitment to European defense or that might force Britain to choose between existing NATO arrangements and a European scheme. He thus rejected a "European clause" for the Multilateral Force and the Atlantic Nuclear Force, arguing additionally that it would imperil East-West détente, since the Soviet Union was so strongly opposed. The Labour leader has also had to mollify those in the left wing of his party who feared any German participation in a nuclear plan. But with the winds of change blowing in Europe, Wilson could easily modify his policy toward a European nuclear role, particularly if it strongly increased the chances of success of his broader European gambit.

Of course, an Anglo-French nuclear accord would not necessarily lead directly to a European nuclear force. One can imagine many in-between stages, as one can imagine a bilateral cooperative arrangement that would lead to little else. The entire concept of a European deterrent is fraught with complexities and difficulties; it cannot be examined here. Still, it will lurk in the background of Britain's European policy in the 1970s. If Britain wants to help shape the new Europe, she will want to take a greater role in its defense, and her natural role will be nuclear. Should the strategic conditions and the political will permitting a European deterrent emerge, Britain would have to be admitted as a full participant into Europe. One cannot envisage a European nuclear force without her inclusion, nor can one imagine such a force without a considerable degree of political integration. For the United States, which may have to choose between aiding a European deterrent or not, the preferred alternative may be to provide nuclear assistance if it wishes to maintain its influence in the future affairs of Europe.

Britain's Technological Contribution to Europe. Advanced technology offers one of the most important contributions that Britain can make to Europe and also one of the greatest opportunities that Europe can offer to Britain. The United Kingdom is the strongest technological power in Western Europe; she would thus bring an impressive scientific and technological dowry to the European Economic Community. At the same time, British technology is increasingly handicapped by the limitations of its available markets. Advanced technology requires large-scale markets and resources. An excellent recent study concludes that "Britain is a supreme illustration of the limitations, in the most advanced defense technology, which scale imposes on the European nation-state. It still has the greatest technological potential in Europe in advanced defense industries. But its small size has made it quite unable to bring that potential to fruition." [20] Joining Europe would make it far easier for Britain to realize her full technological potential.

Britain has the largest research and development base in Western Europe and continues to spend more money on research and development than does any Continental power. In such fields as computers, electronics, nuclear energy, and air transport, Britain retains the lead in Europe. The British aerospace industry is more than double the size of France's (though not twice as productive).

[20] Christopher Layton, *European Advanced Technology* (London, George Allen and Unwin, 1969), p. 54.

Britain is especially strong in defense technology, and much of the reason for her general capabilities in advanced technology is attributable to comparatively large defense expenditures for a nation of her size. Britain only gradually adjusted to her reduced role in the world, and her previous expectations were reflected in large defense budgets. For most of the period from World War II until the early 1960s, Britain attempted to remain on the frontier of defense technology and aimed to possess an independent, self-sufficient weapons industry that could produce almost the same range of weapons as the superpowers produced, although in far smaller quantities.[21]

The Labour government has not overlooked the fact that the strength of British technology is a trump card in its bid for entry into the European Community. Wilson proposed in 1967 a technological community of the EEC plus Britain and called for the creation of a European Technological Institute. Though progress on these proposals has been blocked, Britain has shown her interest in technological cooperation with the Continent by her involvement in a number of bilateral or multilateral projects.[22] London is not unaware that technological cooperation with the Continent leads to a greater influence on European decisions. Moreover, the prospect of additional technological cooperation after Britain's entry into the EEC cannot fail to be attractive to the many Europeans concerned about the growing "gap" between Europe and the United States. The computer industry is but one field in which Britain's potential contribution appeals to continental Europe. American companies control 90 percent of the non-Communist world's computer market. Many Europeans believe that the only means of fighting American domination in computers is through full cooperation with Britain.

Indeed, the notion that Europe must unite its technological resources if it is to meet the American challenge and avoid becoming

---

[21] See C. J. E. Harlow, *The European Armaments Base: A Survey*, part 2, no. two of *Defence, Technology and the Western Alliance*, Alastair Buchan, ed. (London, Institute for Strategic Studies, 1967).

[22] These include, among others, projects on multiple-role combat aircraft, helicopters, the Concorde, computers, nuclear reactors, space, and the Folkstone-to-Calais "chunnel."

still more inferior to the superpowers in industrial and technological terms is hardly a novel one today. To this, Victor Basiuk has added the useful insight that Britain, France, and Germany—the three principal technological powers of Western Europe—are complementary in their strengths and weaknesses. If in the 1970s Britain should join the Common Market, the resulting catalytic effect could result in a major takeoff in scientific and technological progress.[23] This would not, however, occur automatically after British entry into the EEC but would depend on further economic and political integration.

Joining the EEC would help British industries, particularly the defense-related industries, to find a market sufficiently large to sustain them. It would also help generate the capital needed for large research and development projects. As mentioned previously, these are serious problems, and they apply in one form or another to all medium-sized powers that are active in advanced technologies.

The British aircraft industry is a case in point. By most standards it should be the right industry for Britain, a proper area of industrial specialization in the international marketplace. It has a sixty-year tradition of leadership in aeronautics and scientific inventiveness and until very recently retained a highly skilled labor force and excellent airframe-design teams. For the past decade, however, the British aircraft industry has been unable to compete in foreign markets with the American industry, the latter's lower prices having been made possible in part by its far larger domestic market. For the American industry, foreign orders are a welcome bonus, but for the British they are essential to survival. The Plowden Committee, appointed by the British government to examine the condition of the aircraft industry, concluded in 1966 that there was no long-range future for an independent, self-supporting British aircraft industry. Since it thought real collaboration with the American aircraft industry to be unlikely, the Plowden Committee recommended far greater collaboration with Europe, and France in particular.[24] Thus the logic of modern large-scale technology, of

[23] Victor Basiuk, "Future Technology and Western European Security," in this volume.

[24] *Report of the Committee of Inquiry into the Aircraft Industry,* Command 2853 (London: HMSO, 1965).

which defense is an important sector, is inexorably nudging Britain toward Europe.

Inevitably this leads to the idea of a common European arms-procurement program, a concept that has received some attention in Britain. And beyond this, there is the more far-reaching proposition of a European Defense Community, responsible not only for logistics and procurement, but for strategic planning and crisis management as well. Little progress can be expected along these lines, however, until the impasse of Britain's entry into Europe is broken.

Perspectives on European Security. Little has been said thus far about British perspectives on European security, in part because there has not been a distinctly British position on the issue. There has been no British equivalent of West Germany's *Ostpolitik* or France's vision of a Europe "from the Atlantic to the Urals." Rather than being primarily concerned about a European settlement, British thinking has concentrated on a global accommodation between East and West, on summit diplomacy among the major powers, and on arms control and disarmament.

British conceptual thought about European security problems has taken place in an Atlantic rather than a European framework. London's loyalties have been to the United States, whose junior partner she wished to remain, and to NATO. Because of the attractions of her world role and the pull of her commitments beyond Europe, she was never certain as to what her proper role within Europe should be. Accordingly, the British have been somewhat vague in their own thoughts on European security and have tended to adopt prevalent American attitudes. In sum, the British have lacked a clear vision of their own concerning a European political settlement or a new security system.

This is not to suggest that British diplomacy has been inactive. On the contrary, the British have sought to play the diplomatic role of a great power, and on a worldwide scale. First, the British have almost relentlessly sought East-West negotiations "at the top," that is, to bring together the Soviet, American, British, and French foreign ministers or heads of state. Macmillan was especially interested in this, but all the prime ministers have known that a "step toward peace" was good politics at home. The British have also acted as though they were more convinced than most Westerners that political settlement could be reached with the Soviets if the issues were calmly discussed among reasonable men. A recent survey of European attitudes found that "more than any of their Western allies, the British of both major parties think it is important to keep up negotiations with the East."[25]

Second, the British have consistently advocated various arms control measures and played an active role in the negotiations leading to the test ban and nonproliferation treaties. Perhaps some of the most imaginative Western proposals for disengagement in Central Europe came from Hugh Gaitskell and Anthony Eden in the 1950s.[26] More recently, the British have supported such measures as nuclear-free zones, limitations on production of fissionable material for military purposes, and a total ban on biological-warfare research. In addition, Whitehall has sponsored technical studies on the feasibility of establishing observation posts in NATO and Warsaw Pact countries as a means of providing reassurance on capabilities and intentions for both the East and the West.[27]

Third, the British have attempted to play the part of an "honest broker" in mediating differences or in bringing opposing parties to the conference table. In this role the British have sometimes seen themselves as the mediator not only between non-Communist and Communist nations or between opposing Commonwealth partners, but also as the link between the United States and a more independent and assertive Europe.

But these British efforts at high-level diplomacy have not been particularly successful or rewarding—at least as seen from continental Europe. The British may feel that their efforts to bring forth

[25] Bruce M. Russett and Carolyn Cooper, *Arms Control in Europe: Proposals and Political Constraints,* University of Denver, Monograph Series in World Affairs (Denver, 1966–67), p. 32.

[26] It may be interesting—and rewarding—to reexamine in the 1970s some of the proposals of fifteen years earlier. For an analysis of early proposals, see Michael Howard, *Disengagement in Europe* (London, Penguin Books, 1958); also Eugene Hinterhoff, *Disengagement* (London, Stevens, 1959).

[27] See Lord Chalfont, "Value of Observation Posts in NATO and Warsaw Pact Areas," *European Review,* Autumn, 1966.

détente, to influence the superpowers, have not been unproductive. Examples such as Attlee's supposed influence on Truman's decision not to use the atom bomb in the Korean War, or the continuing pressures to reach a test ban agreement, can be cited. From the European perspective, however, Britain did not succeed in shaping a diplomacy which was separate from that of the United States or which achieved any independent results. British moves to improve détente, especially through summit meetings, are thought to have had little effect. Those arms control measures which have been adopted are seen as the result of the Soviet-American dialogue rather than as the outcome of British initiatives. And the honest broker role commands little special respect: despite a great deal of activity, the British have been no more successful than others in mediating conflicts such as those in the Middle East or Vietnam.

What does this experience suggest regarding British perspectives in the 1970s? If Britain is to enter Europe and become a partner in good standing, she will most likely need to undergo a major restructuring of foreign-policy priorities and perspectives. Although the world scene will not be ignored, primary attention will be focused on Europe. In recent years there has already been a new concentration on European affairs, which is likely to be accelerated. As a consequence, Britain will pay less attention to maintaining her influence in Washington and more to increasing it in Paris and Bonn. Similarly, in matters involving détente and East-West relations, Britain may align her policies more closely with those of West Germany and France before discussions in Moscow or in Eastern European capitals.

This possible change raises some interesting prospects. In their differing perspectives on European security, Britain has been a status quo power whereas France and West Germany have been revisionists. France has perceived détente as a way to reduce the domination of the two superpowers over Europe and permit the emergence of a pan-European entity (*l'Europe des Patries*). West Germany, too, has sought a fundamental revision of Europe, arising in first measure from a realignment in Central Europe. Britain, on the other hand, has been willing to accept a bipolar world and, unlike France, has always worked to strengthen her own role through NATO. She has sought a détente between the two blocs rather than a disintegration of the blocs. For Britain, détente has been an end in itself rather than a necessary precondition for changing the status quo.

What if Britain should become a revisionist power in the 1970s? At this point, the change is difficult to imagine, as are the policies that would result from such a transformation. One can, however, imagine a scenario in which Britain for the first time takes a position of leadership in Europe. Present-day Europe appears to be at a stage in which, if it is going to make any real progress toward political and military integration, it is going to need a spur. That impetus might come from Britain's adhesion *and* consequent decision to exercise her political imagination with Europe.

So, in the end, one is brought back to Churchill's three circles. Britain is no more likely in the future than in the past to be able to reconcile her European, Atlantic, and Commonwealth goals. If she continues to attempt this juggling act, she may be left muddling through alone. As has been noted, the latter would not be an altogether unattractive alternative, but it might deprive Britain of an exciting new venture in Europe.

POSTSCRIPT: MARCH, 1971

As this is being written, the prospects for British entry into the EEC appear brighter than at any time since the early 1960s. A new and fresh political climate with an air of forward momentum has pervaded the EEC since the Hague summit meeting of December, 1969. Negotiations between Britain and the EEC have been under way since the middle of 1970, and although they have not been without difficulties, the prospective results are promising. The French attitude towards British entry has undoubtedly undergone an important transformation, even if the final French position remains uncertain and, most likely, still undecided. More, perhaps, then any other single factor, the activist foreign policy of the Brandt government in West Germany has reshuffled the European political kaleidoscope. Along with the new *Ostpolitik*, and partially for the purpose of balancing it, renewed support has been given by West Germany to the long-term goal of Western European unity.

Predicting the course of international politics is always a chancy thing and, given the aborted end of the first two British applications for entry into the Common Market, one should estimate the likelihood of success in the third attempt with particular caution. Nevertheless, this author is of the view that the odds are better than 50-50 (perhaps 70-30) that Britain will be in the European Community within the next two years. One possible schedule of entry would be the completion of negotiations in the fall of 1971, signature of the treaty at the end of the year, ratification in 1972, formal entrance into the EEC in 1973, with a five-year period of transition to end in 1978. Such a timetable may be somewhat optimistic, but less uncertain is the significance of the present round of negotiations. The next two years are likely to make or break the entire question of British participation in the EEC. Most observers on both sides of the question in Britain agree that a third rejection, or a collapse of the negotiations because of British-induced reasons, would be fatal.

To a greater extent than in the two previous approaches, the question of British entry may depend more upon attitudes at home than upon the policies of the Continental states. Public opinion polls reflect a substantial decrease of support in the past year for Britain's participation in Europe. Opposition to adhesion to the EEC can be found on both the far Right and far Left of British politics. On the Continent, however, one senses a greater acceptance than in the past of Britain as a European state. The attitudes of the EEC Commissioners themselves are more favorable; the British now have far better relations with the economically powerful West Germans than they did in the days of Adenauer; and French public opinion and business interests are psychologically prepared for London's entry. One might go so far as to say that for many European bureaucrats the problem of British entry is "unfinished business." Because no progress is possible on a variety of national and community plans until it is out of the way, there exists an active incentive to completing the process of entry.

Since it is difficult to see substantial blockage created by any of the EEC members, including France, the more significant question may be whether the British are now prepared to accept the economic sacrifices associated with entry and to make a sufficiently forceful bid. The domestic debate in Britain on the merits and disadvantages of the Common Market is therefore important. Mr. Heath is a committed pro-European and, despite the rebuffs of the past decade, there is no indication that he has altered his conviction. The prime minister views formal entrance into Europe as but the first step in a fundamental re-shaping of Western Europe into a greater force in world politics. Not all in the Conservative party, however, share this view. Mr. Enoch Powell represents a not insignificant opposition on the far Right that eschews the belief that Britain is part of Europe. Philosophically he repudiates any steps towards the diminution of the prerogatives of the independent nation-state. Although Powell may be able to lead forty or fifty Conservatives into the lobby of the Opposition when the issue is put to vote in the Commons, the large majority of Tory Members will undoubtedly support whatever Mr. Heath's cabinet accepts in the Brussels negotiations.

As for Labour, the picture remains considerably less clear. As long as it was the aim of the Labour government to seek entry into Europe, the bulk of the party followed suit. Now there is the natural inclination of those in the Opposition to be at odds with the government's policy. But far more must be considered if the present lukewarmness of Labour towards Europe is to be explained. Many grassroot Labourites *are* provincial in outlook and mistrustful of an involvement with Germans and other Continentals deemed to be less than devoted to democratic principles. Harold Wilson may have undergone a genuine conversion in his attitude towards the Common Market, but he is still far less committed than Mr. Heath. No doubt Wilson will be tempted to lead the Labour party into a position of finding unacceptable whatever arrangement the prime minister is able to present to the nation as an appropriate basis for entrance into the EEC. Labour sentiment has swung quite sharply against the Common Market since the party lost power, and more than one hundred Labour MPs have already announced their opposition. But enough support remains that if Wilson came out clearly in opposition the party would be deeply split. Such a split within the party, reminiscent of the intra-party civil war a decade ago on the question of unilateral nuclear disarmament, would probably make it impossible for Wilson to become prime minister again, and there is no indication that he is reconciled to this as yet. A more likely course is that the Labour Members will be given a free vote in the Commons, one without disciplined party instructions. If this were to occur, a majority of Labour MPs might oppose membership in the market—but enough would vote with the government to assure its victory.

The parliamentary vote will be preceded by a campaign to mobilize British public opinion behind the agreement that is reached in Brussels. Until then, Geoffrey Rippon and his negotiators are in a difficult predicament. They must appear forthcoming to the European governments but not overly eager to the British public. Above all, the impression must be created that a fair bargain has been struck, one not overly detrimental to British interests.

The principal elements of the economic agreement will deal with the size of the British contribution to the EEC budget and the length of the transitional period during which Britain must adjust to the Community's system. The initial British proposal offered to begin by paying 3 percent of the EEC budget, with a rise to 15 percent at the end of five years. In addition London asked for another three years for gradual adjustment to the Community's budgetary system. The Common Market Commission, on the other hand, has recommended that Britain either begin by paying 21.5 percent of the budget or pay initially between 10 and 15 percent, increasing to 20 to 25 percent during a five-year period of transition.

Since the entire issue of British entry into the Community is, in the last analysis, a political one, a compromise will undoubtedly be reached on the economic questions. Within the Whitehall establishment, the Foreign Office remains committed to a role in Europe. The Treasury is understandably less enthusiastic but appreciates the overarching political rationale. Although the economic case for British entry has been greatly reduced in recent years, none of the political alternatives to entry discussed earlier—

NAFTA as an Atlantic scheme, the Commonwealth, or muddling through alone—has become more attractive. The dominant case for Britain's participation in Europe remains political.

An examination of the foreign- and defense-policy preferences of the Heath government confirms that the European orientation of Britain, begun in the 1960s, is likely to continue during the present decade. No longer does one hear of the "special relationship" with the United States. The prime minister now refers to the "natural relationship." The desired implication in this subtle change is that Britain's European allies are no longer excluded from being "special". Beyond this can be found a widespread assumption in Britain that in the future more attention will be given to Europe and proportionally less to Washington. The historical, cultural, and political links will remain, but in the day-to-day activities of government Whitehall will increasingly be concentrating on the European political chessboard.

Similarly, the former east-of-Suez role will not be fully resuscitated. Prior to the election the Conservatives indicated they would halt the Labour government's reductions of military capabilities East of Suez, in particular in the Persian Gulf and Singapore. After a careful defense review guided by Minister of Defence Lord Carrington, the Tory government only found the economic means to retain a minimal British military presence in the area. Reversing its pre-election position, the government announced in March, 1971, that British forces would be withdrawn from the Persian Gulf during the course of the same year and that the treaties giving Britain responsibility for the defense of nine sheikdoms along the gulf's southern coast would be allowed to lapse. Thus the previous policy of the Wilson government was, in effect, adopted.

In Southeast Asia, however, a token British presence will be retained. An infantry battalion will be stationed in Singapore, and five frigates or destroyers will be stationed East of Suez. Although this, too, is far less than Mr. Heath had previously promised, its symbolic significance should not be underestimated. The need to maintain a naval presence in the Indian Ocean to counter the growing Russian activity there has been recognized, and the United States can now be assured of a Western ally in the area. Of perhaps still greater import, the British presence will make it possible for the United Kingdom to participate in a Five-Power Commonwealth defense arrangement. Australia, Malaysia, New Zealand, and Singapore have agreed to join Britain in the creation of a new defense force that will be designed to help assure stability in Southeast Asia.

One can expect that on the multifaceted issues of European security the Heath government will follow the main lines of the previous administration. Priority will be given to those areas where European defense cooperation seems desirable and practicable. After some hesitation, Whitehall is making a substantial financial contribution to NATO's European defense-improvement program, which was decided upon in late 1970. A fresh look has been taken at the possibilities of Anglo-French collaboration on strategic nuclear weapons. Nuclear cooperation will depend upon complex political and military issues such as the outcome of SALT, in particular whether there is a limitation of ABMs, and the evolution of French strategic doctrine. In any case, nuclear cooperation is likely to be a matter of increasing interest in the next years, particularly if Britain is admitted into Europe. American policy on nuclear sharing with its Allies will consequently need to be reevaluated.[28]

Britain's role in the broad spectrum of East-West negotiations which are expected in the 1970s remains uncertain. The SALT negotiations are being closely watched in London, perhaps with a sharper eye than in any other Western European capital because of Britain's own nuclear knowledge. Thus far the process of NATO consultations has been generally satisfactory. If European-based weapons such as NATO's forward-based aircraft or the Soviet IRBMs and MRBMs are brought into the negotiations, however, we can expect that Washington will need to devise a means to bring the Allies more directly into SALT. On such questions as a European security conference, mutual and balanced force reduction, West Germany's *Ostpolitik*, and the Berlin negotiations, the British position has been closer to that of the United States than

[28] See Andrew J. Pierre, "Nuclear Diplomacy: Britain, France and America," *Foreign Affairs*, January, 1971, pp. 283–301.

has that of any other principal ally.[29] A 1970 proposal, made by Michael Stewart, for a standing East-West commission to discuss European problems has been dropped by the Heath government; one senses that the Conservatives are somewhat more skeptical concerning what can be achieved in negotiations with the Soviet Union. Britain's present attitude, therefore, is cautious and somewhat unimaginative. If the United Kingdom were to enter Europe, however, its political leaders might well seek to strengthen Britain's role and improve European security by taking a position of leadership in the continuing quest for a more viable basis for peace in Europe.

[29] See Andrew J. Pierre, "Reconciliation in Europe: A Western Approach to the European Security Conference," *Interplay*, July, 1970, pp. 16–20.

/ Wilfrid L. Kohl

fRance and european security: de gaulle and after

TWO BASICALLY CONTRADICTORY visions motivated General de Gaulle's foreign and security policies. The first vision stemmed from the Gaullist perception that the international system, dominated by the two superpowers, was unstable. The General sought to change that system into another that would provide a more stable world balance. His efforts were directed primarily at transforming the existing state system in Europe and encouraging the emergence of a new Europe that would act as a third world power. De Gaulle was also determined that France be recognized once again as a great power with an important global role. Thus the General attempted to expand French influence in Asia and Latin America and to retain it in Africa. But Europe remained his chief concern, and it was there that he devoted his greatest energies. He sought a union of European states under French leadership, through which, he hoped, Europe would regain its stature on the world political stage and speak with an independent voice vis-à-vis the superpowers. At the same time this expanded European role would serve as a vehicle to augment France's global influence.

This chapter examines how these two visions were reflected in Gaullist policy on European security. Special attention is directed to the role of French nuclear armament, the French position on disarmament and arms control, and the effects of the invasion of Czechoslovakia and France's domestic crisis of 1968 on de Gaulle's European and security policies. The chapter then addresses the early post–de Gaulle period, assessing the future prospects for French security policies and the extent to which they are likely to depart from or perpetuate earlier Gaullist concepts.[1]

PRINCIPLES OF GAULLIST
FOREIGN POLICY

Gaullist France demonstrated both status quo and revisionist tendencies in her foreign and security policies. On the one hand, she was a status quo power in the sense of having no territorial ambitions or conflicts of interests with other nations, no "possession goals." De Gaulle also adhered to an essentially nineteenth-century view of the stability of the international system, based on the preservation of the nation-state as the fundamental unit of world politics. All efforts to downgrade national sovereignty, especially in the direction of supranational integration, were doggedly opposed. Moreover, de Gaulle's diplomacy and diplomatic style conformed to the pattern of the traditional realist school: power is the key to influence; ideologies are only the cloaks of national ambitions; national security is best pursued by traditional methods—balance of power, cabinet diplomacy, coalitions, a concert of the great powers.[2]

More fundamentally, however, Gaullist France was a revisionist power. In accordance with his view of the instability of the prevailing international system, de Gaulle tried to create a new European and global equilibrium.[3] Although his tactics in pursuing this

[1] This paper is based largely on material from the author's book, *French Nuclear Diplomacy* (Princeton, N.J., Princeton University Press, 1971), to which the reader is referred for more extensive treatment. Reprinted with permission of Princeton University Press.

[2] See, for example, Stanley Hoffman, "De Gaulle's Memoirs: The Hero as History," *World Politics*, October, 1960, pp. 140–55.

[3] For a lucid treatment of the Gaullist perception of the international system and its impact on French policy, see Edward A. Kolodziej, "Revolt and Revisionism in the Gaullist Global Vision: An Analysis of French Strategic Policy," *Journal of Politics* (May, 1971), pp. 448–77.

objective were often unpredictable, de Gaulle defined his general aims with considerable clarity and pursued them with remarkable consistency in his policies. Starting with the division of Europe, each half of which was under the strong influence of a superpower, de Gaulle sought a reunification of the European continent in a loosely confederal system—a "Europe of the states," extending "from the Atlantic to the Urals." According to his design, this would be a "European" Europe independent of the two super-power hegemonies. Such a transformation of the European system would require removal of the American military presence (and, therefore, direct political influence) from Western Europe and withdrawal of Soviet troops from Eastern Europe, coupled with Moscow's consent to an evolution toward liberalization and na-tional autonomy in its former satellite countries. In de Gaulle's view, a new system of all-European security would then be created —presumably "balanced" by the Soviet Union in the East and France in the West, buttressed by the nascent French nuclear force. This new European security equilibrium would then be the basis of a multipolar realignment of global power.

The broad outlines of this Gaullist vision for the future of Eu-rope are visible in an often quoted passage from the third volume of the General's war memoirs (written during the years 1957–1958). De Gaulle described his goals for French policy as follows:

To ensure France's security in Western Europe by preventing a new Reich from menacing her again. To collaborate with the West and the East, constructing alliances with one side or the other as necessary, with-out ever accepting a position of dependence. . . . To encourage the po-litical, economic and strategic grouping of the States bordering on the Rhine, the Alps, and the Pyrenees. To establish this organization as one of the three world Powers and if it should one day be necessary, the ar-bitrator between the Soviet and Anglo-Saxon camps. Since 1940, my every word and act has been dedicated to establishing these possibilities; now that France is on her feet again, I am going to try to realize them.

To this vision was added a larger image of Europe, presumably a longer-term objective. The General hoped that all of Europe would eventually find peace and equilibrium "by an association among Slavs, Germans, Gauls, and Latins." This would provide the basis for a unity of the European peoples "from Iceland to Istanbul, from Gibraltar to the Urals." [4]

The second vision permeating Gaullist foreign policy was the quest for French *grandeur:* de Gaulle insisted that France once again be fitted for special international status as a global power. This idea—stated explicitly on the first page of his memoirs [5]—was in continuous tension with his revisionist design. In de Gaulle's eyes the condition of French *grandeur* was the maintenance of France's independence. Presumably this was his meaning when he wrote that France should "collaborate with the West and the East, constructing alliances with one side or the other as necessary, without ever accepting a position of dependence." [6] On another occasion he explained that independence was the "essential goal" of France's policy.[7] As noted below, this point raises a serious question whether it is possible for a country to work for the achievement of a goal such as the transformation of the European system, which involves cooperation and alliances with other states, without accepting some dependence and loss of freedom of action.

These two Gaullist visions and the tension between them—the revisionist design for the European and world international system and the quest for French *grandeur* and an independent global role —explain the essence of de Gaulle's foreign and security policies, their constructive contribution, and their failure. French nuclear armament was an important element in both of these visions.

[4] Charles de Gaulle, *Mémoires de guerre: Le Salut* (Paris, Plon, pocket edition, 1959), pp. 57–58; 210–11.

[5] Charles de Gaulle, *Mémoires de guerre: L'Appel* (Paris, Plon, pocket edition, 1954), p. 5. "Toute ma vie, je me suis fait une certaine idée de la France. Le sentiment me l'inspire aussi bien que la raison. . . . Bref, à mon sens, la France ne peut être la France sans la grandeur." De Gaulle did not define *grandeur*. He confined himself to the observation that France was destined for greatness and that "vast enterprises" were necessary to compensate for the internal divisions that characterize the French people.

[6] De Gaulle, *Le Salut*, p. 210.

[7] Press conference, October 28, 1966, *Speeches and Press Conferences*, no. 253A, distributed by French Embassy, Press and Information Division, New York. According to André Fontaine, Couve de Murville told him at one time that the aim of Gaullist policy was *indépendence en soi*. Fontaine argues the contrary, contending that de Gaulle developed a "constructive and original policy" directed at achieving European reunification and the disengagement of the blocs. See Fontaine's article, "What Is French Policy?" *Foreign Affairs*, October, 1966, p. 68.

ROLE OF FRENCH
NUCLEAR ARMAMENT

Gaullist assumptions on nuclear force derive from the General's view that the nation-state is and must remain the basic unit of world politics and that the indispensable characteristic of any sovereign state is national defense. The point was made succinctly in his 1959 speech at the Ecole Militaire. For de Gaulle, the general, an effective defense had to include the most modern armament. In this respect the *force de frappe* was the logical postwar extension of his effort in the 1930s to modernize the French Army and French strategy on the basis of a mobile, mechanized armored corps of professional soldiers, as described in one of his early books. But even more important for de Gaulle, the statesman, were the political consequences of atomic armament. He saw nuclear weapons as a fundamental ingredient of a nation's political power and influence in the present era of world politics. "A great state which does not possess them while others have them, does not dispose of its own destiny." [8]

Strategically, the *force de frappe ou de dissuasion* rests on the principles of proportional deterrence and massive anti-city retaliation, which are familiar and will not be analyzed here. A basic assumption of French strategy for many years was that the French force would augment overall deterrence because it might serve, in case of an extreme provocation against France or Western Europe, as a "trigger" of the American nuclear arsenal. Later, with the decline of the Soviet threat of aggression and the development of détente, plus the shift in focus of active United States–Communist world confrontation to Asia, the notion of triggering became less relevant. France's concern shifted, as she took pains to guard her independence and avoid being drawn into any hostilities in Europe which might grow out of a Soviet-American conflict elsewhere, for example in Vietnam.[9]

[8] Speech at Strasbourg, November 23, 1961, as quoted in André Passeron, *De Gaulle Parle*, vol. 1 (Paris, Plon, 1962), p. 357.

[9] The Gaullist regime has also presented economic and technological arguments to defend its military nuclear program. For a discussion of these points see *French Nuclear Diplomacy*, chapt. 5.

In de Gaulle's eyes, however, nuclear weapons were also the key to his attempt to modify the bipolar structure of world politics based on the strategic predominance of the superpowers. As the General said in 1959, "Probably the sort of equilibrium that is establishing itself between the atomic power of the two camps is, for the moment, a factor in world peace, but who can say what will happen tommorow?" [10] Obsessed soon after his return to power by the specter of a Soviet-American conflict enveloping the world, and later by the possibility of a Soviet-American political deal on a European settlement as the Cold War diminished, de Gaulle asserted that France, in equipping herself with an atomic force, was promoting world equilibrium by according Europe once again the means for her own security and an independent political role. He implied, of course, that French nuclear weapons were at the service of Europe.

According to the Gaullist view, then, French nuclear armament was seen as the foundation for France's independent foreign policy and global role, as well as a factor of stability in a multipolar world order growing out of a new strategic and political equilibrium in Europe.

ELABORATION OF EUROPEAN
AND ATLANTIC POLICIES

In retrospect, the evolution of de Gaulle's strategy and his security policies in the European and Atlantic areas can be viewed in four phases. Variables that influenced the contours and timing of these phases include French perceptions of the rise and decline of militarist Soviet policies in Europe and of indirect American threats to French sovereignty and status, the course of Western European integration and United States Atlantic policy, development and deployment of French nuclear arms, and French domes-

---

[10] Press conference, November 10, 1959, in *Major Addresses, Statements and Press Conferences of General Charles de Gaulle, May 19, 1958–January 31, 1964* (New York, French Embassy, Press and Information Division, 1964), p. 61.

tic political and economic constraints (e.g., the Algerian war; later, France's economic and political crisis in 1968), plus other factors affecting the international climate and European power relationships.

The initial phase centered on the General's efforts to achieve Anglo-American acceptance of his 1958 proposal for tripartite coordination of world strategy. In effect, this proposal would have extended the scope of NATO while at the same time elevating France's role and status in the alliance. The persistence of a hostile Soviet attitude toward Western Europe—as revealed, for example, in the 1958 and 1961 Berlin crises—made it necessary for de Gaulle to rely heavily on the United States and NATO during this period to preserve French security, especially since this was a time of French domestic weakness and unrest caused by the Algerian war. But the General had made clear his dissatisfaction with the organization and scope of the Atlantic alliance and had demanded coequal status with the United States and Great Britain in the formation and conduct of global strategy. It was argued that the forthcoming French nuclear arsenal would put France on an equal footing with the Anglo-Saxon powers and thus justify her participation in a special triumvirate grouping to oversee Western security interests around the world.

Had the tripartite scheme been accepted, the result would have been the consolidation of a system of East-West bloc politics; France, however, would have achieved special status in the Western bloc. Probably anticipating that his demands would not be met, de Gaulle had at the same time planted the seeds for French withdrawal from NATO when the reduction of the Soviet threat in Europe would allow it. He undoubtedly planned this withdrawal many years in advance, for French disengagement from a close military alliance with the American superpower was a prerequisite for the achievement of de Gaulle's pan-European design.

An Anglo-Franco-American directorate would have institutionalized discrimination within the Atlantic alliance and probably destroyed all hope of Western European unity. In this respect, the Gaullist national objective of reinstating France as a great power with worldwide interests, based on the development of French nuclear capability, would have been served; it appeared that the objective of French *grandeur* and special international status took precedence during this phase over the idea of transforming the East-West power alignment in Europe into a different European equilibrium based on an independent European role. However, if the tripartite proposal is viewed primarily as a tactical instrument, acceptance of which de Gaulle never really expected, but which provided the foundation for France's later withdrawal from NATO and the pursuit of an all-European policy, then it also served the longer-range Gaullist goal of revision of the European system after French disengagement from the Western military alliance.

By 1960 de Gaulle had begun to speak of his design for a "European entente from the Atlantic to the Urals," but he concentrated initially on achieving an "organized cooperation between states" in Western Europe in the fields of politics, economics, culture, and defense.[11] In his view, a strong grouping of states in Western Europe was a prerequisite for a new all-European equilibrium that would include the states in both halves of Europe. This concept led him to encourage actively the contruction of a political union in Western Europe on the model of the Fouchet plan during 1961–1962, the beginning of *the second phase* of his policy, and to resist President Kennedy's grand design for an integrated, Atlantic-oriented Europe in close partnership with the United States. After the Fouchet negotiations failed in April, 1962, when Belgium and the Netherlands refused further discussion until Britain had secured entry into the Common Market, de Gaulle's response was to make a start toward Western European organization on a more modest scale on the basis of the Franco-German Treaty of January, 1963, which was the Fouchet plan writ small.

De Gaulle later explained how Western European unity fitted into his long-range pan-European design:

The union of the Six, once achieved and all the more if it comes to be supplemented then by new European memberships and associations, can and must be, toward the United States, a valid partner in all areas, I mean powerful and independent. The union of the Six can and must also be one of the piers on which will gradually be built first the equilibrium,

[11] See, for example, his address of May 31, 1960, in *Major Addresses*, p. 78.

then the cooperation and then perhaps, one day, the union of all of Europe, which would enable our continent to settle its own problems peacefully, particularly that of Germany, including its reunification, and to attain, inasmuch as it is the main hearth of civilization, a material and human development worthy of its resources and its capacities.[12]

As part of his plan for a Western European grouping of states, de Gaulle urged the creation of a European defense system around the nucleus of the French atomic force.[13] It was implied that French atomic arms would be placed at the disposal of Western Europe when political unity was achieved. On this basis, he attempted to woo West Germany and the other European allies away from close defense ties with the United States. However, the concept of Europeanization of the French force was purposely left ambiguous.[14] There was never any indication of French willingness to share control of the *force de frappe* with her European neighbors. Rather, de Gaulle tried—largely unsuccessfully—to use the advantage of an evolving French nuclear capability as a political card in France's relations with Germany and other European states. If any serious discussion of the organization of Western European defense ever developed, France would thus preserve the leading role as the only Continental nuclear power. Thus, de Gaulle's concern for special French status took precedence over his concern for a coherent European role in a revised international system.

The Gaullist pursuit of *grandeur* and French leadership in Western Europe was manifested in other ways. France continued to oppose trends in the direction of supranational integration in the European Communities, as reflected by her resistance to expanding the EEC Commission's authority during the 1965–1966 crisis over agriculture and her refusal to support increased cooperation in Eur-

[12] From his press conference, February 21, 1966, *Speeches and Press Conferences*, no. 239.

[13] See, for example, his speech at Strasbourg, November 22, 1964, *Speeches and Press Conferences*, no. 212.

[14] The French position was never defined beyond the following official statement in 1964: "If a political Europe were formed with real responsibilities, France would be willing to study how this French deterrent could be used within the framework of the Europe of tomorrow." *The First Five Years of the Fifth Republic of France, January, 1959–January, 1964* (New York, French Embassy, Press and Information Division), p. 19.

atom when it threatened French national control. The Gaullist stand on European integration also had implications for the future of European defense, since a loose European confederal structure which based its defense on the coordination of national contributions was not likely to deal satisfactorily with the problem of nuclear control. Furthermore, de Gaulle resisted the enlargement of the European Economic Community, as demonstrated in his 1963 veto of British entry (followed by another veto in 1967). He seemed moved not only by a fear of Britain's serving as a Trojan horse for expanding American influence on the Continent, but also by a concern that France's preeminent position in Western Europe remain unchallenged. Yet there was a contradiction here, too, in the Gaullist design, since without Britain it would be difficult to form a "European" Europe sufficiently strong to play an independent role between the superpowers, as the General advocated.

By pursuing a highly nationalist policy in Europe and blocking further steps toward Western European integration, de Gaulle encouraged nationalist tendencies in the German Federal Republic and, indeed, in other countries of the European Community. These tendencies contributed to a politically fragmented Western Europe rather than the increased Western European cooperation de Gaulle sought. The fragmentation guaranteed the perpetuation of the kind of strong American influence on the Continent that the General wanted to combat.

Although maintaining France's participation in the Atlantic alliance during this period, de Gaulle resisted American military domination of Europe by opposing NATO and arguing that the American commitment to defend the Continent with nuclear weapons, in case of Soviet attack, was no longer credible. In his words, the alliance had to be maintained "so long as the Soviets threaten the world. . . . If the free world were attacked, on the old or the new continent, France would take part in the common defense at the sides of her allies, with all means that she has." [15] But NATO, the alliance's organization for military preparedness, was another matter. The General continued to attack the organization on grounds of its limited geographic scope, its domination by the Americans,

[15] Press conference, May 15, 1962, *Major Addresses*, p. 179.

and its "over-integration," which undermined national sovereignty in defense.[16] Similarly, the American proposal for a multilateral nuclear force, the MLF, was opposed as a device aimed at undermining the strategic and diplomatic utility of the French national *force de frappe* and denying Western Europe a fully independent voice over her own defense, since it was to remain subject to an American veto.

French strategy supported Gaullist diplomatic objectives. De Gaulle contended eloquently that, given recently acquired Soviet strategic power, "no one in the world—particularly no one in America—can say if, where, how and to what extent the American nuclear weapons would be employed to defend Europe. . . . American nuclear power does not necessarily and immediately meet all the eventualities concerning Europe and France." [17] In this manner he justified the creation of France's independent atomic force. The General realized that he needed, and indeed benefited from, the presence of the American nuclear umbrella to deter a major Soviet aggression. However, the French nuclear arsenal was held out as a trigger of American nuclear power in case of lesser provocations against which the United States might not be willing to muster a nuclear response. In the words of one Gaullist spokesman, the *force de frappe* was a French *parachute de sécurité* in the face of allied hesitations.[18] More fundamentally, however, French nuclear armament was presented as the core of a future Western European defense independent from American control, the necessary basis for the Gaullist revisionist design for eventual disengagement from the Western alliance and the formation of an independent Western European—and later all-European—political and security identity. Gaullist France had concluded that the American flexible-response strategy, which became the de facto strategy of NATO, not only contained great risks in its emphasis on conventional forces as the first counter to aggression in Europe and on American monopoly of nuclear control but also condemned Europe to a secondary strategic role.

---

[16] *The First Five Years*, p. 18.

[17] Press conference, January 14, 1963, *Major Addresses*, p. 217.

[18] Jacques Baumel, then Secretary-General of the Gaullist party (UNR-UDT), *Le Monde*, October 8, 1963.

Unsuccessful at rallying West Germany and other members of the EEC to his concept of a Western European confederation, de Gaulle turned his attention, beginning in 1965, to developing his Eastern policy of *détente, entente,* and *coopération* and his pan-European design—*the third phase* in Gaullist European and Atlantic diplomacy. Several factors provided the basis for this initiative. There was growing evidence that the Soviet Union had decided on a less militarist policy toward Western Europe. American-Soviet dialogue was on the decline because of differences over the Vietnam war and the MLF, yet the nuclear stalemate between the two superpowers continued and showed signs of preventing any military confrontation (the dangers of which had been highlighted by the 1962 Cuban missile crisis). In the East, the Sino-Soviet conflict had grown more acute and had produced further fragmentation within the Soviet sphere. In the West, France continued to differ with her European allies about the future organization of Western Europe and its relations with the United States. French and Soviet views were converging on a number of issues: Vietnam, Cuba, American intervention in the Dominican Republic, the Congo, the MLF, United Nations financing. Furthermore, Russia seemed to be included in de Gaulle's concept of a Europe from the Atlantic to the Urals, and worsening Franco-German relations plus continued French hostility to NATO simplified Franco-Soviet dialogue.

The initial basis for a warming trend in Franco-Soviet relations was probably the General's statement in February, 1965, on the reunification of Germany—in his view a purely European problem, dependent upon the recognition of Germany's present eastern frontiers and the limitation of its armament (the implication being that this would include no nuclear weapons).[19] Evidence of Moscow's approval of these views was quickly forthcoming during the friendly visit of Foreign Minister Gromyko to Paris in May. His visit was followed by the appointment of a new high-ranking ambassador to Paris, Valerii Zorin, who soon after his arrival spoke of the Soviet Union and France as "the great continental European powers . . . called upon by their very location to play an impor-

[19] Press conference, February 4, 1965, *Speeches and Press Conferences*, no. 216.

tant role in guaranteeing European security." [20] Meanwhile, Franco-Soviet trade was increasing, and an agreement was signed in March, 1965, on the joint exploitation of the French system of color television.

A fundamental step in this phase of Gaullist policy was the French withdrawal from NATO military structures, first announced in the General's press conference on February 21, 1966. This move, which de Gaulle must have contemplated for a long time, was necessary for France's pursuit of a pan-European policy that included among its aims the creation of an all-European security system. It had finally become possible because of what de Gaulle termed "new conditions," most important among which were the reduction of the Soviet threat in Western Europe and trends toward a peaceful and polycentric evolution in Eastern Europe. As de Gaulle observed, "the Western world is no longer threatened today as it was at the time when the American protectorate was set up in Europe under the cover of NATO." [21] In place of a threat from the East, the French leader spoke of the danger that America's involvement in extra-European conflicts, especially Vietnam, might engulf Europe in a conflagration, given American domination of NATO strategy and the American military presence on European soil. Another new condition noted by the French leader was the fact that France was becoming an atomic power (the first-generation weapons of the *force de frappe* were almost fully deployed) and would now begin "to assume itself the very extensive strategic and political responsibilities that this capacity involves." [22]

Another major factor behind Gaullist policy was the French perception, not limited to Gaullists, that the United States had become the dominant world power and would automatically seek to extend its hegemony. This perception was based not only on American strategic power but also on growing American economic and technological strength, now expanding rapidly into European markets. American superiority in high-technology industries, such as

[20] As quoted in W. W. Kulski, *De Gaulle and the World* (Syracuse, N.Y., Syracuse University Press, 1966), p. 304.
[21] Press conference, February 21, 1966, *Speeches and Press Conferences*, no. 239.
[22] Ibid.

computers, and in the management of large-scale international corporations was making it difficult for French and other European firms to compete.[23] In French eyes the international system was seen as gravitating toward a unipolar system, which was menacing the international balance. In place of a Soviet military threat, the French now saw subtle new forms of indirect threat in rising American power. The Gaullist response was to combat American influence wherever possible. Thus, "the struggle against the ally" became an overriding French objective, and differences between France and the United States multiplied and encompassed almost every area of their relations.

France's withdrawal from NATO seemed carefully timed to underpin de Gaulle's eleven-day trip to the Soviet Union in June, 1966, the high point in the French flirtation with Moscow. Despite a lavish reception and a spirit of growing détente, the General's journey to Moscow achieved only modest results. No new ground was broken on the German question. The Soviet leaders repeated their insistence on recognition of the German Democratic Republic, but de Gaulle refused to go along. The principal fruits of the trip were a Moscow-Paris hot line and new Soviet-French cooperation in trade, science, and technology, peaceful uses of atomic energy, and outer-space exploration.

At the end of 1966 de Gaulle claimed that "the cold war that lasted for twenty years [was] in the process of disappearing." Continental rapprochement, he said, was the goal of France's Eastern policy. Its purpose was the creation of a European Europe in order to "re-establish the peaceful equilibrium indispensable to the world" and to allow Europe to "take its place again at the forefront of human progress."[24] In the months that followed, the French president and his senior officials expanded France's contacts and relations with Eastern Europe through a number of visits to Eastern European capitals.

French strategy during this period seemed intent on keeping

[23] See J.-J. Servan-Schreiber, The American Challenge (New York, Atheneum, 1968); also, Robert Gilpin, France in the Age of the Scientific State (Princeton, N.J., Princeton University Press, 1968).

[24] New Year's message, December 31, 1966, Speeches and Press Conferences, no. 255.

open France's military options in order to preserve her independence and to support détente and cooperation with the East. Thus France remained aloof from NATO and refused to commit herself in advance on the conditions under which French forces might cooperate with NATO troops in the event of a European conflict. France would collaborate with her Atlantic allies in case aggression against one of them was "not provoked," but the French government would determine whether or not that was the case when the aggression occurred.[25] Gaullist leaders frequently reiterated that France would not be drawn into any Soviet-American hostilities in Europe that might develop out of the Vietnam conflict, which the French government condemned. Talks between French Chief of Staff Charles Ailleret and NATO Commander Lyman Lemnitzer that were supposed to clarify this situation produced no result.

In this new context the French nuclear force became an instrument to preserve France's freedom of action. The point was underscored by General Ailleret at the end of 1967 when he asserted in an article that France should develop a system of defense that was worldwide in scope (*tous azimuts*) based on megaton-warhead ballistic missiles with intercontinental range. Ailleret argued that "an a priori alliance" could no longer provide France with a general guarantee of her security "since it is almost impossible to foresee what could one day be the cause of a serious conflict, and what would be the distribution of the powers between the various sides, or what hold, even unauthorized, any power would have over the territory of any other power." [26]

The main points of Ailleret's exposition were confirmed in the following months by General de Gaulle himself and by Defense Minister Messmer.[27] France appeared to be laying the groundwork for an ambitious extension of her nuclear-weapons program in the

[25] See, for example, "La France et l'alliance atlantique," *Note d'information*, no. 17, (Paris, Ministère des Armées, August, 1966).

[26] "Défense 'dirigée' ou défense 'tous azimuts,'" *Revue de Défense Nationale*, December, 1967, pp. 1923–32. The quotations are from the English translation which appeared in *Survival*, February, 1968, pp. 38–43.

[27] See de Gaulle's speech at the Ecole Militaire, *Le Monde*, January 30, 1968; Pierre Messmer, "L'Atome, cause et moyen d'une politique militaire autonome," *Revue de Défense Nationale*, March, 1968, pp. 395–402.

1970s and eventual withdrawal from the Atlantic alliance—the logical next step toward de Gaulle's espoused objective of French leadership of an all-European grouping of states independent of the two superpowers. At the basis of this conception was the evolving French nuclear arsenal, which de Gaulle hoped would make France one of the guarantors of a future all-European security system.

The Gaullist design for a reconstituted European system based on a reunified Europe independent of the superpowers contained positive elements for any future European settlement. However, it was also beset with a number of contradictions, stemming especially from de Gaulle's insistence on a special French status in the new European order that was clearly beyond French capabilities.

On the positive side, the Gaullist vision—in contrast to several alternative Atlantic designs—called for a developing Western European identity with much reduced military ties to the United States as the first step toward interesting the Soviets in the process of all-European engagement (i.e., removal of Soviet troops from Eastern Europe, to be followed by increased cooperation between the states in both halves of Europe and eventually by some kind of all-European confederation). This diplomatic strategy does have merit, for it is difficult to understand why the Soviet Union should ever disengage itself from the Eastern half of Europe as long as the Western half remains dominated militarily by the United States. The chances for serious negotiations with the Russians at some future time on arms control in Europe and new European security arrangements will be greater if Western Europe is allowed to develop its own identity and its own foreign and defense policies.

France's expansion of contacts with the Eastern European states, aimed at breaking down the blocs (described here as the third phase of the General's European policy), was also an important contribution to the development of East-West détente politics in the middle 1960s. In several respects, Gaullist initiatives helped prepare the way for the *Ostpolitik* launched by West Germany's Grand Coalition government in 1967, as well as for President Johnson's policy of "bridge-building."

But the Gaullist vision of a Europe of states extending from the Atlantic to the Urals was weakened by inconsistencies and paradoxes. First, the Soviet Union's position in this new European system was not clear. De Gaulle often spoke of a European Europe independent of the superpowers. In this formulation Russia would seem to be excluded from the system (just as the United States would be) in order that the new European grouping could wield an independent policy. On the other hand, if this Europe were to extend to the Urals, Russia would necessarily be included.[28] Other Gaullist utterances bear out such a conclusion and are based on the assumption that Russia was expected to play a balance-of-power role, along with France, in containing Germany and preserving the stability of the new European order.

Among other ambiguities in the General's all-European design, it is not clear how a loosely organized European confederal system could contain Germany. As Pierre Hassner has pointed out, "The overall weight of Germany as compared to France, and the other medium European states, constitutes the disruptive factor in any continental European system, and most strikingly so in such a system based on control by a Franco-Soviet concert."[29] It seems much more probable that the European balance will be determined by the nature of the relationship between Germany and Russia and that France, given her slender resources, will play a less important role. Developments in German-Soviet relations in the post–de Gaulle period tend to confirm this point.

Furthermore, the General's tactics and blunt diplomatic style frequently infuriated his allies, left France in isolation, and generally worked against the realization of his European design. During a

[28] André Fontaine commented in 1966: "In the Elysée it is increasingly clear that the entente must embrace all Europeans, including the Russians. Like all French schoolboys, de Gaulle learned that Europe extends 'from the Atlantic to the Urals.' But since he went to Novosibirsk he has been forced to persuade himself that the Urals, which are practically invisible from an airplane, are no more significant as an ethnic or political barrier than as a geographical one. Thus in his toast at the farewell reception in the Kremlin, he spoke of Europe 'from one end to the other.' This is more vague and cuts short many speculations caused earlier by his too scholastic vocabulary." See Fontaine's "What Is French Policy?" p. 73.

[29] Pierre Hassner, *Change and Security in Europe*, part 2, Adelphi Paper no. 49 (London, Institute for Strategic Studies, 1968), p. 30.

period when Western Europe's defenses (including the French nuclear force) were generally weak, France had to rely as much as her neighbors did on the protection provided by American troops stationed in Western Europe, as well as on the American nuclear umbrella, to guarantee European security in case of a change in Soviet policy. In order to achieve first a strong, independent Western European group of states and then later his longer-range goal of all-European reconciliation, de Gaulle also required American cooperation. Yet the French leader engaged in a series of Olympian actions over a period of several years, always without prior consultation, that served only to alienate the United States. These actions were marked by opposition to and public contempt for American policies everywhere in the world.

IMPACT OF INTERNAL AND
EXTERNAL CRISES IN 1968

The Gaullist European vision, and the hope that through it France would achieve a special European and global role, were abruptly jolted by two events in 1968. The economic and political crisis which shook France as a result of the "events" of May weakened the stability of the Gaullist regime and undermined France's international standing and hence her claim to leadership on the Continent. The Soviet invasion of Czechoslovakia in August was sudden proof that the General's all-European design was premature and based upon an overly optimistic assessment of Soviet policy toward the Eastern European countries. These developments caused several shifts in French positions toward Europe and the Atlantic, marking the beginning of the *fourth and final phase* of Gaullist foreign policy. Among the most important changes were the postponement of the Gaullist pan-European vision, a reassessment of France's relations with her European partners, and a warming in French policy toward NATO and the United States.

The intervention in Czechoslovakia challenged several assumptions of de Gaulle's all-European policy of détente, entente, and cooperation. It raised serious concern about a new militarist attitude in the Kremlin and doubts about Soviet tolerance of liberalization and national autonomy in the Eastern European states and greater independence in their relations with the West. De Gaulle first condemned the Soviet invasion as a return to the policy of the two blocs, begun at Yalta; he then reasserted his intention to work toward a dismantling of the blocs, détente, and European engagement, despite the setback of Czechoslovakia.[30] It was soon clear, however, that progress toward European reconciliation along Gaullist lines would be postponed for a long time. De Gaulle's premise that contacts could be expanded and good relations developed simultaneously with Moscow and with the Eastern European states had been proven false. In the months that followed, government statements, though indicating that the goals of France's Eastern policy remained unchanged, nevertheless acknowledged a major revision in the time frame necessary for achieving French objectives.

The domestic crises that shook France in 1968 weakened her political strength in the eyes of the world and thus affected the means for carrying out French foreign policy and the chances for its success. Student unrest and industrial strikes shook the very foundations of the regime. De Gaulle survived the crisis with an impressive victory in the June elections by appealing for law and order in the face of an exaggerated Communist threat. He increased industrial salaries and promised reforms ("participation") in French government and university structures. But then he fired the man who had done most to surmount the disorder, Premier Georges Pompidou. When in November the French franc came under heavy speculative pressures and the government was forced to take new measures of economic retrenchment, these measures added to the declining trust of Frenchmen in the stability of the Gaullist regime.

For a time after the invasion of Czechoslovakia de Gaulle suspended all Franco-Soviet contacts, but he resumed them in January, 1969, when a delegation headed by Deputy Premier Vladimir Kirillin visited Paris to discuss questions of trade and scientific co-

[30] See de Gaulle's press conference, September 9, 1968, *Speeches and Press Conferences*, no. 1128.

operation. Subsequently, French Minister Galley traveled to Moscow in May for more detailed talks on cooperation in the area of atomic and space research and other scientific projects. An agreement signed the same month called for a doubling of Franco-Soviet trade during the period 1970–1974. Nevertheless, there were new limits to how far the Gaullist regime was willing to go in relations with Russia. No further forays were made by French leaders into Eastern Europe. In April, 1969, at the twentieth-anniversary meeting of the North Atlantic Treaty alliance in Washington, French Foreign Minister Debré agreed with the United States position that the time was not ripe to accept the Budapest appeal issued the previous month by the Warsaw Pact states for the convocation of an all-European security conference.[31]

The invasion of Czechoslovakia and the French domestic difficulties led to a reappraisal of Soviet intentions and an unequivocal statement that France planned to remain in the Atlantic alliance.[32] Liaison with NATO was stepped up, and renewed efforts were made to cooperate with NATO forces in Europe and in the Mediterranean, where Soviet naval activity was rapidly expanding. Friendlier relations were also reestablished with the United States, spurred by the American decision to begin negotiations on a Vietnam settlement, by American backing of de Gaulle's determination not to devalue the franc, and by the advent of the Nixon administration.

Although the declared aims of France's defense policy, like her Eastern policy, were unchanged at the end of 1968, there was a setback in the timetable of several military programs. The budgetary pressures arising out of France's domestic troubles in May and June, plus the international monetary crisis in November, forced a reduction in the military budget and postponement of the 1969 nu-

[31] See the speech by Foreign Minister Debré before the National Assembly on October 2, 1968, *Le Monde*, October 3, 1968; Debré's speech at the UN General Assembly, October 7, 1968, *Speeches and Conferences*, no. 1141; and his speech before the National Assembly, November 7, 1968, *Le Monde*, November 9, 1968. See also Defense Minister Messmer's speech to the National Assembly, December 5, 1968, *Le Monde*, December 7, 1968.

[32] See Defense Minister Messmer's statement before the National Assembly, *Le Monde*, December 7, 1968.

clear tests. The greatest impact of this budgetary reduction was felt by the ground forces, whose long-promised modernization was further postponed. Officially it was admitted that ongoing nuclear programs would be delayed about a year and that long-range plans for the period 1971–1980 (which were to include intercontinental ballistic missiles) would be "revised and amputated." [33] Some considerably longer delays actually occurred. The development of ICBM's was postponed indefinitely. Paradoxically, all this happened in the same year in which France successfully tested her first two hydrogen bombs in the Pacific.

By the end of 1968 it was reported that French officials had approached NATO to discuss conditions under which France, which lost the use of American tactical nuclear weapons after her withdrawal from NATO commands, might be guaranteed tactical nuclear protection in case of a European conflict.[34] There were also rumors that France had made overtures to Washington offering to coordinate targeting of the *force de dissuasion* with that of American nuclear forces. That these subjects could even be raised was due to the removal of several important Franco-American differences.

The positive turn in Franco-American relations was given further impetus by the coming to power of Richard Nixon, a long-standing admirer of General de Gaulle. Mutual respect between these two men was renewed during Nixon's cordial visit in Paris soon after his inauguration, which reportedly included discussion of possible new defense cooperation between the United States and France. American policy seemed to be shifting toward a new tolerance of independent Western European identity. Nixon said later that he shared the General's view "that Europe should have an independent position in its own right." The United States, he observed, no longer needed to be the dominant partner in the Atlantic alliance.[35]

A significant change in French strategy announced in March,

[33] Defense Minister Messmer before the National Assembly, *Le Monde*, November 1 and December 7, 1968.
[34] *Le Monde*, April 4 and 5, 1969.
[35] President Nixon's press conference, *New York Times*, March 5, 1969.

1969, seemed to signal additional French interest in a new kind of relationship with NATO. Lecturing before the Institute of Higher Defense Studies at the Ecole Militaire, General Michel Fourquet, the new Chief of Staff, declared that henceforth French military doctrine would contemplate a "series of graduated actions" to test out the strength of an eventual aggressor before recourse was made to a "strategic response." [36] This meant that French strategy was now moving toward the concept of flexible response based on the use of tactical nuclear weapons, a concept which NATO had adopted many years earlier despite French opposition. General Fourquet made no mention of the *tous azimuts* strategy of his predecessor, the late General Ailleret; instead he spoke specifically of an enemy "coming from the east." French forces, he said, would act in close coordination with allied forces in meeting an aggressor. Thus, France was reverting to a much more modest strategy. The foundation had been laid for future defense cooperation with NATO and the United States.

If the Gaullist concept of a Europe from the Atlantic to the Urals had been shaken by the Soviet occupation of Prague, other events in 1968 had moved de Gaulle to reassess his relations in Western Europe. In particular, the refusal of West Germany to revalue the mark at the November international monetary conference in Bonn was a sharp reminder to a weakened France of the growing political influence of the Federal Republic. It was probably this realization that moved de Gaulle to make a substantial overture to Britain in his talks with the British ambassador, Christopher Soames, in Paris in February, 1969. De Gaulle's suggestion that London and Paris discuss bilaterally the idea of Britain's joining a more loosely organized and broadly based economic association in Europe with an inner political council of four (France, Britain, Germany, and Italy) was misunderstood in London. However, it appears that the General was seeking a way to promote British entry into an *Europe des Etats*, unhampered by traces of suprana-

[36] "Emploi des différents systèmes de forces dans le cadre de la stratégie de dissuasion," *Revue de Défense Nationale*, May, 1969, pp. 757–67; an English translation appeared in *Survival*, July, 1969, pp. 206–11.

tionality, in which Britain could help provide a counterbalance to West Germany's rapidly expanding economic, and hence political, power.[37]

GAULLIST POLICY ON DISARMAMENT AND ARMS CONTROL

The policies of the Gaullist Fifth Republic on disarmament and arms control also were anchored in de Gaulle's two visions of the international system. Gaullist France viewed with suspicion all efforts by the Soviet Union and the United States to negotiate agreements on nuclear arms. The de Gaulle government refused to participate in arms control accords that protected the nuclear monopoly positions of the superpowers and discriminated against smaller states. This corresponded to basic Gaullist hostility toward a bipolar international system dominated by Moscow and Washington. Gaullist arms control policies, which favored efforts toward complete disarmament and the destruction of nuclear stocks and delivery vehicles, were designed to help break down this bipolar system and move toward a multipolar world order.

Another aspect of Gaullist policy in this field supported the General's second vision for a rebirth of France's *grandeur* and a French global role in politics and security. Thus, from 1961 onward, France declined participation in the eighteen-nation disarmament conference because it included nonnuclear states, the presence of which could only dilute French prestige and impede discussion of meaningful disarmament measures. Such measures could be based only on agreement among the nuclear powers. As in the case of the 1958 tripartite proposal, which would have given France equal recognition with Britain and the United States in matters of global security, France was unwilling to settle for less in international arms control and disarmament negotiations and

[37] See the revealing account of the "Soames affair" by André Fontaine, "Comment avorta le dialogue Franco-Brittanique," *Le Monde Hebdomadaire*, March 13–19, 1969.

would participate in such discussions only if her role as a global nuclear power would be clearly recognized. As de Gaulle said in 1962 when he explained France's empty-chair policy at Geneva:

Of course, if there should one day be a meeting of States that truly want to organize disarmament—and such a meeting should, in our mind, be composed of the four atomic powers—France would participate in it wholeheartedly. Until such time, she does not see the need for taking part in proceedings whose inevitable outcome is . . . disillusion.[38]

Similarly, Gaullist France opposed all arms control efforts that would hinder her own nuclear development, the keystone of the global security mission she saw for herself.

French policy has attached high priority to disarmament ever since World War II, as France sought to prevent discrimination against the smaller powers and to reassert her international role.[39] When de Gaulle regained power and pressed forward with the development of a French atomic arsenal, French pronouncements increasingly emphasized steps toward total disarmament. Any arms control measures which threatened the development of the French nuclear program were opposed. Thus the General said in 1959: "If the Anglo-Saxons and the Soviets agree among themselves to halt their tests, France can only approve. But, if anybody wished to ask France to renounce atomic weapons for herself, while others are in possession of them and are developing them in tremendous quantities, there is not the slightest chance that she would accede to such a request." [40] Speaking as Premier in 1967 before the National Assembly, Georges Pompidou likewise spoke disapprovingly of "the system in which the two great powers, overarmed with nuclear weapons—the United States and the Soviet Union—would organize the disarmament of the others." He saw this situation, in which the disarmed countries would be forced "to separate into two blocs, each huddling under the protective wing that it would have chosen," as menacing to world peace.[41] At the same time,

---

[38] Press conference, May 15, 1962, *Major Addresses*, p. 182.

[39] See, for example, Wolf Mendl, "French Attitudes on Disarmament," *Survival*, December, 1967, pp. 393–97.

[40] Press conference, November 10, 1959, *Major Addresses*, p. 61.

[41] Premier Pompidou before the National Assembly, April 20, 1967 in *Textes et Notes*, no. 2000 IT, May 2, 1967 (Paris, La Documentation Française, 1967).

Gaullist officials repeatedly stated that France would renounce atomic weapons if the other nuclear powers did likewise and agreed to destroy their existing stocks of nuclear arms and delivery vehicles, but only on that condition.

It followed that Gaullist France would oppose the two major international arms control agreements of the 1960s. In refusing to sign the test-ban treaty of 1963, de Gaulle termed the treaty "of only limited practical importance" as long as the existing nuclear arms of the United States and the Soviet Union, as well as their right to continue manufacturing more atomic arms, were not affected.[42] The treaty, it was held, discriminated against France, which was just beginning to acquire a nuclear arsenal. As Foreign Minister Couve de Murville explained, "What is at stake is not to disarm those who are armed, but to prevent those who are not armed from arming, and that is what we, as far as we are concerned, cannot find satisfactory." [43]

France viewed the nonproliferation treaty in a similar light. When the United States and the Soviet Union submitted identical draft treaties to the Geneva conference in August 1967, France confirmed her intention not to sign what she viewed as not a true disarmament measure.[44] After Soviet-American agreement was obtained and the final version of the treaty was presented to the United Nations General Assembly, the French government, expressing its sympathy for the principle of nonproliferation, said it would conduct itself exactly as would signatory states. But France abstained in the UN vote on the treaty and refused to sign it. The treaty did not touch on what she considered to be the real problem: the necessity for the nuclear powers to join together and agree on steps toward abolishing nuclear arms through prohibition of their manufacture and destruction of existing stocks.[45] In French eyes the nonproliferation treaty was yet another measure that

---

[42] De Gaulle's press conference, July 29, 1963, *Major Addresses*, pp. 237–38.

[43] Interview on France-Inter radio network, January 7, 1967, *Speeches and Press Conferences*, no. 256.

[44] *Le Monde*, August 27–28, 1967.

[45] See the statement by Armand Berard, French Permanent Representative, before the General Assembly, June 12, 1968, No. 1100 (New York, French Embassy, Press and Information Division, 1968).

strengthened the monopoly positions of the superpowers at the expense of the smaller states.

The French approach to disarmament was primarily political and was linked to the Gaullist position on East-West relations and a European settlement. In the Gaullist revisionist perspective, the major requirement for world peace and international stability was a political settlement by the great powers of the fundamental issues of Europe's division, especially the future of Germany. De Gaulle's policy of détente with the East was aimed at gradually creating the climate for such a settlement. In this context, disarmament was subordinated to the resolution of Europe's political conflicts. In contrast to the superpowers, for whom arms control measures represented instruments of détente, the French view was that détente had to precede arms control and disarmament efforts.[46]

The one notable exception was the case of Germany. For it was an axiom of the Gaullist revisionist design that the stability of an all-European security system depended upon preservation of Germany's nonnuclear status. This was the one kind of arms control that France insisted upon immediately, for it was necessary that Germany be subordinate to France in the military field if France were to become a leader and guarantor of an all-European security system.

FRENCH SECURITY POLICIES
AFTER DE GAULLE

President Georges Pompidou lacks his predecessor's sweeping foreign-policy designs. Since his election in 1969, he has moved cautiously to scale down France's international objectives and to define for his country a more modest conception of national interest, in greater harmony with France's resources and capabilities. Several reasons underlie this change. First, Pompidou does not enjoy de Gaulle's immense personal prestige and respect. More im-

---

[46] See speeches by Couve de Murville, April 30, 1959, *Speeches and Press Conferences*, no. 144, p. 6; and September 29, 1965, *Speeches and Press Conferences*, no. 229.

portant, France is a country with serious domestic problems, which caused even de Gaulle to modify his policies before his retirement. There is also the different temperament and personal style of Pompidou, an intellectual and technocrat turned politician, a man used to the procedure of pragmatic negotiation.

Pompidou has taken personal charge of policy-making in most areas, with the partial exception of economic and social affairs— apparently designated the domain of Premier Jacques Chaban-Delmas. On foreign and security matters, Pompidou is at the center of governmental decision-making. However, he has had to reckon with the presence in his cabinet of arch-Gaullist Michel Debré, Minister of Defense. By his initial actions, it would seem that Pompidou continues to implement Gaullist concepts in some fields of foreign and security policy, while adapting Gaullist policy in others to changing French and world conditions. So far, Pompidou's policy has been characterized by a contraction of global aspirations and concentration on carving out an active middle-power role for France in two key areas: Europe and the Mediterranean.

Western Europe. Pompidou's greatest departure from traditional Gaullist ideas is revealed in his approach to Europe. De Gaulle's political vision of a Europe of states "from the Atlantic to the Urals" is not part of the parlance of his successor. Instead of pressing for reconciliation of the two halves of Europe, Pompidou appears to assign first priority to the organization and strengthening of Western Europe so that it can resist the power of the East. His professed goal is a Western European confederation, to be formed on a pragmatic, step-by-step basis. After playing a leading role in the Hague summit conference of the Common Market in December, 1969, Pompidou reached a compromise with Chancellor Willy Brandt in early 1971 on the basis for launching the first stage of European economic and monetary union, to be achieved by 1980. Pompidou has already sketched how a future confederation might evolve and develop some powers of its own, building on the Council of Ministers. His goal is an independent Western Europe that can find its own place in the world. Like the General, Pompidou is cautious about infringing on the identity and sovereignty of the member states. Unlike his predecessor, Pompidou appears ready to build on the existing Community framework, extending it first in the economic, later in the political and defense fields, rather than circumventing it as de Gaulle tried to do.[47]

The other fundamental change in the attitude of the Pompidou government has been on the issue of enlarging the European Community. France agreed with her partners at the Hague conference to open negotiations with the British government in July 1970. After publicly affirming his support for British entry, the French president reached a wideranging understanding with Prime Minister Heath on the future of Europe at their historic meeting in Paris, May 20–21, 1971. This cleared the way for the successful conclusion of the accession negotiations at Luxembourg a month later. Agreeing on the need to develop "distinctively European policies," first in economic matters "and progressively in other fields," the two leaders also reached common views on the future development and functioning of Community institutions, based on the unanimity rule. Assenting to participation in European economic and monetary union, Britain accepted the principle of the Common Market agricultural policy and gave France assurances on the future role of sterling. Defense and nuclear matters appear not to have been part of the bargain. Cooperation in these areas, it was agreed, would be discussed thoroughly later on. For the time being Pompidou seems to have accepted London's special defense ties with the United States, but Paris probably hopes to interest the British in European defense cooperation when the construction of Europe is further advanced (and when French and British nuclear forces are more equal in strength).[48]

In accepting British entry, the Pompidou government has doubtless recognized the need for British participation in the European Community to help balance rising German power—a factor which de Gaulle came to perceive before retiring from office. France's relations with West Germany have taken on a different character in

[47] See Pompidou's press conference, January 21, 1971, no. 71/9 (New York: Ambassade de France, Service de presse et d'information); also his June 24, 1971, television interview, reprinted in *Le Monde*, June 26, 1971.

[48] The quotations are from the joint communiqué issued at the close of the Heath-Pompidou talks, May 21, 1971, *Le Monde*, May 23–24, 1971.

the post–de Gaulle era. Although regular consultations and exchange visits have proceeded in a cordial atmosphere under the Franco-German treaty, neither country seems intent on the kind of special Franco-German relationship once sought by Adenauer and de Gaulle. The relationship now is more likely to be one of equals, in view of Germany's economic strength and Brandt's willingness to take foreign policy initiatives. Since the European policies of the two countries are now more parallel, there is a basis for considerable Franco-German agreement on key issues. New hopes have been expressed for military cooperation between the two countries, as well as cooperation in industrial projects and civilian nuclear technology. Neither Paris nor Bonn is pressing for supranational integration in Western Europe and the French government has in principle declared its support for Brandt's *Ostpolitik*. However, Brandt has moved so rapidly on this front that tensions could easily develop as each country begins to compete for favored relations in the East. The new self-assertiveness in Bonn, highlighted by *Ostpolitik* and again by West German determination to float the mark in the spring 1971 currency crisis, has removed any possibility of French domination of a West European grouping, an objective sought by de Gaulle.

East-West Relations. Pompidou has not discarded the Gaullist policy of détente and cooperation with the East, aimed at breaking down the Cold War division of Europe. However, he seems to have no illusions about the time required to achieve that goal. Moreover, Pompidou appears to have no precise blueprint for an all-European political or security framework nor for the role France should play in it. Although Bonn has seized much of the initiative in this area, Paris can be expected to persist with its Eastern efforts. But Pompidou is differentiating more carefully than did his predecessor in his relations with the Soviet Union and with the Eastern European states. As evidenced by Pompidou's trip to the Soviet Union in the autumn of 1970, followed by Brezhnev's visit to France in 1971, France now finds it prudent to favor Moscow.

In December, 1969, France pressed for and obtained the assent of her partners at The Hague to the principle that a Europe of the

Six, eventually enlarged, should serve to promote rapprochement among the peoples of the entire European continent. France has supported the Soviet-proposed European security conference, but with the provisions of careful diplomatic preparation and prior evolution of the East-West climate to the point where a conference would promise more than simply a confirmation of existing blocs.

NATO and Franco-American Relations. It is unlikely that France will rejoin NATO. But her intention to remain a member of the Atlantic alliance has been emphasized. Moreover, Pompidou, in contrast to de Gaulle, has asserted that France wants American troops to remain in Europe.[49] French cooperation with NATO has recently increased in a number of areas. Building on an earlier agreement between General Ailleret and NATO Commander Lemnitzer, contingency planning has been undertaken regarding the employment of the two French divisions stationed in Germany. The French have allowed NATO the continued use of a pipeline and certain communication facilities in France and have granted rights for military overflights of French territory. French military liaison with certain NATO headquarters has increased, and the French participate in the NADGE early-warning system and, in more limited fashion, in NATO air defense planning and some NATO exercises, including naval maneuvers.

Recent statements by French leaders, including Defense Minister Debré, have underscored France's willingness to cooperate with the alliance. It is possible that bilateral cooperation between France and NATO could be stepped up in the coming years without formal reentry into NATO. A clearer agreement might be reached, for example, on use in a crisis of French forces stationed in Germany and on their relationship to NATO forces and strategy. Eventually, coordination of French tactical nuclear weapons with those of NATO units may be discussed, as France approaches deployment of the Pluton tactical missile. The French strategy elaborated by General Fourquet (*la réplique graduée*) should facilitate such coordination. France might even establish some relationship with the NATO Nuclear Planning Group. There are other areas of

[49] *New York Times*, February 25, 1970.

potential cooperation, including: assured availability of certain areas of French territory for support facilities and air space; assured availability of the petroleum pipeline in time of war; expanded joint maneuvers and assignment of French officers to NATO headquarters; and consultations on nuclear strategy. In a number of fields—such as tactical nuclear strategy and participation in the NATO satellite communication system—it will clearly be in France's interest to increase her cooperation with NATO.

France continues to pursue warmer relations with the United States, a trend begun by de Gaulle. Pompidou's state visit to America in February, 1970, underscored this objective. There are several kinds of potential military cooperation with the United States in which the French government has shown signs of interest, ranging from conventional weapons projects all the way to the sale of computers and the sharing of missile and nuclear-related technologies. Another possibility, and one that might easily be managed, is the coordination of the *force de dissuasion* with American nuclear forces. The sharing of American information on missile guidance or nuclear warheads would obviously be a more difficult matter to resolve, given the test ban treaty, the nonproliferation treaty, and past American policy with its bias against France. Much will depend on the evolution of French policies toward NATO and the outcome of SALT. The Nixon administration is trying to improve Franco-American relations and may be sympathetic to cooperation in some of these areas.

The Mediterranean. In 1969–1970 President Pompidou boldly seized the initiative in North Africa and the Mediterranean where he moved swiftly to strengthen France's presence. Through a series of visits by Foreign Minister Maurice Schumann, France revived friendly relations with Algeria and Tunisia and reestablished normal relations with Morocco. Weapons and military equipment may be delivered to these countries. Most spectacular, however, was the announcement that France had agreed to sell 110 Mirage jets to Libya. A smaller number of these planes will also go to Spain and possibly to Greece.

Officially, it was explained that this new thrust in French policy is designed to reinforce France's economic and cultural interests in the states of North Africa, particularly in her former colonies, with a military sphere of influence aimed at preventing further super-power (especially Soviet)penetration in the area. Libya and other countries of this region are important sources of oil for France and other European countries. For both strategic and political reasons the south shore of the Mediterranean is viewed as the vulnerable "underbelly of Europe" which France has taken upon herself to protect.[50] It remains unclear how this French initiative will affect the Arab-Israeli conflict and the chances for a Middle East settle-ment, which, France insists, depends on Four-Power accord. Pompidou's Mediterranean policy was dealt a severe blow in the spring of 1971 when nationalization of French oil company assets produced a major crisis in French-Algerian relations.

The Nuclear Deterrent. As had been anticipated, the direction of military nuclear programs remains basically unchanged under the Pompidou regime, but the pace has been slowed by continuing budgetary pressures. A few days after the formation of his government, Premier Jacques Chaban-Delmas declared in a radio inter-view that French nuclear policy was both *irréversible et orientable*. Continuity was emphasized by the appointment of Gaullist leader Michel Debré as Minister of Defense. The term *orientable* implied two things: first, that the French nuclear effort would be cut back to some extent in view of pressing domestic economic and social needs, and great care would be taken to avoid unnecessary expen-ditures; second, that France was interested in the possibility of cooperation with Britain in the nuclear field. On the latter point, the premier said that if Britain entered the Common Market, a nuclear accord might be reached "which would seriously modify the conditions of the [French] national effort, which would cease to be national in order to become European."[51] The British Labour

---

[50] Pompidou's interview with C. L. Sulzberger, *New York Times*, February 15, 1970. For further discussion, see: André Fontaine, "Pompidou's Mediterra-nean Policy," *Interplay*, April, 1970, pp. 12–14; also Edward A. Kolodziej, "French Mediterranean Policy: The Politics of Weakness," *International Af-fairs*, July, 1971, pp. 503–517.

[51] As quoted in *Le Monde*, June 29–30, 1969.

government responded negatively to this French overture. However, the subject could easily be raised with the Tory government,
given Prime Minister Heath's longstanding interest in the idea and
British entry into the European Community. But Pompidou has
stressed that France will not rejoin NATO, and this places strict
limits on any prospective nuclear collaboration.[52]

The tightening of budgetary constraints on the French nuclear
program, begun by de Gaulle in 1968, was carried further in President Pompidou's first military budget adopted by the National Assembly in the autumn of 1969. Representing only 3.4 percent of
GNP and 17.6 percent of the total national budget, military expenditures in the 1970 budget (NF27.19 billion) were proportionately
the lowest in over a century. Within this budget, nuclear forces
continued to receive priority over conventional forces. Nuclear
tests were resumed in the summer of 1970, but funding of planned
missile programs was scaled down. In place of the twenty-seven
land-based missiles previously announced, only eighteen were provided for, and the launching of the fourth nuclear submarine was
postponed. According to the usual practice, the exact amount of
money earmarked for nuclear programs was left obscure. Government figures were in the neighborhood of NF6–7 billion, but other
estimates ran into the range of NF9 billion. Characterizing the
1970 military budget as an austerity budget unacceptable over the
long term, Defense Minister Debré insisted publicly that the strategic nuclear force will be "constantly adapted and modernized." [53]

Important indicators of future plans for the *force de frappe* are
contained in the third military program-law for the period
1971–1975. Passed by the National Assembly in the autumn of
1970, this law reflects a determination to continue development of
the nuclear force but at a slower pace than de Gaulle—or even his
still active disciple, Michel Debré—probably would have liked.

[52] For discussion of the prospects for Anglo-French nuclear cooperation and
the possible forms it could take, see the author's *French Nuclear Diplomacy*,
pp. 349–53, n., p. 373; also Ian Smart, *Future Conditional: The Prospect for
Anglo-French Nuclear Cooperation*, Adelphi Paper, no. 78 (London, Institute
for Strategic Studies, 1971).

[53] Information in this paragraph is derived from *Le Monde*, November 7,
11, 12, 14, and 19, 1969.

Setting the tone, a high French defense official noted that France begins the 1970s without any immediately visible threats to her security. In this context, "compromises appear possible, taking account of the available financial means, between the needs of defense policy and those of the economic and social development appropriate for the country." [54] In proportion to French GNP, the defense budget is scheduled to decline from 3.44% in 1970 to approximately 3.0% in 1975, a figure never before attained in the history of the French Republic. President Pompidou, who reportedly desires to allocate to defense "all it is due, nothing more, nothing less," declared that, beginning in 1971, defense will cease to be accorded the largest piece of the national budgetary pie and will be surpassed by expenditures for education.[55] The application of new programming and budgeting techniques in the Ministry of Defense will, it is hoped, yield a more efficient use of resources within the strict limits set on future military expenditure.

Out of a projected total of NF93.5 billion to be authorized for military programs under the third program-law, about one-third (NF30.9 billion) will be earmarked for strategic and tactical nuclear systems, according to official figures. Production and deployment of eighteen SSBS landbased missiles is to be completed, and tactical nuclear arms (short range Pluton missiles for the Army and small tactical bombs to be carried by the Air Force's Jaguar aircraft) will be produced for service sometime in 1973 or 1974. Nuclear tests will be continued to "militarize" thermonuclear warheads for use in SSBS and MSBS missiles in the second half of the decade. The launching of a fourth nuclear submarine and initial construction work on a fifth is anticipated by 1975.[56] Within these carefully set limits, the priority given nuclear programs under the third program-law will undoubtedly mean further postponement of the modernization of conventional forces, which have already suffered severely during a decade of nuclear priorities. This may

[54] Marceau Long, "Financement de la politique militaire française," *Revue de Défense Nationale*, April, 1970, p. 537. Long is Secretary General for Administration in the Ministry of Defense.

[55] *Le Monde*, July 30, 1970.

[56] This compares with about NF34 billion spent on nuclear programs during the preceding six-year period, 1965–70. See *Le Monde*, July 31 and August 8, 1970. Also Defense Minister Debré's press conference in *Le Monde*, July 31–August 1, 1970.

cause increasing resentment among officers of the career services.[57]

If current plans are successfully implemented, France's already existing nuclear force of thirty-six Mirage IV bombers (plus additional reserve and trainer aircraft) will be complemented in the mid-1970s by less than two dozen rather vulnerable land-based missiles and three missile-carrying submarines. At that time the British force of four nuclear submarines will be somewhat more imposing, in view of its superior missiles with thermonuclear Polaris A-3 warheads and somewhat longer range. By the end of the decade, however, France could increase the number of her nuclear submarines to five and improve their missile warheads and penetration devices. On the face of it, such a French nuclear submarine force should be moderately impressive.[58]

Arms control. Just how impressive the French force will be depends on how fast superpower weapons technology develops. The scale of Soviet ABM deployment will be particularly important. For this reason defense officials in Paris can be expected to give close attention to the outcome of SALT, which will determine the relative strength of the French (and the British) nuclear capability for years to come. The first SALT agreement reached between the Soviet Union and the United States in May, 1972, limiting their ABM deployments to 200 launchers (100 to protect each country's national capital area and 100 to defend one field of ICBM launch sites), will prolong French nuclear credibility. Moscow, it is true, will be more difficult for the French to hit, although not totally impossible with sophisticated penetration devices.[59] Other major Soviet cities will presumably remain unprotected and hence vulner-

[57] In the spring of 1970 the chief of staff of the French Navy, Admiral Patou, resigned his post after a dispute with Defense Minister Debré over a cutoff in funding for the modernization of an antiaircraft cruiser.

[58] The French submarine force will also have significant shortcomings, among them vulnerability to Soviet hunter-killer subs (France will probably have only one nuclear submarine base at Ile Longue and, so far, plans no hunter-killer subs), the limited range of its missiles, and the probability of having only one VLF (very low frequency) communications center.

[59] Official French analysts have played down the potential effects on the French nuclear force of Soviet ABM deployment. French missiles, they argue, could penetrate a Soviet ABM system because "saturating tactics" could be used and because Soviet radar would have difficulty in detecting them, given the short distance they must travel and their low-altitude trajectories.

able to attack by even a small missile force such as the French are acquiring.

In order to maintain a credible deterrent over the longer run, especially as the superpowers increase their MIRV deployments, the French will have to augment considerably the number of planned missiles in their nuclear arsenal and improve their warheads and penetration aids. Faced with this expensive prospect, France might be forced to conclude that she does not have the resources to keep pace with Soviet and American advances in weapons technology, and therefore to abandon her nuclear effort by the end of the decade. Alternatively, and more likely, she could be moved to merge her resources with those of allied countries to form some kind of European nuclear arrangement. Such an arrangement would most likely be based on French and British nuclear technology.

As for French arms control policies, there has been little change under President Pompidou. France continues to boycott the Geneva disarmament conference, while approving some of its results—for example, the treaty outlawing nuclear arms on the seabed. The French government has not altered its position against signature of the nonproliferation treaty, although agreeing with the principle of that accord.

The persistence of the Gaullist approach of subordinating arms control measures to détente and the prior settlement of fundamental political issues associated with Europe's division can be seen clearly in the French stance on the question of mutual balanced force reductions (MBFR). France opposes any East-West negotiations on this issue at the present time, especially on a bloc-to-bloc basis. Uncertain as they are about Soviet policy in Europe and the fragility of détente in the present period, the French are disposed to maintain a strong defense posture and are urging their Western European neighbors to do likewise. United States forces, in their view, should remain in Europe. Any MBFR agreement, they suspect, would probably give the Soviets military advantages in a situation where the present lineup of Western and East bloc military forces is barely in balance. Paris is favorably inclined toward the convening of a European security conference to discuss East-West cooperation and the possible attenuation of the political confrontation in Europe between the two blocs.

In short, French security policy under Pompidou is based on a more modest conception of France's role in Europe and the world. The principal objective is to promote France's status and enhance her security in Europe by increasing cooperation with her Western allies, especially in the European Community. France's ties to the United States will be maintained, as will her membership and limited cooperation within the Atlantic Alliance, even though the French will not rejoin NATO. Infringements on French sovereignty and independence, however, will be kept to a minimum, for the present time. The Gaullist vision of an all-European security system does not seem within easy reach, given Soviet military power and Moscow's tight hold on the policies of East European regimes. While continuing to expand French cooperation with the Soviet Union and Eastern Europe, present leaders in Paris realize that East-West détente will be a long-term process and that France can only play a limited part.

/ *Catherine M. Kelleher*
and Donald J. Puchala

GERMANY, EUROPEAN SECURITY, and ARMS CONTROL

THE AIM of this chapter is to survey the Central European political environment,[1] with particular attention to the new trends in West German foreign policy, Eastern reactions to them, and the resulting implications for East-West political settlement and arms control.

Despite the firmest commitment to scholarly objectivity, analysis of ongoing international events invariably amounts to a combination of inadequate evidence with goodly doses of speculation. This paper must be somewhat indefinite because many of the policies and events discussed have not yet made their full impact upon world politics. Nevertheless, the authors have considerable confidence in their findings, mainly because most alternative conclusions were proven inaccurate by sequences of events in Central and Eastern Europe during the summer of 1968 and in the months that followed.

Six major conclusions follow from the paper's analysis:

[1] As used in this chapter, "Central Europe" denotes Germany (East and West), Austria, Poland, Czechoslovakia, and Hungary. "Eastern Europe" denotes the four Communist states mentioned above plus Albania, Bulgaria, Rumania, and Yugoslavia. "The East" denotes Eastern Europe plus the Soviet Union.

1. Only a settlement of the problem of a divided Germany can significantly alter the Central European status quo. But since there is no conceivable solution to this problem that would not now and for the next few years demand intolerable concessions from either the East or the West, de facto acceptance of the status quo will continue.

2. The Eastern policy, *Ostpolitik*, of the Federal Republic of Germany is a somewhat uncertain variable in the Central European political system. There is little evidence that this West German self-assertiveness is contributing toward a settlement in Central Europe on a basis other than the status quo, and virtually no evidence that the Soviet Union will allow any significant movement to follow from the Bonn initiatives. Nevertheless, although there is no reason that the Federal Republic should expect major new political payoffs from its *Ostpolitik* in the foreseeable future, neither is there any good reason why it should discontinue or lessen its efforts vis-à-vis the East.

3. West German foreign policy is entangled in a web of interrelated contingencies in three operational theaters: the Atlantic community, the EEC, and the Communist East. Bonn's dilemma is that its primary interests in these three arenas are equally important but are, at least in potential, mutually contradictory. In any event, its success in any one of these arenas depends upon variables beyond the Federal Republic's control.

4. Contrary to the assumptions of many Western observers, Eastern Europe and Eastern European national policies are not, and in the conceivable future will not be, truly independent variables in the Central European international system. Although clearly preceded by some hesitation, the invasion of Czechoslovakia emphasized once again that the Soviet Union will continue to insist on strict hierarchical control in the Central European Communist states. This insistence stems from orthodox political, military, and economic concerns overlaid with the ideological orthodoxy which, especially over the past several years, has characterized Soviet decision-making.

5. Although some installments have already been paid, settlement in Central Europe implies high political costs for the West.

Refusal to pay these costs and settle on Russian terms means extending the status quo indefinitely. On the other hand, conceding to the Soviet Union probably would mean formalizing new arrangements that would be even less comfortable for the West than those of the inherently tense present.

6. The current political-military situation in Central Europe opens few easy opportunities for arms control and disarmament. Continuing political tensions nurtured by unsettled issues demand that East-West military equilibrium be maintained in Europe. Hence, the only arms control measures practicable in the existing situation would be measures taken to buttress the existing military arrangements. Such measures would necessarily be of the "freeze" variety: to freeze the deterrent balance in Europe through agreements concerning qualitative and quantitative force limitations, and to control West Germany with agreements guaranteeing that German military potential will not become German military power. Other and more ambitious arms control schemes for Europe are of course conceivable. But they are probable only in the context of definite movement toward the settlement of major political issues, and such movement seems unlikely.

For specific reasons, this report scans the Central European environment from two vantage points—Bonn and Moscow. Rather than offering a grand and general overview of the whole European landscape, the chapter focuses more closely upon the most basic developments in Central European international politics, namely, the unfolding of Bonn's *Ostpolitik* and the clarification of Soviet attitudes toward Eastern Europe.

Bonn's policies of attempted conciliation toward the East were born in 1966, if one does not quibble about antecedents, with the Grand Coalition of the CDU and SPD led by Chancellor Kurt Kiesinger and Foreign Minister Willy Brandt. The actual changes in West German policy implied in *Ostpolitik* are notable; to some, the changes which Brandt and others have wrought and to which they still aspire verge on the revolutionary. Bonn's policies deserve close scrutiny, not least because the impact of their failure could be almost as dramatic as the results of their success.

The clarification of Soviet attitudes toward Eastern Europe

came, of course, in the aftermath of the invasion of Czechoslovakia. Several years of Western (and perhaps Eastern European) miscalculation and wishful thinking ended abruptly when the Russian armies marched into Prague. Both the fact of the invasion and the results of the Soviet-Czechoslovak settlement must now weigh heavily in any assessment of the possibility of a Central European settlement.

Adding the implications of *Ostpolitik* to those of the invasion of Czechoslovakia should produce some insights into how conditions in Central Europe may affect opportunities for arms control in the 1970s.

THE UNFOLDING OF
OSTPOLITIK: *1966–1968*

For both observers and participants, the principal change in Central European international politics in recent years came with the launching of *Ostpolitik*, a set of West German initiatives aimed at détente. From its formation in December, 1966, the Grand Coalition consistently and painstakingly sought the "normalization" of its relations with the Eastern states, including both the Soviet Union and the German Democratic Republic (GDR). Bonn publicly acknowledged what had long been admitted privately, that reunification—or more precisely, the solution of the German question—was not imminent; it would be reached, if at all, only in the far future and then only as the last step in a broader European settlement. Moreover, primary responsibility for any current movement in this direction would have to be borne by an increasingly self-assertive Federal Republic.

Nascence of Ostpolitik. In certain respects, the shift in West German policy was hardly surprising, representing merely a long-delayed adjustment to the dictates of political reality. Whatever their declaratory policies, by 1962 each of West Germany's principal allies had implicitly accepted the country's division as an estab-

lished fact for the foreseeable future.[2] There had indeed been minimum fulfillment of basic West German demands: no formal recognition of the GDR, and pious NATO pronouncements of broad support for the goal of reunification. But with the United States in the
lead, there had been mounting pressure for a more flexible German approach, for a quiet burial of the legalistic dogmas and in-
cessant demands for reassurance that had marked the 1950s
and early 1960s.

Moreover, the shift clearly did not emerge fullblown from the
head of the Grand Coalition. Its direct antecedents were the cautious Erhard-Schroeder "policy of movement" toward the East and
the *Politik der kleinen Schritte* advocated by the then Mayor of
Berlin, Willy Brandt. Of only somewhat less significance were the
debates and proposals which emerged after the building of the
Berlin Wall in 1961—in intellectual circles, within the churches, in
the liberal media, and in the business community, to mention only
the most obvious sources. Precedents and patterns could even be
found in traditional German policies toward the East, especially
the economic-cultural thrusts in 1890 and 1936.[3]

What was unique about the *Ostpolitik* inaugurated in 1966 was
the clear political decision, supported by a broad consensus, to revise the priorities and content formerly assigned to Germany's
well-known triad of foreign policy goals—Atlantic security, Western European integration, and reunification. As all major political
leaders hasten to declare, assigning a higher priority to *Ostpolitik*
did not imply any lessening of belief in the ultimate mutual interrelation of all three goals. It was simply that for the present neither the Atlantic nor the Western European arena promised much
further development in line with German interests.

Belief in some degree of immediate mutual interrelation was suggested by the *Ostpolitik* tinge given to many West German moves
in the Atlantic and European arenas. At North Atlantic Council

[2] Many would view this acceptance as dating from the failure of the Moscow Conference of Foreign Ministers in 1947.

[3] For the seminal discussion of these events and their contemporary parallels, see William E. Griffith's "Germany and Eastern Europe," published
through the Center for International Studies, M.I.T.

meetings, for example, then Foreign Minister Brandt made it clear that any further reduction of American troops in Germany—perhaps to the new "magic" level of two divisions—would be tolerable if effected within the framework of East-West balanced force reductions. In part, this was clearly a tactic aimed at making sudden unilateral decisions more difficult. But it also represented a new effort to extract maximum national advantage from the seemingly inevitable. The West German effort was for the first time backed up by serious studies and proposals as to the types of manpower and armament cuts that would be realizable, acceptable, and politically beneficial.

Similarly, the Kiesinger-Brandt government agreed to French demands to postpone any immediate broadening or acceleration of EEC development, but only with the clear proviso that serious future consideration be given to the how and when of Eastern European association with the EEC. For the moment, West Germany demanded joint action to provide long-term trade credits to the East and to relax Community barriers to Eastern commodities such as agricultural products.

Ostpolitik: *Aims and Impacts.* In its push toward the East, the Kiesinger-Brandt government emphasized another triad of mutually interdependent yet distinct policy areas: relations with the Soviet Union, with the Eastern European states, and with the "other part of Germany." "Normalization" of all three, leaders repeatedly declared, would be essential for a future peaceful order in Europe. Despite the accepted interdependence of the three operational areas, Bonn's goals, strategy, and timing in each varied significantly in accordance with past legacies, present opportunities, and future designs.

Relations with the Soviet Union. Endeavors vis-à-vis Moscow to move away from the hostile, minimal efforts of the Adenauer era and well beyond the tentative probes of Erhard clearly met with limited success, if any. Starting very slowly, the German political leadership found even its most tentative efforts toward new understanding with the Soviet Union halted both by intra-coalition opposition from the CDU-CSU ranks and by continuing Soviet intransigence. Despite the friendlier tone in German appeals for improved relations and some tactical shifting as diplomatic exchange followed upon diplomatic exchange, there was almost no observable change in Soviet–West German relations during the period of 1966–1968.

On the one Bonn-proposed discussion point picked up by the Soviets—the exchange of pledges renouncing the use of force—the coalition demonstrated considerable flexibility in the face of steadily escalating Soviet demands. It moved from the concept foreseen in the March, 1966, Erhard "peace note"—exchanges between the Federal Republic and the Warsaw Treaty area as a whole—to that of April, 1968—a network of interlocking bilateral treaties with each state, including a still-not-to-be-recognized GDR. Bonn increasingly emphasized that the first exchange should be with Moscow, as leader of the Eastern alliance, to be followed by a jointly scheduled program of negotiations with the other members. And this, the coalition emphasized, would make German ratification of the nonproliferation treaty—unquestionably a major Soviet goal—a far easier and swifter process.

The coalition showed even greater flexibility in its response to Soviet proposals regarding a new European security system. Bonn did conform to the basic Western position on two central points: the time for a European security conference was not yet ripe, and any new system must proceed from, not abolish, existing alliance systems. Yet the Federal Republic repeatedly asserted its continuing interest in such proposals and indicated its agreement on certain Soviet stipulations for the "European peace order" to be achieved, namely, respect for the different social and economic systems involved and mutual renunciations of force among all participants.

Most radical of all, the coalition's position with respect to the steps needed to create such a system virtually mirrored Eastern arms control proposals, particularly the Rapacki and Gomulka plans. Foreign Minister Brandt foresaw a two-stage reduction of direct military confrontation in Europe: first the balanced withdrawal of foreign troops from both parts of Germany, then a balanced reduction (but perhaps involving a different nuclear-conventional combination for each side) of all forces in the Central European (i.e., Rapacki-designated) area. The removal of atomic warheads and delivery vehicles could be treated as a "natural" consequence of troop cuts or as a "separate" element. Further, before final agreement on such steps, "mitigating" measures against surprise attack could and should be taken, such as the creation of fixed or mobile observation posts, the exchange of special observers or missions, and pledges of mutual renunciation of force.

Clearly, much of this could be interpreted as gestures toward the Western gallery and as moves designed at least as much to dampen popular Eastern European fears of German revanchism as to affect Soviet attitudes. No German leader, not even during the auspicious days of the Brandt-Tsarapkin talks in the winter of 1968, really expected major reversals in Soviet policies on reunification, the future European role of the Federal Republic, or the clustered preconditions for any serious discussions on reunification and Central European problems.

To a significant degree, the intermediate-range German strategy looked like an attempt paralleling the Soviet Union's own ambivalent or "options open" policy toward the Federal Republic. On the one hand, Bonn stressed détente, offering limited political retreats and economic deals as concessions to open a dialogue with the Soviet Union. Correspondingly, Bonn hinted at further positive interactions and presumed converging interests with Moscow. On the other hand, the Bonn government pursued protection, seeking to prevent its isolation in the West and to minimize direct confrontation with the Soviet Union in its search for influence in Eastern Europe.

Relations with Eastern Europe. It was in the Eastern European area, prior to the invasion of Czechoslovakia, that *Ostpolitik* was most visible and most successful in the short-run normalization and expansion of Bonn's economic, cultural, and political contacts. The four trade missions previously set up by Schroeder and the one established in Prague in 1967 provided a framework for continuing negotiations on, for example, further trade liberalization, German participation in Eastern joint ventures, and the provision of investment credits and technological opportunities. Moreover, official visits eastward increased at least fourfold between 1966 and 1968 and "private trips" grew by a radically larger factor. The Federal Republic established full diplomatic relations with Rumania and Yugoslavia and reached agreement with the Dubček government on the consular powers of the Prague trade mission.

The Grand Coalition also moved, directly and indirectly, to revise certain uncompromising juridical dogmas of the past. Whatever the legal acrobatics performed, the renewal of relations with Belgrade marked the end of even the "birth-defect" version of the Hallstein Doctrine on recognition of European regimes that also recognized the GDR. Each round of negotiations did see disagreement on a few legal formulations, particularly on the proper designation of the Federal Republic of Germany and on the inclusion of the so-called Berlin clause.[4] But the Rumanian and Yugoslav accords constituted a new model: they contained both common declarations regarding the agreement and separate national statements on differing fundamental policy positions, principally positions on the recognition of the GDR.

Despite refugee protests and over some CDU-CSU objections, the German stance on border questions became more flexible. From its inception, the coalition declared that although final designation must await an equitable European peace settlement, it regarded the Munich agreement of 1938 as "no longer valid" and well understood Poland's desire for "secure borders" in the interim. Unofficially, government spokesmen, particularly those from the SPD, went much further. At a 1968 SPD conference, for example, Brandt called for "recognition and respect of the Oder-Neisse line" as one of postwar Europe's "realities"; there were also reportedly private offers to Dubček's government regarding "repudiation from the outset" of the Munich pact.

However great were the intangible improvements in atmosphere and the allaying of justified mistrust, the Kiesinger-Brandt government admitted that it garnered few substantive political gains and

[4] In all its trade agreements (except the "informal" agreements with the GDR), Bonn insisted that products produced or consumed in Berlin be considered no different from those produced or consumed in West Germany. This implied, of course, acceptance of Berlin's status, not as the legal capital of the GDR, but as the eleventh *Land* of the *Bundesrepublik*.

no really spectacular successes. Poland remained obdurate. Despite their repeated expressions of interest in full diplomatic relations and pledges of mutual renunciation of force, Hungary and Bulgaria and even a liberalizing Czechoslovakia deferred (with varying degrees of reluctance) to increasing Soviet and East German pressure regarding absolute preconditions for normalized relations, namely, recognition of the GDR and final acceptance of the present German borders. Even in the most receptive states the gravitational pull of West German economic and technological strength, though substantial, proved less than all-determining. Similarly, the greatly increased cultural exchanges notwithstanding, official utterances still contained familiar castigations of the "revanchist," "nuclear-mad," "neo-Nazi" West Germans.

Relations with East Germany. Bonn's most significant and at the same time most frustrated initiatives under *Ostpolitik* were changes in its approach to East Germany. Perhaps the most striking departure was the clear determination on the part of all major political groups in the Federal Republic to pursue "normalization" even in the face of adversity that formerly would have been intolerable. Continuing Soviet and East German pressures were applied in Eastern Europe to frustrate improvements in West German–Eastern European relations. All of these met with dogged, continuing West German efforts and expressions of understanding and respect. Failure to achieve agreement on any given problem led to what was for Bonn swift tactical reconsideration and renewed emphasis on other negotiable points, however minor.

Unquestionably, the most revolutionary aspect of *Ostpolitik* was the decision not to leave basic intra-German relations to the outcome of Four-Power negotiations (as under Adenauer) or of a direct West German campaign to isolate the GDR (as during Erhard's last years). Publicly and privately, the GDR would be considered an "existing, governing political order on German soil," and an integral (albeit special) member of the Eastern alliance. However great its disapproval of the current East German regime and its interest in ultimate reunification, Bonn would make every reasonable effort to achieve interim "normalization," a modus vivendi (Brandt's *geregeltes Nebeneinander*) for the two "constituent states" of the divided German nation.

During its first eighteen months, the Grand Coalition gave unprecedented substance to the long-declared priority of human concerns vis-à-vis the 17 million East Germans over efforts to achieve juridical unity (*Freiheit vor Einheit*). On the simplest level, the government smoothed or halted many provocative or irritating practices rooted in previous precepts of "no recognition under any guise." In its approach to the failing intra-German trade, the coalition stressed the mutual benefit at stake and praised the recent East German *Wirtschaftswunder* and, albeit without success, also prepared many new measures designed to facilitate and consolidate future agreements.

Of greater importance were the constant West German calls for negotiations on other "practical matters of German existence," leaving aside all political and legal questions on which "agreement is not possible." In his 1967 letters to East German Premier Willi Stoph, Kiesinger proposed talks—virtually anywhere, on any level —on sixteen specific points concerning greater personal mobility and communication, greater cooperation on mutually beneficial technical projects, and broader cultural and information exchanges. The only caveat was that these or any topics suggested by the GDR were not to be the subject of "inordinate" or "maximal" demands.

Even the coalition's consistent refusals to meet Ulbricht's basic demand of full recognition evidenced significant departures from the past. Bonn's explicit reference was always to recognition under international law, which did not exclude consideration of the GDR's "state-like" character. There were far fewer mentions of Bonn's role as sole legitimate representative of the German people, and these only in terms of a political-moral duty as spokesman, conservator, or "keeper of the faith" for the future.

Moreover, the principal thrust of Bonn's argument shifted radically from the "undemocratic," "illegitimate," "puppet-like" nature of the GDR to the "fact" that it was not a foreign state, but part of the German nation. A number of unofficial statements (mainly from the SPD and left CDU ranks) implied that the GDR already possessed some legitimacy and would acquire more, probably to a degree that made at least interim recognition possible, through progressive political liberalization. Although not going as far as did advocates of immediate unconditional recognition, a few officials hinted privately that any measurable movement toward change might be enough to prompt a West German statement of intent.

All of these "interim changes" clearly signaled changes in official perceptions of the ultimate goal, reunification, or, as many officials interviewed in Bonn during June, 1968, expressed it, "reassociation of the German nation." Government statements went little beyond observations about the length and uncertainty of such a process and pledges that the Federal Republic did not seek the complete political disappearance of the GDR or a complete dissolution of its Communist system. Within the coalition parties and outside them, private estimates of what was possible ranged along a unitary-confederated-divided continuum, with ever increasing weight concentrated on the latter alternatives. For the majority (whatever their public stance) it was a question of evolutionary change within and among existing institutions leading to an unforeseeable new system, German as well as European.

Basically, therefore, Bonn's all-German policy was to pursue détente and normalization in hopes of convergence and evolutionary change. But despite the coalition's truly dramatic softening of policies vis-à-vis the GDR, no real reciprocity was elicited from Ulbricht. To be sure, some hints were dropped during the spring of 1968. Notably, Ulbricht uttered some ambiguous phrases about "technical talks" a few days prior to the invasion of Czechoslovakia and, for the first time, he did not link the idea of dialogue directly with the perennial demand for recognition. But, even before the invasion, most observers viewed these moves as principally the spillover from the GDR's game with Moscow and Moscow's game with an ever more liberalizing Prague.

Pre-Czechoslovakian **Ostpolitik** *in Overview.* Whatever its successes or disappointments, Bonn's Eastern strategy up to August, 1968, remained the same. On the simplest level, its concern was the seizure of new opportunities in an area of traditional German economic and political influence. What the precise limits of "normalization" or of the economic offensive would be, no one could accurately foretell. What concessions would ultimately be demanded from Bonn and what concessions Bonn would actually be willing to make were questions seemingly left to the evolving situation and never carefully mapped or thoroughly debated. The general hope among quite disparate groups, the point of consensus in *Ostpolitik*, was that any progress on any issue in any area would be a gain over the frozen past.

Then, too, *Ostpolitik* was founded in the general Western conviction (never enunciated but relatively visible in Bonn as in Washington) that present favorable engagement in Eastern Europe constituted the back door to any future European settlement—or at least the "can opener" for improved relations with the Soviet Union and the GDR. Clearly, the Kiesinger-Brandt government took great pains to avoid any frontal attack on Soviet political, strategic, and economic stakes in Eastern Europe or on the continuation there of the Communist system. Rather, the coalition argument seemed to be that, objectively, Moscow would not long be able to resist Eastern European pressures for political normalization and economic reassociation with the Federal Republic. The Soviet government would be faced with a choice between paying unacceptable costs to ensure conformity among its restive clients (e.g., intervention or massive Soviet economic and technological infusions) or relaxing some of the restraints on their political flexibility and its own. Furthermore, without Soviet support, Ulbricht would confront a similar dilemma: the danger of self-isolation and uncontrolled, disruptive contagion from his contemptuous neighbors or the risk of accommodation to the wind of the future and some major concessions to preserve his role as a primary arbiter of "German relations" with Eastern countries.

All that has been said to this point should enable the reader to share the image of 1966–1968 *Ostpolitik* that the authors' analysis impressed on them: the policy was new, imaginative, and probably politically healthy for the Federal Republic, both domestically and internationally. But even before the Czech invasion, it brought forth only minimal responsiveness from the East and no tangible political results. In brief, it was a network of short, one-way streets terminating, essentially, in a series of dead ends. There is more to be said on the future of *Ostpolitik*, but it must follow an exploration of the reasons why neither the new West German self-assertiveness nor any of the various similar attempts at Western bridge-building gained the expected and predicted responsiveness from the East. An understanding of Eastern nonresponsiveness emerges from looking over the Central European theater from the vantage point of Moscow.

THE FUTURE OF EASTERN
EUROPE IN THE 1970s

Lessons of Czechoslovakia. Perhaps the best place to begin any investigation of the Eastern European future is with the most recent failure in predicting it, Western misassessments before the Soviet invasion of Czechoslovakia. From this experience the analyst can, one hopes, gain insights into not only specific Soviet-imposed constraints on future development but also the problems of Western (including West German) assumptions and assessments. For it was in these respects that the events of August, 1968, seemed the most surprising and contradictory. Soviet and Western analysts were probably in fairly close agreement concerning happenings in Eastern Europe in the months before the invasion of Czechoslovakia. Movements toward political liberalization under Dubček, expanding Rumanian trade with Western countries, proliferation of business deals and cultural interactions between Eastern Communist states and their non-Communist regional neighbors, steady Eastern European inchings toward greater national economic autonomy, and West Germany's penetrating *Ostpolitik* were all as observable in Moscow as in Western capitals. Where Soviet and Western analyses parted was on the future of Eastern European trends toward national autonomy. Specifically, the Western assessment of Eastern European economic and political movements prior to the Warsaw Treaty Organization's invasion of Czechoslovakia departed from what became the Soviet-imposed reality at three major points.

The assumption that increasing liberalization in Eastern European countries and rapid fragmentation of the old bloc represented a unidirectional, irreversible movement toward diminished Soviet authority in this area was proved false. In part, these preinvasion analyses were only giving a "most favorable" reading of what was without doubt an unclear, uncertain pattern of Soviet decision-making. But, more than anything else, the fact of the invasion underlined the fallacy of conjectures concerning a new definition of Communist unity among the Warsaw Pact states. "New" elements —greater emphasis on consensual decision-making in Warsaw Pact affairs, greater Soviet permissiveness concerning Western economic contacts and unorthodox domestic developments—could and can exist only within certain narrow, specific limits. And these elements were clearly of secondary importance to the only basic definition of Communist unity that the Soviet Union would accept: continued commitment to the Warsaw Pact, continued Communist party control, and continued acceptance of Soviet political, economic, and military suzerainty in Eastern Europe.

Over the next few years the limits within which this definition will be enforced will vary, perhaps the most basic distinction in interpretation being between the "crucial" states of Central Europe and the lesser partners such as Rumania, Yugoslavia, or Albania. The exact threshold of Soviet permissiveness will also depend on whether the general hardening of Soviet internal policy—observed by some critics since late 1967—continues unabated. But for the foreseeable future, under the Brezhnev doctrine the CPSU has reserved for itself the right to judge the orthodoxy of Eastern European client parties and the right to condemn and punish deviation, by the unabashed use of military force, if necessary. Eastern Europe still is a Soviet camp and will remain so, whatever the Eastern European disgruntlements, until the Soviet Union decides to accept a new modus vivendi.

Western estimates concerning the relative prominence of military, economic, political, and ideological factors were proven too limited or simply wrong. Here analysts face the dangers of engaging in infallible postdiction and of demanding greater Western perspicacity when, in fact, the Soviet leadership itself had not yet reached (and perhaps had temporarily rejected) the final decision. Yet the basic calculus which led the CPSU to bear the high costs of defending strict hierarchical unity within the East seems to have been sharply etched in several crucial areas.

That the leadership of the CPSU was clearly most concerned with domestic stability within the Soviet Union and therefore most sensitive to developments in Eastern European countries that could affect this stability seems a sound contention. However small the domestic audience, the Soviet leadership feared the contagion of liberal ideas and models that were already generating calls for emulation. This fear greatly increased when the liberal ideas emanated from other Communist countries and bore the implicit message, "This, too, can happen under Communism." What the CPSU eschewed was not liberalization per se but rather any movement toward liberalization that outpaced its own erratic limpings and, more importantly, any experiments that suggested dilution of party authority.

After concerns for its own tenure and authority, the Communist party was concerned with the military security of the Soviet Union. To this end, the Russians insisted upon unhampered and unhamperable military mobility, support, and supply in Eastern Europe, particularly Central Europe, where they placed their first line of defense for the Soviet Union's western frontier. Russian officers continued to give ground invasion from the West a high priority in their military contingency planning, and they saw their effectiveness in defense resting on bastions in the "northern tier" or "iron triangle" zone of Eastern Europe, i.e., in East Germany, Poland, and Czechoslovakia. Consequently, the Russian military and through them the CPSU leadership viewed with extreme alarm any development in an Eastern European country that might reduce that country's reliability as a Warsaw Pact member or otherwise hinder the defense of the northern tier. In short, for the Soviet Union questions of deviation from political orthodoxy prescribed by Moscow easily became questions of military security.

Third in order among CPSU concerns for tight alignment in the Eastern sphere was Moscow's fear of liberal contagion within Eastern Europe itself. There never was and never would be any question of the Soviet Union's political-ideological isolation within its own Communist domain. More realistically, however, Moscow owed

Kadar, Gomulka, Zhivkov, Ulbricht, and their respective cliques a substantial political debt for unswerving good behavior in the form of constant and enthusiastic support for CPSU policy over many years. It was not a situation where the hard-liners might threaten deviationism if the Soviet Union failed to grant them favors. But domestic forces would have made life a great deal more difficult for the hard-liners if Moscow had toned down its insistence upon orthodoxy within its sphere. Moscow therefore owed its orthodox friends protection from liberal forces and some assurance of continued tenure.

After these major concerns for conformity in the Eastern camp, three additional factors cluster at a somewhat lower level of importance. There was the Soviet insistence upon economic dominance in Eastern foreign trade, involving both Soviet dependence upon some basic Eastern European commodities and Soviet fear that loosened political control over its sphere would send Eastern Europeans flocking westward for capital and markets.[5] Further, there seemed clear psychological grounds for the CPSU's distaste for unorthodox views in the Eastern alliance. The ideologue typically thinks in an either-or framework and includes among those not to be trusted anyone who deviates in the slightest from orthodoxy. Neither the CPSU leadership nor Walter Ulbricht, for example, trusted Dubček during preinvasion meetings despite the latter's strong and apparently sincere commitment to Communism and his repeated assurances of loyalty and good faith. Even if the CPSU leaders had no stronger reason for insisting upon orthodoxy in their sphere, they most probably would still have wanted it in order to avoid the psychological discomforts of having to live and work with men whom they could not bring themselves to trust.

Finally, intraparty politics in the CPSU was surely a determining factor in Soviet policies toward Eastern Europe. It is extremely

---

[5] For example, closer Eastern European economic relations with West Germany would probably exacerbate domestic problems in East Germany, reduce East Germany's influence in the Eastern alliance, work against Moscow's interest in buttressing the GDR government, and increase traditional Soviet fears regarding German influence and penetration in its political-economic domain. Then, too, achieving competitive equality in Western markets could ease the political turn westward by Eastern European countries.

difficult to specify at any time how intraelite competition in the Soviet Union directly reinforces a particular policy stance. One likely possibility in this case is that forces opposing greater economic liberalization in the Soviet Union raised the specter of diminishing central control for the Communist party and that this pressure led to a more adamant ideological position. Another possibility is that conservative military influence was on the upswing in Soviet policy-making. A third possibility is a combination of the two just mentioned, an orthodox alliance of the military and the party ideologues against the economic pragmatists and reformers.

In sum, the Soviet invasion of Czechoslovakia was not difficult to understand in the light of CPSU concerns for conformity in the alliance. Dubček's internal experiments and external leaning focused Soviet fears and discomforts at a single point. Where fears of contagion or perceptions of military insecurity, concern for the positions of orthodox allies, or economic, political, or psychological penalties, taken separately and singly, probably would not have aroused the Soviet Union to such extreme action, all of these factors combined into a highly and inevitably explosive amalgam. The analytical shortsightedness in the failure of Westerners to predict the move on Czechoslovakia followed not so much from failure to see deep Soviet concerns in the Czechoslovak situation, but rather from failures to gauge the real depth of Soviet concern and the potential explosiveness in a situation that was simultaneously detrimental to a wide range of the Soviet Union's most vital interests.

The growing optimism in the West about compatible movements toward political settlement in Central Europe was proven ill-founded or at least premature. Before August, 1968, it looked to some analysts as if a framework of minimal détente was emerging in Central Europe. Again, Western weighting of the factors that might add to a European settlement was inaccurate. Westerners placed too much reliance on the image of settlement emerging from piecemeal movements of certain Eastern European states westward, and they gave too little attention to Soviet resistance to these movements. They also attributed too much significance to minimal Eastern European receptiveness to Bonn's *Ostpolitik* and attributed too little to Russia's condemnation of Bonn's policies. Furthermore, they valued Rumanian and Czechoslovak conciliatory attitudes too highly and East German obduracy not nearly enough. Finally, Westerners focused too much on the idea of East-West normalization in Europe and underplayed the primary importance of superpower détente in any such settlement.

Prognosis for the 1970's. The importance of superpower détente being reserved for later discussion, what is the prognosis for Eastern Europe in the 1970s? Peering into the future even at this distance from the 1968 invasion must still be a highly speculative undertaking. Nevertheless, the Soviet concerns reemphasized by the invasion suggest several important points about the probable evolution of the Eastern European situation in the 1970s.

The first point has already been discussed: the Soviet definition of Communist unity in Central Europe remains a definition of superpower dominance. The value of the Eastern European domain in Soviet political and strategic decision-making has not diminished with time, and there is no reason to believe that it will diminish greatly in the near future.

Second, Eastern Europe is a zone of Soviet influence by Soviet design, not by Eastern European choice. For the short run at least, Eastern Europe will have to be considered a dependent variable in any equation for Central European political change.

Third, the forceful reassertion of Soviet interest in suzerainty has discouraged or at least sharply curbed would-be liberalizers throughout Eastern Europe. For a time (probably quite a long time) one can expect few dramatic or abrupt moves toward liberalization within Eastern European countries and no more probing for the outer limits of Soviet tolerance. The hand of the orthodox, pro-Moscow leaders has been strengthened, if only because they can again confront their more liberal internal and external antagonists with a very persuasive "look what deviation brings" argument.

Although most clues to the evolution of the Eastern European situation are contained in the Soviet interests that prompted the invasion of Czechoslovakia, further hints about the probable future are shown in Eastern European reactions to the harsh tactic of Soviet invasion and in Eastern European reactions to the repressive settlement imposed upon the Dubček regime.

The Soviet move, because it was a military move and a move against an ally, carried costs that cannot be easily ignored. First, the splits between Moscow on the one hand and Bucharest and Belgrade on the other were greatly exacerbated by the invasion, to the point where Moscow found even greater continuing, open, and embarrassing Communist criticism of many of its global and sphere policies. The Russians, therefore, faced the predicament of living with outspoken opposition within their camp, searching for compromise with Ceausescu and possibly Tito, too, or imposing coerced conformity upon Rumania and perhaps also Yugoslavia. During the years since the invasion, despite occasional feints, Moscow has essentially pursued the first course. But whether this is the result of tactical considerations, of longer-range cost-benefit calculations, or of indecision among the Soviet leaders is far from clear.

If there is any substance to Western press reports, the invasion of Czechoslovakia also stirred up much popular ill-will in all Warsaw Pact countries, even in those countries whose governments joined the Soviet Union in the military move. It is true that diffuse popular will has little influence on official policy in Communist countries and that the direct sense of outrage has been a rather transitory phenomenon. Still, one can assume that Communist credibility has been somewhat tarnished, and one can hypothesize that, for the present, Communist rule by compliance is going to be more difficult.

Clearly, the settlement in Czechoslovakia is going to influence greatly the Eastern European situation for a long time, though perhaps not as long as that of Hungary in 1956. On one level, the Soviet Union has apparently gained virtually all of the alterations in Czechoslovak policy and personnel which it initially sought, and perhaps more. Indeed, the most obvious lesson of Czechoslovakia seems to be the Soviet Union's ability to quash in systematic, often "indirect," phases the roots of Czechoslovak reform. With armed presence a constant reminder of Soviet determination and an instrument of pressure, the liberal leadership was forced to discredit itself. The conservative successors have retrograded gradually but effectively. Perhaps most important in the long run is the Soviet blessing of conservative Slovak nationalism, a divisive force not without parallels in other Eastern European states.

But on another level the Soviet course in Czechoslovakia has not been totally smooth. Deep popular resentment exists, surfacing erratically in response to specific decrees or incidents, and is likely to continue as a source of tension and uncertainty throughout the 1970s. Moreover, as Poland in December, 1970, again dramatically illustrated, neither Soviet insistence upon strict suzerainty nor its predisposition to preserve Leninist orthodoxy by military force will make any positive contribution toward solving the economic suffocation that caused the Czechoslovak liberalization in the first place or toward bridging the "generation gap" that exists throughout Eastern Europe. Finally, these efforts can at most only dampen the new attentiveness westward that has characterized all levels of Eastern European public opinion during the last several years.

With respect to the Eastern European future, therefore, one would expect in the short run that the obvious lesson from the Czechoslovak experience of 1968 will be the more potent; that would-be liberalizers will retreat, conservative elements will move toward consolidating their positions, and CPSU prescriptions will become Eastern European desires. In the longer run, however (five to ten years), ambiguities from the Czechoslovak situation will probably lead to new probings for the limits of Soviet tolerance and to new liberal experiments, in the absence of explicit proscriptions. Uncertainties in the Czech settlement, the "Polish problem" of fulfilling simultaneously the requirements of both economic necessity and ideological orthodoxy, will provide grist for continuing debate between ideologues and pragmatists in all Communist systems, including the Soviet Union.

Nonetheless, there seemingly will be few major changes in the near future, unless fairly wild assumptions about radical shifts in the Soviet leadership or popular upheavals in Eastern Europe are made. Some Eastern European regimes have again begun inching toward greater national autonomy. Hungary is in the cautious lead; the Gomulka-Gierek transfer in Poland was a most dramatic straw in the wind. Still, even in fairly long-run terms, there is no reason to expect any fundamental movement away from orthodoxy in East Germany, no good reason (save an unlikely change in Western or Soviet policy well beyond the outer limits or dreams of *Ostpolitik*) to expect Ulbricht's successors to allow any meaningful softening of the hard line toward the West, no reason to expect much dramatic movement in Hungary, either. As far as Czechoslovakia or Poland is concerned, what "orthodoxy" is going to mean cannot be determined until the situation stabilizes. It is, however, not likely to mean new, far-reaching liberal reforms like those of the Prague Spring.

Central European Settlement. Realistically speaking, political settlement in Central Europe is no farther away now than it was before August, 1968. Before the invasion of Czechoslovakia, a settlement depended upon reconciliation with and concessions to the Soviet Union and East Germany; it still does. If anything has changed for the worse as a result of the invasion, it is the political atmosphere in Central Europe. Not only does settlement still appear distant, but now even talking seriously about it appears distant.

The direct relationship between this chapter's extended analysis of the Eastern European political environment and the question of East-West settlement in Central Europe can be pinpointed in two propositions: first, the separate and independent national wills of Eastern European states will influence settlement in Central Europe only to the extent that they are congruent with CPSU political-ideological interest and Russian national interest; and second, no settlement in Central Europe is possible unless and until Russian interests in Eastern Europe are recognized and accommodated.

In one sense, the first proposition greatly simplifies the search for a settlement. It suggests indeed that the West never really had any Eastern European cards in its diplomatic hand to play against the Soviet Union and is unlikely to get any in the future that will make any great difference in the final outcome in Central Europe. To the extent that pre-Czechoslovakia *Ostpolitik* and indeed American bridge-building were conceived as levers to pry the Soviet Union from obduracy by nurturing moderation in Eastern Europe, these Western policies were destined for disappointing conclusions from the outset. Enticing Eastern Europe is simply not the same as persuading or moving the Soviet Union. Despite the images of improving relations projected by advocates of the "soft line to the East," the Soviet Union did not accept the conciliatory nature of Western intentions, and the Russians saw no explicit or implicit concessions to Soviet interests in the Western bridge-building policies. With regard to *Ostpolitik* particularly, the Russians saw and will probably continue to see no West German intentions to recognize permanently Soviet predominance in Eastern Europe, and in general no West German willingness to pay any significant price for settlement in Europe. Clearly, there is a high risk of bankruptcy in bridge-building policies and a strong indication in Russian attitudes and behavior that the pathway to Central European settlement does not lead to Moscow through Eastern Europe.

On the other hand, eliminating an independent Eastern European role makes the problem of a Central European settlement considerably more difficult. When the possibility of an intermediate and moderate Eastern European position is erased, Soviet and Western interests emerge in direct confrontation and the finding of a new European settlement reverts to a problem of accommodating incompatibilities. Unless either the West or the Soviet Union makes substantial concessions, the stalemate in Central Europe and the division into recognized spheres of influence will continue indefinitely.

This brings the discussion to the second proposition: the Soviet demand that its predominant interest in Eastern Europe—indeed, its suzerainty in the region—be recognized, accepted, guaranteed, and perpetuated in any formal European settlement. The Russians will almost certainly continue to insist for the foreseeable future that the Communist regimes of all Warsaw Treaty countries be indefinitely preserved and protected; that Soviet–Eastern European economic interdependence remain undisturbed and unchallenged even if buttressed through Western capital investment; that the Soviet Union be guaranteed military predominance in Eastern Europe and "security" against ground attack from the West. It is hard to conceive of much change in the existing European settlement that will still meet all these requirements.

To focus specifically on the German question, the declared heart of *Ostpolitik:* the Soviet Union may indeed consider German reunification in the context of a very loose confederation in the distant but foreseeable future. But a primary condition will seemingly still be a framework that leaves the authority of Ulbricht's successors in what is now the GDR basically unrestricted. Moreover, there is every reason to assume that Moscow will continue to delay as long as possible on any significant progress. It will probably continue to ignore or not accept as valid any West German fulfillment of its stated and restated preconditions for serious discussion about reunification: namely, recognition of the GDR; final acceptance of the present borders of both Germanies; recognition of West Berlin as a "special political unit"; renunciation of German access, in any form, to control over nuclear weapons; and suppression of all "antidemocratic," "neo-Nazi" elements in the Federal Republic. In short, Moscow's essential backing of Ulbricht's policies seems certain for some time to come.

This is not to suggest that overt Soviet behavior, particularly in continued calls for the swift convening of a European security conference, will not be even more cordial and enticing towards Western Europe than it has been since August, 1968. Quite apart from the traditional Soviet approach of carrot-as-well-as-stick, there are a number of objective bases on which Moscow might pursue conciliation: the oft-cited desire to secure peace in the West, given the conflict with China; to gain Western economic and technological assistance in the interest of industrial growth at no sacrifice of domestic defense spending; and, indeed, Moscow's new freedom of maneuver, given the relative obedience and discipline the Czech example continues to ensure even on the part of the Rumanians. But the basic conclusion remains: these are second-order considerations expendable whenever any threat or risk to the presently preferred settlement in Central Europe is perceived.

BONN, THE WEST, AND THE
CENTRAL EUROPEAN DILEMMA

The present situation in Central Europe, consolidated again after the invasion of Czechoslovakia, is really an informal version of nearly the kind of European status quo that the Russians would like to formalize. Since Soviet price tags are not likely to change in the foreseeable future, what are the probable Western responses and policy perspectives? Before turning to the specific post-Czechoslovakia fortunes of *Ostpolitik*, it might be well to consider the stance of Bonn's principal Western allies and perhaps eventual competitors, the United States and France.

American Interest in Détente. As President Nixon has emphasized in every major foreign policy statement since he assumed office, the primary American goal is the search for superpower agreement. The pace has not always been swift; the promise of "negotiation, not confrontation" has not always been met, especially in the Middle East or even regarding Southeast Asia and the Vietnam wind-down. But neither occasionally blunt demonstrations of national will nor even a repetition of the Czechoslovak moves within the Soviet sphere will alter the critical strategic realities on which global Soviet-American cooperation has been explicitly based since 1962. In this sense, SALT is the principal short-run arena, the framework within which the search for significant expansion of the "limited adversary" relationship is being pushed.

This relationship has not precluded some firming-up of the American position vis-à-vis Europe—a repetition, in minor key, of 1956 and 1962. The autumn, 1968, NATO meetings saw both American promises to defer troop withdrawals and real concern about the dictates of flexible response in the face of primed Warsaw Treaty forces and new Soviet deployments in Central Europe. Affirmations of American commitment to NATO defense with or without MBFR have been repeatedly voiced by Nixon administration spokesmen—as recently as February, 1972. Too, the new economic burden-sharing efforts of the European allies, even though largely restricted to new incremental expenditures, have been welcomed as contributions to a "significant security community" of the 1970s.

Over the longer term, however, the firming-up will probably amount only to temporary recementing of the more obvious cracks which NATO has shown since 1965. The basic American goal will remain the gradual alleviation of tensions within Europe, but only within the context of overarching Soviet-American agreement. Support for ultimate reunification "in peace and freedom" will still be proclaimed; Washington will still defer to Bonn in matters concerning relations with the GDR. But changing the status quo in Europe or in Germany is not likely to assume any higher priority in American policy-making in the immediate or foreseeable future, and the gradual reduction of the American physical presence in Western Europe is almost sure to continue.

Moreover, at least as perceived by the Europeans, the psychic distance between Washington and the Continent seems likely to grow. Among European journalists in 1970, for example, a popular image was of America as a sick giant—ravaged from within, introspective and unsure, and unable to serve as either a model or a protector. More significant was the gap that yawned between the preferred American and German timetables for Four-Power discussions on Berlin and the resulting brief but strident public unpleasantness in both countries. At issue were clearly divergent goals: the United States was anxious to further agreement with the Soviets but not at the cost of bargaining advantages or even saliency within SALT and other forums; the West Germans were committed to achieving significant progress on Berlin before ratifying the Russian and Polish treaties or making any further *Ostpolitik* advances.

French Ambitions and Options. Similarly, there will probably be little change in the long-range goals of another (though less significant) bridge-builder, France. Even without de Gaulle, French interest lies in eliciting Soviet cooperation in the containment of the German problem and the lessening of direct American involvement (domination, in French eyes) in European affairs. For the present there are fewer direct probings and attempts to exploit France's limited financial resources for political gain in Eastern Europe. As recent Brandt-Pompidou talks once again affirmed, Paris also will not directly challenge Bonn's stance on any one issue of Eastern policy.

But for all of French intentions and ambitions, French bridges to the East cannot support Soviet obduracy and suspicion any better than can American or West German bridges. The Pompidou government will almost certainly not undertake any action which might threaten even future Franco-Russian entente. In the last analysis, France's only operational alternative at the moment, if it persists in nursing the Atlantic-to-the-Urals dream, is to sit and wait.

Ostpolitik: *Present and Future.* Central to all these considerations, however, is the future direction of West German foreign policy. To a striking degree, given the frozen past, official Bonn seemed to have internalized some of the "lessons of Czechoslovakia" before the actual invasion. Official contacts during the Prague Spring were always considered, cautious, and of a careful, decidedly nonprovocative character. Even as the Federal Republic became the Soviet-designated villain of the Czechoslovak "counter-revolution," Bonn remained cool, patient, and interested in further "natural" normalization in Central Europe.

The past months have witnessed considerable outward reward for this patience. In August of 1970, after long months of careful negotiation, Willy Brandt, now Chancellor, flew to Moscow to sign a Treaty on the Renunciation of Force and on Cooperation. Five months later, he arrived in Warsaw to initial an agreement acknowledging the inviolability of Poland's present frontiers, including the long-disputed Oder-Neisse line. Further, the SPD-FDP coalition government is now engaged in the serious negotiation of similar agreements with all remaining Eastern European states except Albania. Perhaps Brandt's most innovative moves have been vis-à-vis the GDR: his government has resumed active negotiation and communication, including two spectacular direct meetings between Brandt and East Germany's Willi Stoph, one on GDR soil, and a last-minute meeting of the minds on the 1971 Berlin agreement.

One clear reason for this success is simple steadfastness, first shown by the Kiesinger-Brandt government which, in the face of some domestic outrage and in the absence of any truly viable alternative, refused to bury the Eastern policy after Czechoslovakia. "We shall continue our efforts to work with any of our Central and Eastern European neighbors that so desire," Chancellor Kiesinger told the Bundestag in August, 1968. Despite invectives flowing westward, repeated invitations to negotiate about political problems were directed from Bonn eastward during 1968 and 1969. The principles and peaceful intentions of Ostpolitik were stated, restated, and stated again by Kiesinger, by Brandt, by Luebke, and by Heinemann, in Bonn, in Washington, in Paris, and even in Tokyo. Tactically, Bonn redirected the thrust of its Eastern policy: Moscow became the immediate target for improved relations; the wooing of Eastern European states was to be temporarily de-emphasized.

Whether intentionally or fortuitously, Bonn's persistent efforts toward reconciliation with the East converged in 1969 with the Russians' efforts to cleanse their international image, tarnished by the invasion of Czechoslovakia. For reasons that are not yet entirely clear, during the spring of 1969 the Soviet government decided that East-West relations could begin to be improved. Bonn reacted favorably but cautiously to the results of the Budapest conference of Warsaw Pact countries in March. The image of a European security conference and the theme of "all-European dialogue," projected from Budapest, were echoed by the Federal Republic in a series of direct invitations to bilateral meetings. Moscow was approached first, then Warsaw, and finally East Berlin. Although informal contacts between Soviet officials and West German party delegations as well as West German–Polish trade negotiations took place during the summer of 1969, none of Bonn's invitations to political meetings gained favorable responses from the East until after the Federal elections in October.

Without question, a second major factor in West German success was the accession of the Brandt-Scheel government which, on re-placing the Grand Coalition in 1969, essentially elevated *Ostpolitik* from an emphasis to a preoccupation. *Ostpolitik* is now officially labeled the policy on the opening to the East and has been pursued—despite numerous domestic maelstroms and several severe setbacks from the East—through an adroit, careful but still imaginative diplomatic offensive. Most efforts have borne Brandt's unmistakable personal stamp and have evidenced the chancellor's continuing commitment to an ending of the tattered legalistic remnants of World War II and the reemergence of peaceful German involvement in all-European affairs. His Nobel Prize was perhaps prematurely awarded but was clearly honestly deserved.

The chancellor's successes have come despite a small and potentially ever-diminishing *Bundestag* majority and despite the carping, increasingly savage opposition of the CDU and, most particularly, of Franz Josef Strauss's CSU. The first problem is resolvable —at least theoretically—because the German Basic Law requires a "constructive" vote of no confidence, that is, the election first of another chancellor by the presently highly improbable two-thirds majority in the *Bundestag*. The second problem has been affected by the continuing crisis of succession within the CDU-CSU and the many unresolved regional and religious intraparty cleavages activated by the not yet conclusively decided leadership struggle. Moreover, the proven failure of the *Ostpolitik*-as-sellout theme during state electoral campaigns to date as well the evident *Ostpolitik* support tendered by Schroeder or even Barzel, now CDU chairman, has muted most attempts to present a credible CDU-CSU alternative program toward the East.[6]

In terms of SPD-FDP electoral hopes as well as more general German interests, a continuation of this opening to the East would

[6] As this essay undergoes final revision, the CDU-CSU has indeed won at least a short-run victory in a negative upper-house (*Bundesrat*) vote on the first reading of the Russian and Polish treaties. The SPD-FDP coalition, however, does have sufficient votes in the *Bundestag* to override this opinion, and might even gain *Bundesrat* strength in upcoming state elections. And if the nonproliferation-treaty debate in Germany is any guide, the CDU-CSU's penchant for political irresponsibility tends to increase in direct proportion to an issue's "inevitability."

seem to offer prospects for Central European settlement that are no worse, and perhaps somewhat better, than those offered by other West German policy alternatives.

Resumption of the German search for broader Atlantic partnership is possible, but it promises few benefits beyond those already gained. A post-Vietnam revival of American interest in resolving the intractable problems of NATO consultation, control-sharing, or strategy to Germany's satisfaction seems doubtful. To maintain the present *Bundeswehr* level and the present level of American troop support payments already seems to many Germans an undue and unfair economic burden. To maintain it in the face of further American (and other) withdrawals will risk incurring little military benefit ("What can we do alone?") and considerable political liability. Bonn is all too aware that many of its allies share Soviet fears about a reunified and armed Germany of 77 million people. And it is determined to extract the maximum possible concessions from the East—preferably in the form of mutual balanced force reductions (MBFR)—before it will even grudgingly agree to significant American cuts.

Prospects for further cooperation in Western Europe are indeed somewhat more favorable for the early 1970s than they were for the late 1960s. Bonn's strong support for British entry into the European Economic Community, and the German initiatives that resulted in the far-reaching European summit agreement at The Hague in November, 1969, partly account for the current revitalization of Europeanism. Too, de Gaulle's exit seemingly removed at least symbolic barriers to integration. Still it must be pointed out that Britain is not yet a proven firm supporter of integration, and much of the positive tone of the meeting at The Hague emanated from discussions about "what should happen in Europe by 1976." National governments already appear to be having second thoughts about the desirability of these projected integrative happenings, as the failing progress on coordinated foreign policies as well as the cautious construction of even a rudimentary monetary-fiscal union well demonstrates.

Then, too, even the most optimistic among integrationists foresees little beyond enhanced supranationality and broadened cooperation in the economic sector in the 1970s. For West Germany this would promise greater prosperity and perhaps heightened influence in regional and global economic and monetary affairs. But Western European economic integration does not open a pathway to German reunification. Nor does it become a vehicle for Central European political settlement. Nor, for that matter, does it contribute greatly to West German security while the Central European environment remains unsettled.

To many outside of Germany, the 1970 Bonn-Moscow treaty suggested new credence for the often discussed possibility of a new Rapallo, which, however, seems to bear little relation to the post–World War II world. Clearly, if any of its aims in Central Europe are to be realized, the Federal Republic must seek—now more urgently than before—some accommodation with the Soviet Union. But it is still hard to imagine that an increasingly self-assertive Federal Republic would be willing to pay the necessary price for a new Rapallo or to undergo the contingent risks simply for the sake of uneasy unity with a "socialist state." It is even harder to conceive of a superpower Soviet Union, whatever its particular paranoia about Germany, perceiving any significant gain in such an agreement. Moscow now holds most of the cards it needs through other relationships, particularly that with the United States, and its intermittent approaches to "democratic" German elements seem to be only so many softening-up tactics.

The prospects in a fourth arena—a nationalistic turning inward —are somewhat more difficult to assess. Recent years have witnessed certain suggestive signs, such as the assertions of the lately diminished NPD regarding national pride against foreign slurs and exploitation, or the attraction of a neutral, satisfied life for much of the German middle and student classes. But even if its allies and opponents would allow such a strategically located vacuum, the Federal Republic would still not be Switzerland. Given traditional German difficulties in finding a point of political equilibrium, the intense frustrations which caused such a turning inward might easily be turned outward again.

However, we must reemphasize that *Ostpolitik* will offer only somewhat better prospects for the German future in the 1970s and beyond. Without question, the conception and execution of this policy have marked the end of Germany's postwar rehabilitation and the beginning of a far more independent role in European affairs. Even under the Kiesinger-Brandt regime, *Ostpolitik* represented a maximum departure from the calls for reassurance and feelings of dependence and frustration within the West which characterized the late 1950s and early 1960s, and stood in marked contrast to the often painful invective and imagery heard contemporaneously with respect to the nonproliferation treaty. Through a very interesting sequence of events, Brandt has in effect been able to reverse the scenario of a decade ago. It is Bonn which is pressing a change, at least in environment, through negotiation, whereas the Western allies have assumed the role of brakes, of the residual guardians of the German nation and the guarantors of an equitable settlement of World War II's divisions.

There have also been a number of specific and quite spectacular gains over the past. A de facto peace treaty with the East, similar in character to that signed with the West in the 1954 agreements on NATO and WEU, is now close to conclusion. The emotional and propagandist image of the "revanchist, Nazi-filled" Federal Republic has essentially been swept aside, and partnership possibilities (at least in the economic area) have once again been established. Last, the explicit framework for discussion of European security and the German question has been painstakingly defused, and a partial catalogue of common concerns, procedures, and terms developed.

But there, at least for the foreseeable future, the benefits would seem to end. West Germany has gained new opportunities for economic and technological input into the East; the Mercedes truck arrangement with the Soviet Union was only a foretaste of more significant things to come. But surely once there seems political utility in raising the specter of "indirect penetration" à la Czechoslovakia, stringent limits will spring up, whatever the "objective" Eastern economic needs. Normalization, too, will not indefinitely be of sufficient benefit as either a goal or a condition. Moreover, there would seem some truth to the criticism that Bonn's potential vulnerability, if not instability, is now more painfully exposed than ever. Once the Federal Republic has essentially accepted the status quo in Europe and sold its birthright for a relatively limited amount of economic pottage, these critics declare, what else does it have to bargain? And does this still somewhat tenuous democratic system, indebted to continuing economic prosperity for a good measure of its popular and elite support, really possess resources necessary to sustain a European or domestic equilibrium in the face of the predictable pressures, threats, and attempts at political blackmail?

Such tasks will be ever more difficult if *Ostpolitik* continues to engender suspicion and criticism among Bonn's principal Western allies. Some of the adverse reaction during the past two years has clearly been the product of pique or simple discomfort with Germany's new-found role. But particularly that stemming from Washington and Paris has been more concerned with perceived threats either to the pattern of past relationships (e.g., France's ambitions vis-à-vis the East) or to preferred future outcomes (e.g., the American linking in 1970–1971 of SALT and Berlin). Despite repeated, seemingly sincere German assurances that only *Westpolitik* (in the EEC as well as NATO) has made the opening of the East possible, each new action has brought further criticism or has further strengthened the U.S. Senate proponents of troop withdrawals from a self-sufficient Europe. Given the present array of political forces, it is hard to imagine that the future will witness any greater trust of German motives or any greater confidence that Bonn can secure Western interests without the need for intervention or protection on the part of its allies.

Less clear is the future cast of Soviet interests in relationships with the Federal Republic. Our earlier analysis dealt only with the limits of Soviet tolerance demonstrated in Czechoslovakia; what its more positive goals are, particularly vis-à-vis the West, seems susceptible to several interpretations. In one view, the Soviet Union is still primarily interested in clear political dominance on the Continent, to be achieved by de facto isolation of the Western European states (and specifically West Germany) from the United States. Perhaps the polar opposite is the belief that the Soviet Union is now basically uninterested in Western Europe; that, given the magnitude of other problems, Moscow finds the present situation relatively tolerable, and is only interested in limited political gains to secure its own Eastern pattern. Whatever the more accurate estimate, Bonn's future success still depends on crucial variables which are at best only dimly apparent now and are not subject to much independent influence.

Most telling of all are the constraints which the Federal Republic, merely by proclaiming the continued existence of one German nation, places upon its own future freedom of maneuver. For example, in attaching the Berlin precondition to final ratification of both the Soviet and Polish treaties, Brandt did much to undercut domestic cries of a sellout, to mollify allied demands for recognition of residual occupation rights, and to affirm again the far future goal of German unity. Yet his action also brought dramatic repeated demonstrations of the disruptive abilities of the GDR, of the talents of Ulbricht and then Honecker as master tacticians within the Eastern group, of the mixed nature of Soviet motives, and of the willingness of Bonn's Western allies to indulge in a little polite blackmail upon occasion. So long as there is no formal recognition of the GDR, so long as Bonn defines even a few issues as unresolvable until a formal European settlement is reached, such actions will in all probability continue because, most simply, they serve the political interests of all the other nations involved.

Despite these complications, however, we return to our central point: a continuation of *Ostpolitik* even at a minimum level offers prospects no worse and perhaps somewhat better than the other alternatives presently open to Bonn. Should the stated German goals become more ambitious and more precise, there is the possibility of failure, with rather significant consequences not only for the Federal Republic but for the rest of Western Europe as well. Given the cautious optimism of Brandt and the tactical brilliance of German diplomacy since Czechoslovakia, such a development appears unlikely. If anything, *Ostpolitik* as a policy is likely to remain in much the same state—an options-open attempt at movement, testing the national mood as well as probing the patience and tolerance of ally and opponent alike.

POLITICAL-MILITARY SETTING
FOR ARMS CONTROL

Available Alternatives. As noted earlier, it is possible to envisage a number of arms control arrangements that would, if introduced, buttress military stability and enhance security in Central Europe. It is also possible to envisage arms control measures that would complement phased movement toward political settlement in Central Europe. It is not possible, however, to see arms control as the first step or impetus toward Central European settlement. Furthermore, as might be gathered from the paper's negative conclusions regarding the reimposition of Soviet will in Eastern Europe and the new tensions along the dividing line between East and West, low probabilities must be assigned to formal arms control arrangements in Central Europe in the next five to ten years. Arms control strategies, after all, are intended and designed to complement states' security policies. Therefore, as long as Russians, Eastern Europeans, and West Germans (and Americans and Frenchmen), continue to define their security at least partially in terms of one another's insecurity, mutually acceptable arms control arrangements are unlikely to evolve.

The problem of arms control in Central Europe is part of the larger problem of Central European security. In the authors' thinking, "Central European security" would be a state of relatively stable military-political equilibrium among actors concerned with Central European issues. Here, military-political equilibrium means relative military safety for actors and relative political satisfaction among them. The fundamental dilemma for Central European arms control at present is that military safety and political satisfaction cannot be made compatible for all actors.

East and West meet in Central Europe in a military equilibrium that has remained remarkably stable for two decades despite manpower and missile gaps, several shifts in strategic and tactical doctrine, and considerable qualitative and quantitative advances in the arms race. This equilibrium may not represent a true balance of capabilities, but at least in the actors' perceptions the capabilities on either side have appeared sufficient to ensure stable deterrence. While it is an exaggeration to say that states feel militarily safe in the Central European military equilibrium, it is fair to say that most of them hold direct conflict to be highly improbable, largely because of this military balance. And most of them expect the equilibrium to continue—both in the Central European theater and on a global scale.

The drawback in this situation is that the military equilibrium frames, and to a considerable extent "freezes," a political status quo that is discomforting to all actors in varying degrees (see Table 1). Here the dilemmas begin to compound.

Since dissatisfaction with the status quo varies and the Russians are the least dissatisfied, initiators of movement toward political change are immediately placed at a bargaining disadvantage. Far from any East-West common interest in directions of change, there is no real common interest in change per se, so that political concessions are implicit in the very raising of the question. Once such concessions are made, the Pandora's box of incompatible substantive concerns is opened. Since hardened differences exist on the critical Central European issues—the status of Berlin and East Germany, the nature and status of a united Germany, the security of boundaries, and the size and functions of foreign garrisons, to name only a few—the probability of settlement is low and almost directly proportional to the number of issues raised and the number of actors negotiating.

Hovering above all this is the fact that most conceivable changes in the political status quo imply major perturbations of the military equilibrium. If settlement in Central Europe is not to be simply a formalization of the present patterns (i.e., a Versailles for the 1970s, as Franz Josef Strauss has charged), then it must raise the risk of German movement eastward, westward, or into unpredictable neutrality. Any one of these alternatives would jeopardize the existing or any conceivable military equilibrium in Central Europe. Pressed to a choice, most states with a stake in this area—the superpowers almost definitely—would select military safety over

Country	Attitude Toward Status Quo	Reasons for Satisfaction	Reasons for Dissatisfaction
USSR	Relatively content	Hegemony in Eastern Europe maintained. West Germany kept under wraps. American problems with allies exacerbated.	Political debts contracted with Ulbricht, and others. High economic costs in defense and occupation, and economic support.
German Democratic Republic	Partially content	Perception of world status rising with time. Perception of special status with Moscow. Conviction that future will bring all of Germany into Eastern alignment.	Berlin: unfulfilled leadership ambitions within Eastern sphere.
Poland, Czechoslovakia, Hungary	Partially content	West Germany kept under wraps. Relatively secure internal tenure.	Soviet hegemony objectionable, crushing to "national" aspirations. Economic dealings with West curtailed, hopes for modernization dashed, as a result of Czechoslovak invasion.
United States	Partially content	Acceptance of status quo opens ways to greater détente with USSR, supports US global interest.	Frustrations in status quo challenge the American "European design," damage American–West German relations; American presence required under status quo expensive, damages American–French relations.
France	Discontent for the most part	German unification still considered threat; Status quo facilitates overtures to East.	Status quo means continuing division of Continent into Soviet and American spheres of influence.
Federal Republic of Germany	Discontent		Status quo means continuing division of Germany and continuing frustration of FRG attempts to foster movement toward political settlement in Central Europe.

political satisfaction, as they have been doing for the past several years.

Current Possibility for Arms Control in Central Europe. Given these conditions of military equilibrium and unresolved political differences in Central Europe, the authors can see few possible changes in the military-political status quo that would open avenues to arms control and can recognize only a scant possibility that arms control arrangements might stimulate political movement. Therefore, questions of possible arms control arrangements really become questions of needs and opportunities existing within the framework of the current military-political situation. Here at least two avenues are partially open.

First, since it is reasonable to expect continuing political tension in Central Europe, efforts could well be made via arms control arrangements to fortify the deterrent balance against possible political disturbances. Such arrangements might be called political-storm-weathering devices. Their purpose would be to discourage intensification of the arms race during periods of political tension and rapid military escalation during acute political crises. In short, arms control might attack the relationship between political fervor and military panic. One arrangement to this end might see the superpowers agreeing to a qualitative and quantitative freeze on their regional conventional and nuclear deployments at current or "acceptable" levels, and the regional powers committing themselves to restraint—as in the nonproliferation treaty—with respect to their local deployments. Such arrangements would strengthen the deterrent balance by preventing ambiguities concerning military capability and commitment. In so doing they would operate to constrain military initiatives during periods of political strain. In addition, they would eliminate sources of possible local disturbance in the military equilibrium by committing regional powers to good behavior.

Second, the authors would like to resurrect the disengagement theme here, fully aware of its rather dismal history in Central Europe. They reintroduce it without fully believing that conditions have changed to a point where ideas unacceptable several years ago may be currently feasible. But even with the questions of defense strategy and alliance cohesion that it raises, disengagement has an attraction in its promises of damage control, localization, and retarded escalation. In addition and most important, reducing capabilities symmetrically may effectively remove some of the "terror" from the military balance but leave deterrence intact. Arrangements in the direction of qualitative disengagement could take the form of superpower agreements to reduce (symmetrically or perhaps even asymmetrically) such items as firepower, manpower, and operational range, preserving the power balance while cutting the magnitude of power balanced. Here again the agreement would have to be of a dual nature in that it would involve superpower agreements to disengage and regional power commitments to refrain from tampering with the military equilibrium as disengagement proceeds.

Albeit within a quite different context, a limited disengagement scheme might also lead to an easing of certain American-European tensions. In effect, the United States would solemnly agree to be something like the "holder of the balance," that is, to maintain a minimum Continental presence, a presence proportional to the efforts of both its own allies and the East. Such firmly fixed "magic numbers" might be expected to be somewhat more reassuring than quadrennial presidential pledges.

Political Realities and Arms Control. The major and probably fatal flaw in virtually all arms control arrangements possible within the existing military-political status quo in Central Europe is that they all contribute to formalizing, legitimizing, and perpetuating this status quo. To argue that arms control arrangements buy time for diplomacy rings hollow in the light of barriers to political settlement and of diplomacy's record in Central Europe over the past century. Stated most forcefully, freezing arms in Central Europe means further freezing the political status quo; controlling arms means controlling West Germans. While the superpowers can find convergent interests in legitimizing the Central European status quo via arms control, West Germany's only interest in arms control must be in its possible instrumental value for changing the status quo. French, and for that matter Eastern European, interests also must rest in arms control as an instrument for changing the status quo. Therefore, arms control arrangements currently possible carry strong implications of intra-alliance dissension. Still, there is an outside chance that proposing and discussing schemes to legitimize the existing situation could make the status quo more acceptable to all concerned by underlining the unattainability of alternatives.

In short, the outlook for the 1970s is less than encouraging. Barring the accidents and surprises with which history is dotted, there must be major changes in several varieties of political calculus before any change in the basic Central European array will become a significant political probability.

/ Annette Baker Fox

domestic pressures in north america to withdraw forces from europe

AMERICANS HAVE NEEDED constant reminders that their national-security decision-makers do not have a blank sheet on which to lay out their policies but instead operate within an international system in which important and relevant decisions are made by relatively autonomous actors outside their state. They are less often reminded of restraints arising from inside their country. The relative weight of internal pressures compared to needs generated from outside the country may differ from one state to another, but both sets of pressures operate in every state. They narrow a government's range of choice from opposite directions—sometimes to the vanishing point. Any examination of possible contributions of the North American NATO allies to possible European security systems of the 1970s can be expected to find that estimates of what the domestic traffic will bear will strongly affect the ability of the United States and Canadian governments to meet external demands.

Since the commitment of armed forces to the defense of Europe represents for both countries a special burden traditionally borne only in time of war and since their own territory is only indirectly involved, one might expect that domestic pressures would play an equally important part in shaping the commitments of each country. But such a commitment represents expenditures not only in money and men but also in attention, and the capacity to attend to security problems outside the borders of a country is one measure of that country's power. Thus, in the formation of their respective NATO policies domestic considerations may have less impact on the government of a superpower than on the government of its middle-power neighbor.

CONTRASTS IN WORLD POSITION:
THE UNITED STATES AND CANADA

In some ways Canada and the United States stand at opposite extremes within the Atlantic alliance as far as essentiality is concerned. A comparison of the domestic pressures on force commitments in these contrasting countries may therefore help in understanding the importance of such factors in the other countries whose future contributions to NATO require assessment. In some ways Canada resembles the smaller allies, especially those in the north, where the sense of being only marginally significant to the alliance is strong. However, unlike Canada, neither Denmark nor Norway has forces on the central front. Like them, Canada is by no means a poor country, and the scale of its resources available for collective defense only looks small when compared to that currently possessed by England, France, or Germany. In the early days of NATO, Canada was a vitally important member of the alliance as one of the two providers of "mutual aid" to the European allies. Canada had weight even though the Mackenzie King government had earlier chosen not to share in the occupation of Germany when not given a direct voice in occupation policy. As in the Scandinavian countries, there is in Canada a very strong streak of antimilitarism and of longing for a deemphasis on bloc affiliation. Unlike the circumstances of Norway and Denmark, however, the population, area, relatively invulnerable location, and resources of Canada help to qualify it for the rather nebulous status of "middle power." This status was consciously claimed by Canadians in the early postwar years, but by the 1960s, especially with the revival and burgeoning of the European allies, Canada was playing a less prominent role in world politics.

On the other hand, although having only about one-tenth the population of the United States and being in many respects a weak power in comparison with that country, Canada shares so many characteristics that instead of thinking of it as being at one extreme from the United States in relation to other NATO countries, one might regard it as a pale reflection. Distance from Europe, the second or third highest living standard in the world, and a culture so similar to that of the United States that Canadians constantly struggle to maintain their distinctiveness—all these might classify Canada and the United States together in assessments of domestic pressures for reducing force commitments to an increasingly affluent Europe. In both, prior to World War II, there were strong leanings toward isolationism, but in both, "Europe" gradually became part of their own political community, and the realization of strategic interdependence underpinned their association with Western Europe. Canada and the United States differed chiefly with respect to their varying perspectives on their roles in NATO and their capacity to fill these roles. Canada could "pass the buck" to the United States but then would have to conform to the consequences.

As the members of the Brussels Pact realized in 1948, an alliance of Britain, France, and the Benelux countries against a potential aggressor would be hollow without the United States joining it. In his own initiative, the Canadian Secretary of State for External Affairs, Louis St. Laurent, showed that Canadian leaders were of the same mind. That both Canada and the United States adhered to the North Atlantic Treaty made the agreement look like a truly Atlantic collective effort rather than some new way for the United States to provide military aid to Western Europe. But as the need for aid tapered off and military technology changed radically, Canada's role in promoting European security became more and more marginal. For some years, however, Canada continued to take important political initiatives in the North Atlantic Council, and high-level Canadian officials played significant parts in NATO affairs.

The decline in Canada's importance coincided with a lessening of the perceived threat to Western Europe from the Soviet Union, especially as compared to other dangers around the world. For both North American countries, questioning about the continuation of their current force commitments to NATO increased, not only among government officials but also within the articulate public. But the doubts expressed in Canada were much stronger, more pervasive, and deeper. A few critics in Canada even questioned the desirability of NATO's continued existence, and more than a few questioned Canada's remaining a member. In neither country were most of the doubters much concerned about strategy and the relation of force levels to it.

As Canadians looked at it, the issue appeared to be less a military than a political question; many believed that their committed forces were small enough in number that Europeans could conceivably have taken over their task. Europeans could indeed have done so, although the very high quality of the Canadian contribution made it valuable militarily. So far as the physical protection of Canada's homeland was concerned, they believed it was going to be defended, whether in Europe or in North America, by virtue of its proximity to the United States, whether or not Canadians asked it to be. In this most important matter of geography, Canada differed from the smaller allies in Europe. Granted the advantages of collective defense, Canadians regarded continuing to maintain armed forces in Europe as useful chiefly to retain the respect of the other allies as well as their own. Of almost equal value was their ability thereby to share in the making of alliance decisions. Some Canadians hoped that their military contribution would help produce a balance through NATO to American domination, because when the United States was negotiating defense questions of concern to Canada it would also in effect be dealing with the whole alliance. But few spoke of other balances, in particular that vis-à-vis German forces.

From the time of the San Francisco Conference founding the United Nations, Canadians have been wont to stress that as a state with significant yet limited power, Canada should follow a kind of functionalist rule, playing its part in collective security or collective defense in accordance with its special capacities. During the period that it has been a member of the Atlantic alliance, Canada has played a distinctive role in other groupings on the world scene, particularly in the United Nations, where it has been one of the most important participants in peacekeeping forces, but also in the Colombo Plan and in the Commonwealth. Although traditionally oriented toward Europe, Canadians have not found a strong stress on regionalism very appealing. Unlike the smaller European allies, they have no neighbors except superpowers. In 1969 Prime Minister Pierre Trudeau began stressing that Canada had Pacific and Arctic interests which would require a reorientation away from an almost exclusive concern with Europe.

The Atlantic alliance originally appealed to Canadians because it linked Canada's two mother countries, England and France, with the North American states and removed an embarrassing need to discriminate among the three greater powers. The entrance of West Germany into the alliance was less welcome in Canada than in the United States, which bore major responsibility for the "forward defense" of the alliance. The tie between Germany and Canada has not grown as strong as between Germany and the United States, so that maintaining forces for defense in Germany has a different meaning to Canadians. The relationship to the United States is so basic to all other foreign-policy considerations that all Canadian considerations of an appropriate role in NATO are weighed in terms of this relationship, consciously or not.

CANADIAN AND AMERICAN
CONTRIBUTIONS TO NATO

So much for the impact of the outside world on the Canadian government and its response. (The story is familiar on the American side, and the inherent contrasts are apparent.[1]) What has been the commitment of Canadian and American forces to European security? What costs have the two governments thereby incurred? As

[1] See William T. R. Fox and Annette Baker Fox, *NATO and the Range of American Choice* (New York, Columbia University Press, 1967), chaps. 3 and 4.

in all discussions of NATO and European security, the American strategic guarantee is taken for granted and the figures presented here are confined, for the most part, to contributions on the central front, because this is where the controversy is focused. Although there have been some shifts in strategic doctrine in the last twenty years, the numbers of Canadian and American troops committed to Europe remained remarkably unchanged until the end of the 1960s. Official doctrinal changes in NATO strategy came slowly, as they required the consent of fourteen allies (Iceland has no forces committed to NATO); force-level adaptations came even more slowly. The difficulties of getting agreement to changes from all the allies were so great that only unilateral erosions from earlier commitments took place. Neither the Canadians nor the Americans were as inclined to dilute their contributions as were the Europeans. The 1967 McNamara-inspired reform in NATO which aimed to correlate strategy, force levels, and resources more effectively has begun to produce greater flexibility and realism. At least domestic pressures have been more formally recognized.

Total United States forces in Europe were estimated in 1971 at between 300,000 and 315,000 men, depending on how they were counted; at their highest during the life of NATO they were about 450,000. United States ground troops in Europe (which means chiefly in Germany) have varied since the early 1950s from about 195,000 to roughly 260,000 men. In the earlier years, between five and six divisions were involved. Other forces, the equivalent of a little more than two divisions, were earmarked and trained for NATO but kept in reserve at home. Following a complicated agreement with Germany and Britain concerning offset compensation for British and American forces maintained in Germany, in 1968 the United States began a limited withdrawal. About two-thirds of a division returned to the United States, where the two brigades were to be kept ready for rapid return while being rotated annually and brought together once a year for exercises. After the Soviet invasion of Czechoslovakia some troops were moved back for exercises ahead of schedule. In the eight years following the buildup due to the Berlin crisis, American forces in Europe were reduced by about 100,000 men; some of this reduction occurred when they had to leave France. Until a change in 1969, Canadian ground forces in Europe totaled between 5,000 and 6,000 men, constituting a highly mechanized brigade. Two battalions, part of the reserves in Canada, were committed to the ACE Mobile Force and were kept ready for immediate transfer to Europe.

Air force contributions of the two countries have fluctuated more and are harder to pinpoint; in the discussions regarding reductions they are less frequently cited. For Canada, contributions have ranged from twelve down to six strike-reconnaissance squadrons of aircraft, their number at the time of the 1969 policy change. They have been stationed in Germany and, until 1966, in France. The six squadrons comprised about 4,500 men, who were trained and equipped to use nuclear weapons. In 1971, United States Air Forces, Europe (USAFE) had approximately twenty-one tactical-fighter squadrons and five tactical-reconnaissance squadrons, based in England, Germany, the Netherlands, and Turkey, as well as in Spain, which is not in NATO.[2] (These figures do not include the four dual-based squadrons, originally pulled back to the United States in 1968 "on call" for immediate return to Europe.)

From the start of NATO until the stepping-up of the Vietnam war, the American ground forces in Europe were of the finest quality in training and equipment, and the numbers formally committed remained constant, although the worldwide total of army divisions varied from about eight in the Radford New Look period to nineteen and two-thirds (1.6 million men) during the height of the Vietnam war. Far more important for Western European security than the number of men was the composition of the American forces in Europe, which varied considerably from time to time and fluctuated in quality.

[2] Figures come from *The Military Balance*, published annually by the Institute for Strategic Studies, London, and from the Senate Committee on Foreign Relations, *Report, Fourteenth Meeting of the North Atlantic Assembly*, 91st Cong., 1st sess. (1969), pp. 28, 61–62. A figure for all United States forces in West Germany and Berlin, furnished by the Department of Defense for early 1970, was 214,000, of which 180,000 were army [House of Representatives Committee on Foreign Affairs, Subcommittee on Europe, *Hearings, United States Relations with Europe in the Decade of the 1970's*, 91st Cong., 2nd sess. (1970), p. 411]. According to an AP dispatch (*Greenwich Time*, June 28, 1971), other air squadrons have been quietly returned to the United States to join those regularly "dual-based," bringing the total to twelve.

In Canada's ground forces, one of its four brigades has been stationed in Europe; two others were earmarked for NATO use. In April, 1969, the Trudeau government announced a projected change that would gradually but very markedly reduce both ground and air forces in Europe while stressing mobility through redeployment to Canada for multipurpose use. The following September more precise figures were published; the projected reduction of all military forces in Europe—air and ground—left 5,000 men equipped only with non-nuclear weapons. The six air squadrons were reduced to three, eventually to carry only conventional weapons. They were to be confined to ground support and reconnaissance roles after an interim changeover period, but in 1971 the government declared its readiness to accept an attack role for all three. These reductions were part of an overall decrease in the armed services, which in turn reflected a marked retrenchment in the total national budget.[3]

To allocate specific American expenditures to the NATO area is very difficult. A joint survey by the Departments of State and Defense reported in late 1968 that United States bases around the world cost about $5 billion annually and that about 30 percent of this cost was in NATO Europe.[4] Senator John Sherman Cooper reported to the North Atlantic Assembly in 1968 that the United States paid for its military commitment to NATO (including all types of contribution) between $12 and $15 billion a year.[5] These latter figures are often cited, as is another estimate of $8 billion, but the annual cost of United States forces in Europe itself, including civilians associated with them as well as the operating costs of the Sixth Fleet, has been reported to be only $2.9 billion.[6] Part of

---

[3] New York Times, September 20, 1969. In December, 1969, the Canadian government announced a reduction of 4,000 men in its reserve armed forces (ibid., December 21, 1969). The White Paper on Defence published in 1971 is summarized in the Canadian Weekly Bulletin, September 8, 1971.

[4] New York Times, April 9, 1969.

[5] Report, Fourteenth Annual Meeting of the North Atlantic Assembly, p. 28.

[6] Hearings, United States Relations with Europe, pp. 33, 411. For a detailed examination of the difficulties in calculating costs, see Edward R. Fried, "The Financial Cost of Alliance," in John Newhouse with others, U.S. Troops in Europe (Washington, D.C., Brookings Institution, 1971), pp. 102–144. The theoretical difficulties are expounded by T. Alden Williams, "Sharing NATO's Burden: Hegemony by Formula," in NATO in the Seventies, ed. Edwin H.

the higher estimates covers overhead, nondistributable and non-negotiable in determining proper burden-sharing. One example is base support for general purpose forces in the United States that are kept mainly for a European emergency. If these latter forces are included, some estimates have run as high as $25 billion.

For Canada in 1962 (a rough midpoint in the lifetime of NATO), total defense expenditure in relation to the GNP was 5.2 percent; Canada thus ranked at about the median among NATO allies, below the United States with its 10.4 percent and Portugal, Britain, France, Turkey, and West Germany, in that order.[7] The Canadian defense expenditure as a percentage of GNP has steadily declined since 1962; in 1967 it was 3.6 percent, falling below not only the ratios of the above countries but of Italy, Greece, Norway, and the Netherlands as well. By 1970 the Canadian percentage was 2.5, only Denmark and Luxembourg being lower.[8] On the other hand, the absolute size of Canada's defense expenditures was exceeded in the period 1961–1964 only by that of the United States, Britain, France, and Germany, and in the next two years, by that of these same countries plus Italy.[9] In 1968 Canadian defense expenditures represented about 16 percent of the federal budget; for the United States, where they included $30 billion for the Vietnam war, they were about 44 percent. American expenditures for 1968 were more than 9 percent of United States GNP, which kept the United States ratio at the top of the NATO list.[10] However, that portion of the United States budget *devoted to NATO* was a smaller percentage

---

Fedder (St. Louis, University of Missouri, Center for International Studies, 1970), pp. 147–75.

[7] Canada, House of Commons, *Special Studies Prepared for the Special Committee of the House of Commons on Matters Relating to Defence* (1965), p. 90.

[8] Senate Committee on Foreign Relations and Senate Committee on Armed Services, *Hearings, United States Troops in Europe*, 90th Cong., 1st sess. (1967), pp. 22–23. The figures in this report and those in the Canadian report cited in fn. 7 are not exactly the same, but the rankings are. For the 1970 figure, see *The Military Balance, 1971–72*, p. 60.

[9] Ibid. Among the smaller allies only the Benelux countries have forces in the Central Europe Allied Command. These include, among others, two mechanized divisions each from the Netherlands and Belgium, plus an artillery battalion from Luxembourg.

[10] Institute for Strategic Studies, *The Military Balance: 1968–69*, p. 56; *The Military Balance: 1969–70*, pp. 57–58; *Washington Post*, May 29, 1969.

of the American GNP than the ratio of some European allies' defense contributions to NATO were to their respective GNPs. And whereas the American defense budget was falling, theirs were rising in 1970.

In 1968 the United States had about 3,500,000 men in its regular (non-reserve) armed forces (8.9 percent of all men of military age) but by late 1971 the number had fallen to 2,600,000. By contrast, Canada with no conscription had 101,600 in its regular forces in 1968, or 2.5 percent of its men of military age. Since then it has cut these numbers in roughly the same proportion as the American reduction; the 1972 authorization was only 82,000, although the next year's projection was for an increase of 1,000.[11]

Prior to a reconsideration of security needs in 1969, American defense planners believed that American forces ought to be sufficient to carry on simultaneously a war with the Soviet Union in Europe, a war with Communist China in Asia, and an "emergency" operation in Latin America. However, defense officials have always declared that outside the United States the core area of concern to them was NATO Europe. When budgetary restrictions forced a review of American strategy in late 1969, the orientation of major-war contingency planning was toward Europe.[12] Forces stationed in Europe are not interchangeable parts, readily available for service elsewhere; militarily as well as politically they have a different significance and communicate another kind of message to friend and foe if they are maintained at home and are redeployed to Europe than if they are located there regularly.

Annually the NATO Parliamentarians Conference (now called the North Atlantic Assembly) has called attention to the need for strengthened forces pledged to NATO, but these complaints applied chiefly to the European allies. Some attrition occurred in the Canadian and American forces, but in general the North American

---

[11] *The Military Balance: 1968–69; Wall Street Journal*, December 27, 1971; *Canadian Weekly Bulletin*, September 8, 1971. *The Military Balance, 1970–71*, gave the total United States armed forces as 3,161,000, representing 8.5 percent of men of military age, and the total Canadian forces as 93,325, with the percentage of men under arms as 2.3. The next year these numbers dropped to 2,699,000 and 85,000 respectively.

[12] *New York Times*, December 27, 1969.

allies were models for the others. During the economizing New Look period in the Eisenhower administration and again when the Vietnam war escalated in the Johnson administration, one effect of American defense policies was some thinning out of American forces in Europe, which exacerbated European fears of a lessening concern with NATO. Numerous Americans were also concerned, despite Department of Defense assurances that the quality of the forces was unimpaired. Critics did not regard such moves as simply "cutting out the fat," but rather as beginning a pernicious cycle of disengagement. Similar criticisms did not greet Canadian attrition.

There has been a marked American tendency to reinvigorate forces committed to NATO after crises generated by the Soviet Union; it is otherwise in Canada. However, the Canadians did respond to the American appeal for a buildup by sending more men to the NATO forces at the time of the 1961 Berlin crisis, but somewhat grudgingly. Canada again dragged its feet after the Czechoslovakian crisis, which in any case appeared to shock Canadians much less than the European allies. This difference in reaction is evidence of the contrasting roles played by Canada and the United States, but it also reflects a different style in international affairs. Canadians (whether English or French) have long had a reputation for being cautious, conservative, and thrifty. Such characteristics may arise as much from role as from culture; they also could be found in Norway and Denmark.

Commitment of ground forces to Europe is only one among many ways in which the United States and Canada give military support to the alliance; another is the joint North American Air Defense (NORAD), which protects the principal strategic deterrent sheltering all the allies. These contributions reinforce each other, but in both countries questions have arisen over which should be given higher priority. In 1969 Prime Minister Trudeau gave precedence to NORAD as his new defense policy emphasized territorial and continental defense, to be supported in part by forces returned from Europe.

In the northwest Atlantic, a thousand miles off its coast, Canada makes a significant naval contribution, which costs it about twice as much as Canadian forces in Europe and 30 percent more than its share in NORAD.[13] Canada also participates in the small Standing Naval Force Atlantic and in various NATO naval maneuvers that involve Canadian naval units committed to NATO. The giant contribution to various NATO naval groups is from the United States, including the Sixth Fleet in the Mediterranean.

To return to North American forces in Central Europe, what are the issues? Ideological opposition to NATO itself can be disregarded, as opponents are politically weak in the United States and even in Canada. The choices facing the two governments relate to the purpose or needs of the alliance and what the governments seek from it. In recent years NATO's strategic goal has shifted from deterrence of westward expansion by the Soviet Union alone to a combination of this aim with preparation for peaceful reunification and stabilization of Europe. A latent but well-understood function of North American forces in Central Europe is to quiet other allies' fears of a resurgent, uncontrollable Germany; both the Germans and the other NATO members desire the presence of these forces, but to some extent for different reasons. Other political, economic, and technological changes induced the two North American governments to reconsider the military requirements of the alliance and how their respective countries should meet them. Americans have discussed at length the framework of adjustment, especially the desirability of a strong "European" pillar, an approach and idea which inevitably leave the Canadians cold. The *practical* political choices include those involving the size, composition, deployment, mobility, and functions of American and Canadian forces in Europe as well as the timing and prerequisites for adjustments. The most political choice to be considered here is burden-sharing: Who is to do what? (The question cannot be easily separated from the equally important political question of control over nuclear weapons. On this question the Canadians, unlike many other allies, have tended to stress not so much participation as non-participation in any NATO plan for sharing in the physical possession of such arms.)

Over the years several patterns have been revealed by statements of Americans who were concerned about these issues; the

[13] Peter Dobell, "Canada and NATO," *ORBIS*, Spring, 1969, p. 316.

patterns are especially evident in hearings held by various Congressional committees. The first and most critical public debate on assignment of ground forces to Europe was that staged jointly by the Senate Foreign Relations and Armed Services Committees on the Wherry Resolution in early 1951. From then onwards a common complaint has been that the Europeans were not doing enough for themselves (Canada was not involved). When the Vietnam war escalated, these complaints were often linked with observations that its European allies were not helping the United States in Southeast Asia and that American forces committed to Europe were needed in Vietnam. A different theme related to nuclear technology: Had it not reduced the usefulness of conventional forces in Europe, and what new combination of forces was then required by technological change? Budgetary burdens on the economy and, since 1959, the adverse effect of foreign-based forces on the American balance of payments have been other concerns. The importance of having American troops in Europe to bolster European confidence in the United States guarantee is a perennial subject: How many troops are necessary if their only function is to be hostages and how many if they are also seriously intended for fighting if armed conflict erupts? Would token forces signify token interest? Continual doubts about the viability of NATO, prompted by each of its crises (they began almost with its birth), have raised questions about the justification for American forces in Europe. The constant rumors of withdrawals have usually produced two responses from administrative officials in the United States. They reassured Europeans that the stories were baseless, until the late 1960s, when this line was abandoned for its opposite. They told members of Congress that if American forces were reduced, European troops would not be increased to compensate for them. Instead, the American reduction would give the signal for reduced European contributions, for the allies would accept the leader's estimate that a reduction was safe.

One facet of these interrelated issues is the cost of maintaining American forces on the central front. Both the balance of payments and the budget are involved. Since 1967 Germany has agreed to compensate the United States for part of the balance-of-payments deficit due to American troops being stationed there, a loss estimated in 1969 to be about $950 million a year. In the first two annual agreements, a large part of the compensation was provided through purchase of treasury notes and other fiscal measures, an improvement on earlier American requirements that Germany buy large quantities of military equipment from the United States regardless of German estimates of need or other allies' markets or the similar problem posed to Britain by the maintenance of *its* forces in Germany. In the agreement of July, 1969, a complicated bargain which included German dollar credits for German investors in the United States, the United States secured a two-year arrangement that covered more of the deficit (about 80 percent, of which about 61 percent would be compensated for by purchases of services and goods in the United States, primarily military goods, but including some civilian items).[14] Critics point out that such arrangements, useful in temporarily reducing the balance-of-payments deficit, only paper over the difficulty and do not meet the American budgetary problem.

Among the reasons that Germany has in the past been unwilling to pay outright for the maintenance of these forces, whether British or American, is the feeling that paying for them would make them appear to be occupation forces. This principle was breached for the British in 1971, but not for the Americans. The Federal Republic has, however, provided the installations housing the American forces as well as other contributions and late in 1971 agreed to make a cash payment for improvements in Germany. The Germans say that their own forces are protecting the alliance in general, as are the forces of other allies stationed on German soil. Since the

---

[14] *New York Times*, July 10 and 22, 1969; *Atlantic Community News*, September, 1969. After prolonged bargaining, a new two-year agreement was announced December 10, 1971. Besides the usual provisions for procurement of military supplies in the United States, to help cover the balance-of-payments deficit with Germany it included for the first time a lump-sum cash payment of $184,000,000 to be spent in modernizing the barracks and other residential quarters for American forces in Germany (*New York Times*, December 11, 1971). The Anglo-German agreement of 1971, on the other hand, provided cash payments in equal installments over five years to cover part of the British costs of maintaining the British Army on the Rhine (*Atlantic Community News*, May, 1971).

German forces, all of which are committed to NATO, are worrisomely deficient for lack of financial support, among other reasons, the United States is faced with a dilemma in pressing for higher German expenditures—whether to secure funds for American forces in Germany or to have them spent on Germany's own forces. Too great an insistence looks like intervention in German domestic affairs because of the budgetary and political implications. To withdraw substantial numbers of Americans would reduce the financial cost of maintaining them in Germany in the same way that dropping an insurance policy saves the premiums. A similar dilemma faces the German government, which in agreeing to make a larger compensation was moved by the same hope as the American negotiators, that thereby senatorial pressure for withdrawal might decrease. Large increases in the German defense budget would produce effects undesired by either that government or the United States. But the complexities of the problem elude the notice of some of the proponents of troop removals. Nor have they noticed that the United States bargain with the German government constrains its freedom to pull out troops without risk that the Germans might again turn their dollars into gold.[15]

The patterns on the Canadian side have been somewhat different. No one has seriously raised the question of Germany's compensating Canada for the forces it has kept in Germany. The assertion has been common in Canada that its limited forces would be better employed for United Nations peacekeeping purposes. There has been greater readiness to perceive a détente with the Soviet Union, justifying withdrawal. Some Canadians have even claimed that the existence of North American forces in Europe prevents such détente. The question of Canadian forces in Europe has been mixed up with fears that a nuclear role was being forced on the unwilling Canadians. A little anti-Americanism peeked out from under allegations that the requirements for Canadian forces showed that allied policy was made in the United States. Like some Americans, Canadians have asked in recent years why the af-

---

[15] See Peter Kenen, "The International Position of the Dollar," *International Organization,* Summer, 1969, p. 715 for the other side of a trade to get a short-term monetary advantage.

fluent Europeans could not provide their own military defense. Others, however, have claimed that Canadian withdrawals would simply induce the rest to reduce their contributions and that so long as there are American forces in Europe the Canadians should be there too. The independence-minded Canadian, on the other hand, abhors any European conception of Canadian forces serving as proxies for Americans.

Among those favoring a continued Canadian presence, there have been arguments about the appropriate use of Canadian forces in Europe. Even some of NATO's staunchest advocates have stressed more and more the "Canadian" Article II of the North Atlantic Treaty (which provides for economic and cultural cooperation), desiring to soft-pedal the military aspects of the alliance. As befits a somewhat less affluent nation, Canadians have been more aware than Americans of alternative uses for the money being spent to fulfill their NATO obligations; in spite of disillusionment they still point to their special capacity for UN peacekeeping jobs. The need to modernize the Canadian air force in Europe brought to a head a reorganization so altering its size and role as to make it compatible with forces in Canada itself; this, it was assumed, would enable the government to maintain the same training and equipment for both.[16]

OPINION GROUPS

Who takes which side on these questions about contributions to NATO in the United States and in Canada? Just as the issues differ in the two countries, so do the pressures for accepting one view rather than the other on a particular issue. It must be noted that maintaining forces in Europe involves a number of technical considerations, on which an opinion will be expressed chiefly by those with an interest in and knowledge of defense questions. In the past not many Canadians, especially among the civilian population,

[16] John Holmes usefully summarized arguments about NATO in "The New Perspectives of Canadian Foreign Policy," World Today, October, 1969, pp. 450–60.

have been interested in or trained to evaluate matters of strategy; furthermore, the military in Canada occupy a lower level of influence among those who help to determine public policy than is the case in the United States. Knowledge about defense matters is increasing, however, in part because of Canada's membership in NATO. Many of the pressures clearly articulated by the few who have been concerned with these issues related not to total disengagement but to alternative ways to use Canadian forces, both ground and air, and especially to where they should be positioned.

There have been shifts in interest and changes in the strength of particular views, in both Canada and the United States. At the start of NATO, once the Korean War had destroyed Canadian hopes of confining its alliance contribution to military aid, the Canadian government's commitment of forces to Europe generated relatively little debate; the chief criticism came from some (opposition) Conservative Party members who thought the Canadian contribution should be larger.[17] Like the Americans, however, the Canadians originally expected that Western Europe's need for non-European forces would not endure many years, that Europeans would eventually take over. More than in the United States, the anti-communist appeal associated with the idea of NATO has markedly diminished over the years, and those among the articulate public who shy away from things military have grown more vocal. Coincidentally, Canadians tended to lean, consciously or not, on the United States to do what was necessary in Europe as well as in continental defense, while their country turned to what seemed to be more altruistic roles, especially United Nations peacekeeping and technical aid to countries in the Third World.

Unlike the original Canadian commitment of forces, the first American commitment, under President Truman in the fall of 1950, aroused a "Great Debate." It was inaugurated by ex-President Hoover, who in December of that year delivered his "Gibraltar" speech stating, among other things, that no American troops should be sent to Europe until the European countries were ready

---

[17] Jon B. McLin, *Canada's Changing Defense Policy, 1957–1963* (Baltimore, Johns Hopkins Press, 1967), pp. 19–20. See also Dobell, "Canada and NATO," pp. 312–23 for opinions on Canada's participation in NATO.

to defend themselves. Then followed the joint hearings by the Senate Foreign Relations and Armed Services Committees which provided the last significant gasp of the isolationists such as Senator Taft. From then on, the public oratory took on various shades of internationalism—or interventionism. The tendency to set budget ceilings for defense expenditures because a larger amount would "threaten the economy" gradually diminished. However, the New Look, with its implications for NATO ground forces, was an example of security policy being determined by "economic" considerations rather than by estimates of the foreign threat. Through the years, members of Congress became more and more sophisticated about defense matters and more interested in NATO. At the same time, the early expectations of everyone, including General Eisenhower as Supreme Allied Commander Europe, that the need for American troops in Europe would diminish after the mid-1950s changed to the realization that so long as the United States wanted NATO to be strong and the allies shared this desire, substantial American forces would have to remain in Europe. Especially after the batterings from de Gaulle, members of Congress also showed marked understanding that consultation meant that the United States had to listen to its allies as well as tell them, and there was in general a greater interest in NATO than in the period when the United States had little trouble with its allies. New interest meant increased attention to the size of American forces in Europe and new questioning regarding the need to maintain as many as five divisions of ground troops in view of European capacity and Soviet behavior.

These shifts have taken place at the highest levels, where domestic pressures might be felt in most concentrated form. What about the other end of the spectrum, the amorphous arena called "public opinion"? In Canada, where the matter of forces in Europe had become more of a public issue, there is some evidence that political leaders' views were not representative of those of other groups. For example, in a poll taken in November, 1962 (shortly after the Cuban missile crisis), of 1,500 members of elite groups (party leaders, Members of Parliament, business and labor leaders) plus "voters," only the politicians favored withdrawing forces from Central

Europe, even if some forces from both sides were to be withdrawn. Similar divisions of opinion have appeared with respect to the West's increasing its military strength against Russia and with respect to most nuclear questions.[18] In December, 1968, the Canadian Institute of Public Opinion published a poll directly on the question of the stationing of Canadian troops in Europe as part of NATO. Almost two-thirds of those polled believed that Canadian forces should be kept in Europe.[19] Regional differences were clear, as the figures show:

	National	Quebec	Ontario	West
Continue there	64%	55%	66%	71%
Call back	23	32	22	20
Qualified	3	—	1	5
Don't know	10	13	11	4

Five years earlier, a Canadian Peace Research Institute poll showed 15 percent of respondents satisfied with current Canadian defense policies, 12 percent dissatisfied, and 57.5 *percent having no opinion.* In that poll, however, those interviewed were focusing on questions involving nuclear weapons.[20]

In the United States, a 1963 Roper poll of a "representative sample" of the population contained no question directly on American forces in Europe but had some relevant findings. Of four alternatives on handling the Cold War, 68 percent of those polled favored keeping up United States military strength but simultaneously doing everything possible to build up alliances and strengthen other countries in order to stop the spread of communism.[21] Forty-five percent thought Western Europe the area most important to America's future. Sixty-seven percent wanted to maintain ties or form even closer ties with Europe, whereas 6 percent wanted to pull back as quickly as possible.[22] Among those wishing closer ties,

[18] John Paul and Jerome Laulicht, *In Your Opinion* (Clarkson, Ont., Canadian Peace Research Institute, 1963), pp. 19, 22–24.
[19] *Ottawa Citizen*, December 11, 1968.
[20] Peyton V. Lyon, *Canada in World Affairs, 1961–63* (Toronto, Oxford University Press, 1968), pp. 535–47.
[21] Atlantic Council of the United States, *American Attitudes Toward Ties with Other Democratic Countries* (Washington, 1964), p. 13.
[22] Ibid., p. 15.

the largest group (29 percent) said that they wanted them for military reasons or to stop communism. There was no important difference between Republicans and Democrats on the general desirability of close ties with Europe.[23] Six years later, a Louis Harris poll on American attitudes concerning various kinds of support to selected countries around the world against Communist invasion or attack from within showed general reluctance, varying with the country and kind of support. NATO obligations were not mentioned, but two European allies were included, Germany and Italy. The persons polled showed less willingness to render military aid, including American forces, to Germany than to Canada, Mexico, and the Bahamas (highest in the list). Brazil also ranked higher than Italy! (When aid through a UN force was included in the question, willingness to aid rose substantially, but the rankings did not change.[24])

In neither Canada nor the United States does the symbol "NATO" bear much affect, although when the term is used in American election campaigns, the reference has almost always been positive. In Canada, on the other hand, at least one of the minor parties (the New Democratic Party) has qualified its endorsement by strongly opposing certain kinds of Canadian participation in NATO, most specifically through acquisition of nuclear weapons. As early as January, 1963, one of NATO's strongest supporters in Canada, Lester Pearson, called for a reexamination of Canada's role in it, pointing to the waning of the "collective" aspects of the alliance.

What President Truman wrote of the 1952 election in the United States could be repeated for all subsequent ones: NATO was one project he believed he could pass on to his successor knowing that they shared the same sentiments about it. Throughout the 1950s and 1960s, in each presidential election the platforms of both major parties included favorable references and more or less specific promises about NATO.[25]

[23] Ibid., p. 21.   [24] Time, May 2, 1969.
[25] Except for a minor comment by Senator Eugene McCarthy in April, 1968, Senator George McGovern was the first serious Presidential candidate to include in his campaign appeals a proposal for a sharp reduction in the number of American forces in Europe, in his January, 1972, "alternative defense budget" of greatly decreased military spending.

Specific types of support for NATO, such as where to station ground forces, are not appropriate subjects for campaigning, but even the more general commitment, which partakes of the characteristics of both foreign policy and defense policy, is not one on which elections have turned in the United States. Some issues in these two policy areas could be expected to be crucial to Canadian elections, even if so mixed in with other questions that they cannot be said to have *determined* outcomes. Yet neither NATO as such nor the Canadian contribution to it has been an election issue. As a minor exception the election of 1963 might be cited, for during the preceding campaign there was much discussion as to whether or not the Canadian government should go through with its earlier agreement to arm its air force in Europe with nuclear weapons.[26] As usual, the relationship with the United States became inextricably entangled in the arguments for and against the Diefenbaker government's position, although the candidates for the most part avoided playing directly on this more fundamental theme. As with Americans, pocketbook issues are more interesting to Canadian voters than defense-policy issues. As long as the electorate does not directly feel the pinch from a specific form of Canadian support for NATO, a particular position on NATO forces is unlikely either to elect or to defeat a candidate.[27]

The outcome of the 1968 elections in both countries had an indirect impact on their roles in NATO, but in the opposite directions. President Nixon made a point of "renewing" relations with the Europeans allies during his postinaugural European trip. Prime Minister Trudeau, on the other hand, spun out a suspense story involving a fundamental reexamination of Canada's role in NATO. It culminated in his program for retrenchment over a period of years, as he declared that a military alliance could no longer determine Canada's foreign policy. In neither case, however, could the successful candidate claim that his position represented a mandate

[26] From 1957 up until 1968, years very important in the history of NATO, national elections in Canada were very close in numbers of seats won, and candidates seemed to be willing to politicize almost any question.

[27] In the American case, John Kennedy in 1960 used a campaign argument regarding defense which was indirectly related to NATO (but not to forces there) when he claimed that the Eisenhower administration had neglected to maintain its missile defenses vis-à-vis the Soviet Union.

from the voters. In Canada the Conservative opposition continually called attention to any suggestion of weakening government support for NATO, and leading members of the Prime Minister's own party took more extreme stands on either side than his. Yet Mr. Trudeau had such a solid majority in Parliament (unusual for over a decade) that he had great leeway for new maneuvers if he chose.

As to American parties, in recent years Republican leaders appear to have taken a greater interest in supporting NATO than have the Democrats, although they differ among themselves on the specific reasons and prescriptions for support. A Republican group which is devoted to NATO has existed in the House of Representatives under Congressman Paul Findley for several years. Its members tend to be conservative on many domestic matters. Division between "liberals" and "conservatives" of both parties regarding NATO can be observed. The former, when not preoccupied with domestic problems such as poverty and civil rights, are more interested in the United Nations or in aid to underdeveloped countries. When addressing themselves to Europe, the more liberal leaders focus mostly on ways to promote détente and arms control, and not all of them see NATO as other than an impediment to these activities. For some conservatives of the Goldwater type, NATO has been valued as an anticommunist organization which could be another military arm of the United States government. Liberal supporters, on the other hand, tend to stress the opportunities for political consultation provided by NATO.

The weight of specific private groups which might have influential views on their country's force commitment to NATO is hard to determine. In both countries there are small organizations devoted to the general desirability of supporting the international ties in the "Atlantic Community." Although composed of influential individuals in private life, they have to compete for attention with larger, more emotion-swaying organizations devoted to the United Nations, to disarmament, and to "peace." The latter groups appear to be more successful in catching the eye of leading politicians in Canada than in the United States.[28] Small groups of immigrants

[28] For example, see Lyon, *Canada in World Affairs*, p. 140, where he tells of the uproar when Lester Pearson declared in 1963 that Canada should ac-

from areas taken over by the Soviet Union in World War II may have expressed especially strong anticommunist views to their legislators, but their role has been very limited with respect to a specific NATO obligation. In neither country have there been strong groups opposing commitments to NATO, although in Canada a minority on the Left has been vocal; some of these opponents are in the universities. Certain prominent leaders in private life have advocated severe cuts in Canada's contribution to NATO. In sharp contrast to similar American periodicals, a leading Canadian mass-circulation magazine, *Macleans*, has argued for Canadian withdrawal from NATO. Articulate younger Canadians, who did not experience the early postwar problems or the pride of Canadians in their role in solving them, are less European-oriented than their elders and seem to feel that the NATO compact has no meaning for current issues; their American counterparts have paid little attention to NATO, compared to other issues.[29] The pressure groups which have real impact on legislators and administrators, such as agricultural lobbies, are in fields not concerned with NATO matters.

Differences about NATO among opinion leaders in both countries, especially those in the administrative or legislative branches of government, principally concern how forces committed to NATO should be used, equipped, or positioned. The divisions are more prominent on the Canadian side where, despite vigorous support for NATO by key members of the cabinet, some leaders would have Canada disengage completely. There has been no counterpart in any American administration for Eric Kierens, a former Trudeau cabinet member (Post Office) who said early in 1969: "Instead of a genuine deterrent against a genuine threat, NATO has become a self-justifying deterrent against a non-existent military threat." [30]

---

quire the nuclear weapons for its NATO force which the government had earlier agreed to.

[29] On Canadian youth, see, for example, John W. Holmes, "The American Problem," *International Journal*, Spring, 1969, pp. 232–33.

[30] *New York Times* (Week in Review), February 2, 1969. Although less outspoken about NATO, a cabinet minister of the earlier Diefenbaker regime, Secretary of State for External Affairs Howard Green, also made statements which produced confusion over what was cabinet policy, since they were opposed to the position of the Minister of National Defence. The statements related to nuclear weapons for the air force committed to NATO.

Prime Minister Trudeau, in his first months of office, was tantalizingly ambivalent about Canada's participation in NATO. The result of an extensive and prolonged review was a plan to reduce Canadian forces in Europe by phases and to concentrate more resources on continental defense, while continuing membership in NATO to aid alliance efforts toward détente. Trudeau's predecessor in the Liberal Party leadership, Lester Pearson, apparently changed his own views somewhat over the years. In 1965 he doubted that NATO would be in Canada's best interest in the long run; in 1968 he believed that strong military power was necessary for deterrence and to back up negotiations with the Soviet Union. His competitor, colleague, and Minister for External Affairs, Paul Martin, backed NATO as unambivalently as any cause to which he addressed himself. Differing stands on some aspects of Canada's participation in NATO are always good for parliamentary parry and thrust among opponents within and between parties.

Informed critics in Parliament, in the press, among retired military officers of high rank, and in the scholarly world have raised serious questions of a less political nature. They have dealt with whether Canadian troops should be on the "exposed" front line in Germany, whether they would better serve national security interests back in Canada as a mobile force ready to go to threatened areas, and whether the Canadian air squadrons should have a more defensive role in Europe than the strike-reconnaissance function which they have been performing. The Trudeau government's program for reduced force in Europe with a somewhat different role and its emphasis on mobility reflected these criticisms.

On the American side, within the government the main issue concerns how many Americans troops should be in Europe rather than held in readiness in the United States. One of the principal critics of current policy has been Senator Stuart Symington. Ever since his investigation of "Major Defense Matters" in 1959, he has questioned whether American conventional forces in Europe could have a meaningful role other than as hostages for the American nuclear guarantee and has been acutely worried about the effects on the American economy of maintaining troops in Europe. Senator William Fulbright's concern with the asserted overcommitment of the United States has centered rather on Vietnam, although he has long been suspicious of military views on the needs of national security and of the reliability of the executive branch in properly assessing them. His predecessor as chairman of the Senate Foreign Relations Committee, Theodore Francis Green, was an enthusiastic supporter of NATO and of the continued importance of conventional forces despite advances in nuclear weapons.[31] In general, members of this committee began in the late 1960s to lean away from the strong support of NATO given in earlier years and toward a sharp questioning of the dominant role of the United States in NATO's activities, a change related to more general disillusionment with American military policy.

The most clear-cut challenge to current American deployment of troops in Europe was Senator Mike Mansfield's resolution proposing "substantial reduction," introduced first in August, 1966, and reintroduced in February, 1967, after which hearings were held on it. In various degrees of opposition to Senator Mansfield's campaign to "bring the boys home" were prominent senators, especially Senator Henry Jackson, who has made an important opinion-leading niche for himself through his subcommittee of the Committee on Government Operations, and Senator John Stennis of the Armed Services Committee. On the Republican side, the liberal Senator Jacob Javits, who has worked hard for understanding, support, and reinvigoration of NATO, offered in 1967 a competing resolution to Senator Mansfield's. On December 1, 1969, Senator Mansfield once again introduced his resolution. This time bipartisan support was not in evidence, due in part to Republican loyalty to the administration, which opposed such a move at that time. Yet by early 1970 he claimed fifty-one backers. These names he had quietly gathered, although he was in no hurry to hold hearings. By 1971, however, he decided to force the issue. In May his effort to get Senate approval for cutting in half the number of American forces in Europe was defeated 61–36. He tried again in November to gain acceptance for a 60,000-man reduction and was defeated 54–39.

[31] See his report in Senate Committee on Foreign Relations, *NATO—Autumn 1957*, 85th Cong., 2nd sess. (1958).

Although the resolutions struck a responsive chord among many, especially as domestic problems loomed larger and larger compared to foreign obligations, Senator Mansfield's pressure for troop withdrawal was based on a very personal assessment of the world situation which discounted the importance of strategic questions. The Czechoslovak crisis only temporarily quieted Senator Mansfield, and he was more concerned about the European allies' failure to bear a greater burden than about the buildup of Soviet conventional forces in Europe. By getting just over half the members of the Senate as cosponsors to his earlier resolution he could lead the press to assume that it was as good as passed, and over time he created the impression—denied by other legislators—that public opinion called for it. The 1971 votes told a somewhat different story. The printed record of hearings on NATO does not suggest strong pressures from the Senators' constituencies to withdraw troops.

In assessing attitudes toward NATO in the Senate, one needs to cite particular individuals (even then the assessment might mislead, since a Senator can act unpredictably when the occasion arises). In the House of Representatives the more important influences are likely to be found in specific committees. Hearings of the Subcommittee on Europe of the House Committee on Foreign Affairs, held in the spring of 1966 and devoted to "the crisis in NATO," dealt most specifically with how to meet President de Gaulle's challenge and the continuing threat from the Soviet Union. No one urged withdrawing large numbers of American forces from Europe. Not to be outdone by the Senate, this subcommittee held hearings early in 1970 related directly to the troop-withdrawal issue. Most of the subcommittee were either ambivalent or opposed to sharp reductions, at least in the near future, and most of the testimony they took also was opposed to withdrawals, at least in the near future. One witness, Representative Henry S. Reuss, argued for streamlining the American headquarters structure in Europe in the interest of efficiency and economy. Constituent pressure for troop withdrawals was not evident.

Members and staff of the Senate Foreign Relations Committee

may be more sensitive to other countries' views, but their opposite numbers in the House appear to have less distaste for the military aspects of NATO. (This statement is, however, not true of those who belong to the liberal Democratic Study Group.) As supporters for the administration's policy regarding military commitments, the House Committee on Foreign Affairs has changed places with the Senate Committee on Foreign Relations in recent years; the senators have grown increasingly skeptical of the dominating role of the United States around the globe.

Senators and Representatives who attend the interparliamentary North Atlantic Assembly might be expected to provide support for NATO requirements in their respective houses. The House delegation remains fairly constant in membership, whereas attendance is passed around somewhat more in the Senate. Individual members usually have used their position to pursue their own special NATO-related concerns, not to undermine administration policy on maintaining forces in Europe.

GOVERNMENTAL STRUCTURES
AND NATO ISSUES

Neither in the House nor in the Senate do views regarding NATO commitments divide according to party any more than on any other issue. In both houses, numerous members in each party would be happy about American withdrawals that were matched by reductions of Warsaw Pact forces; they mostly question large *unilateral* reductions of American forces. Inside both the administration and Congress and between the two branches of government there are differing preferences; these reflect concern about the relative power of the various governmental institutions in decision-making as much as about the substance of policies.

It is between Congress and the administration that the outstanding conflicts have arisen in which the power to decide seemed more important than the differing views on forces in Europe. The classic example is the 1951 confrontation on assignment of United States ground forces to Europe.[32] Just as certain senators then sought to limit the President's power to deploy large numbers of armed forces abroad without the Senate's prior consent, so Senators Mansfield and Fulbright indicated in 1967 that they were seeking to prevent the President from making large force commitments abroad, comparable to those made in Vietnam, without Senate approval, since the power to declare war was implicitly involved. (Senator Mansfield has claimed that his desire to reduce troop deployments in Europe antedated the Vietnam escalation.) Although the administration was on the defensive in both cases, in the second they were arguing for the maintenance of forces not much smaller than the average over seventeen years or so, while in the former they were upholding an action the magnitude of which they were compelled to publicize as a result of the hearings. (Secretary of Defense Marshall reluctantly revealed that the whole discussion was about roughly six divisions, relieving many who had feared a large, open-ended commitment.) The Senate resolution on foreign commitments, passed in June, 1969, illustrated renewed Senate demands to participate in administration decisions involving military obligations to foreign countries.

In such proceedings it is natural for the administration to be on the defensive against congressional critics, regardless of the issue. Challenged by the Mansfield resolution, Undersecretary of State Elliott Richardson on January 20, 1970, made an unprecedentedly forthright and comprehensive statement of the need to retain substantial American forces in Europe. In the days of Secretary of Defense Charles Wilson's drastic reductions in the Army, the shoe was on the other foot. Administrative officials always want to make their own cuts. Thus Secretary McNamara in 1966 suddenly withdrew 15,000 specialists from Europe for Vietnam and in 1967 initiated the redeployment of about 33,000 men, to be "on call" for NATO but in the United States; these actions required much ex-

---

[32] An interesting sidelight was the proposal of John F. Kennedy, then Representative, that favored the sending of troops to Europe but suggested they be supervised by the appropriate congressional committees, Senate Committee on Foreign Relations and Senate Committee on Armed Services, *Hearings, Assignment of Ground Forces to Europe*, 82nd Cong., 1st sess. (1951), pp. 424–28.

plaining to Congress. Further reductions of support personnel, projected in 1969 to "streamline" American forces in Europe, were said to have been planned in part to forestall congressional demands.[33] If this was the reason, it may represent a misreading of congressional desires; depending on which members of Congress the administration had in mind, such cuts were either too large or too small. Studies of the need for particular sizes and types of armed forces and weapons systems made by the Nixon administration under Deputy Secretary of Defense Packard and by more than one committee in Congress illustrate the competitive nature of these issues. They also foretell *some* kind of reduction as a result of the contests.

Unlike members of the Nixon administration, Secretary McNamara did not make preemptive announcements, but he took startling steps toward his own reductions, more or less ignoring the need to consult interested members of Congress, to say nothing of members of NATO. One noticeable change from the early days of NATO is that numerous senators and representatives insist that the United States consult with its allies prior to making changes, whereas earlier congressional critics stressed unfettered decision-making by the Americans.

Sometimes the need to defend themselves against congressional criticism has flowed from illogical strategic or economic doctrines adopted by members of an administration. During the days of massive retaliation, the period of "a bigger bang for a buck" and of the stress on nuclear weapons "to compensate for inevitable weaknesses in manpower," many congressmen found it hard to understand the need for substantial conventional forces in Europe. Their administration adversaries often appeared foolish in their efforts to uphold the need for the formally unchanged divisions in Europe while indicating that the real deterrent was America's strategic weapons.

Almost inevitably, administration spokesmen have had to defend the failure of Europeans to pick up more of the burden of European security, even while these same spokesmen have always ex-

33 *New York Times*, January 26 and July 10, 1969.

pressed sympathy with congressmen's complaints about this failure. The almost constant rumors of withdrawal of American forces spread from these (and other) encounters are probably not unwelcome to the administration in many cases. For they exert indirect pressure on Europeans, especially Germans, who are the most common object of complaints.

After so many years, such warnings could have the effect of calling "wolf" once too often. However, by 1969 the British took the threat seriously; they urged the European allies to recognize the likely end of American patience, and increase their own contribution to the alliance. And in 1970 the North Atlantic Council ordered studies on how to adjust to potential reductions in American forces. On December 1, 1970, ten European members announced their intention to do so by adding one billion dollars to their contributions to NATO defenses over the next five years. Two days later President Nixon responded to them—and to senatorial critics —with his pledge that the United States would maintain its force strength in Europe through fiscal year 1972 unless the Soviet Union meantime agreed to a reciprocal reduction. The Soviet Union did not respond but the ten European allies did in 1971. They agreed on December 7 to an additional expenditure of one billion dollars on their defense forces while announcing that the previous year's schedule of improvements was being met.

Regardless of competition between the two branches of government, the recurring patterns of concern about NATO have hardly altered significantly the American contribution to European defense, at least up to 1972. Part of the explanation may lie in the crisscrossing of shared preferences between members of the administration and members of Congress, even between members of opposing parties.[34] One of the sad consequences of the Vietnam war is the erosion of confidence between such informal groups, which inevitably has raised doubts also about the NATO commitment.

Within Congress itself there are not only competing houses but

[34] Thus there was implicit Johnson administration encouragement to Senator Javits when, in early 1967, he introduced his competing resolution to Senator Mansfield's, a resolution which more closely accorded with the government's position. Ibid., February 13 and March 6, 1967.

competing committees within each house which take differing views on the details of the American commitment and which have relatively little contact with each other. These pressures would thus seem inevitably to cancel out each other. To counteract the power of the Armed Services Committees, for example, a bipartisan "Military Spending Committee of the Members of Congress for Peace and Law," was formed in 1969 under Senator Mark Hatfield's leadership; its first report that summer recommended sharp cuts in various hardware projects. It also had its eye on greatly reducing the number of men under arms and in particular the number serving in Europe; other self-constituted groups of congressmen have since made similar suggestions.[35] This issue also becomes involved in tensions between the party leadership and others in the party.[36]

Conflicts of opinion on issues such as United States forces in Europe are less easily exposed in the executive branch. However, the normal concerns of each department pull them apart from an easy agreement on issues relevant to the size of the forces. The Bureau of the Budget and the Treasury will press toward reducing them, or take expediential positions making more difficult their continued maintenance. For example the Treasury has preferred bilateral agreements on sharing the costs of keeping troops in Europe as opposed to more complicated multilateral arrangements for burden-sharing.[37] The Department of State is usually in the position of upholding current dispositions, reflecting, among other things, European preferences. Officials in the Department of State are also more watchful (or critical, when they have opposed the decisions) of the ways in which the Department of Defense carries out its decisions. Within the Department of Defense, civilians have clashed with the Joint Chiefs of Staff on United States forces in NATO,

[35] Ibid., July 10, 1967; March 2, 1970; June 16, 1970; and AP dispatch, *Greenwich Time*, July 16, 1970.

[36] For example, Senate minority leader Everett Dirksen derided a House Republican group visiting Europe in 1965 for a NATO inquiry; Democratic rank-and-file members resented the way in which Senator Mansfield pushed forth his resolution in 1966 (*New York Times*, June 3, 1965, and September 7, 1966).

[37] House of Representatives Committee on Foreign Affairs, Subcommittee on Europe, *Hearings, United States Relations with Europe*, p. 160.

with the latter somewhat paradoxically on the same side with the Department of State.[38] In recent years the problem of the balance of payments has sufficiently impressed the Department of State and especially the Department of Defense that they need no pressure from fiscal authorities to use this argument in urging European allies to do more. Nor does it divide them sharply from congressional critics, some of whom use balance-of-payments and gold-flow problems as rationalizations for pressing shifts in deployment they wanted anyway.

Within the executive branch, the most interesting opposing pressures which relate to United States forces in Europe arise between military and civilian officials. In the course of the last twenty years the military leaders have changed their attitude regarding large numbers of American forces in Europe (or abroad anywhere). At the time the North Atlantic Treaty was signed and for some period thereafter, they were reluctant to have so fixed a commitment. They gradually adjusted to this situation and, in recent years, recognizing that their control over these forces is not significantly lessened, preferred not to make large changes in these force levels. (If a volunteer system replaced the draft and if this should result in a notably smaller number of men available, military leaders might then revise their desire to keep close to five divisions in Europe.) The earlier influence of the Air Force, which in the then-current stage of nuclear-weapon development and deployment had downgraded the importance of ground troops, has in recent years met stronger competition from other services. Unified commands and the strengthening of air transport of troops have changed the rules of competition.

The concern over the effects of reducing the size of the army on United States commitments abroad, which brought Generals Ridgeway, Taylor, and Gavin into conflict with the Eisenhower Chiefs of Staff, has no counterpart in the 1960s. However, their conflict with Secretary of Defense Wilson does resemble, in exaggerated form, the milder differences between the Chiefs of Staff and Secretary of Defense McNamara in the late 1960s over the lat-

[38] New York Times, April 13, 1969, and October 28, 1970.

ter's rotation plan for some United States forces in Europe. While General Wheeler stated in 1967 that there was "no military justification for any reduction of military forces in Central Europe," Secretaries Rusk and McNamara were saying that the planned return of 33,000 men to the United States would not reduce the combat capability of American forces committed to NATO. Military officials have feared that once home the soldiers would never return. Although General Wheeler had his sympathizers in some parts of Congress, the men came home in 1968. Many went back temporarily in 1969, but the physical difficulties encountered tended to support military views that they were no adequate substitute for forces already in place.

In the small Canadian government, competition among whole groups of officials which could affect the Canadian contribution to European security is less evident. (Personal rivalries are another matter.) As in the United States, the big controversies have been over weapons acquisitions and aircraft procurement, in which economic stakes and prestige were involved. The other large issue was the unification of the armed services in 1964. In both types of policy question there were implications for the Canadian contribution to European security. The White Paper on Defence which set forth the unification plan in 1964 explicitly stated that one basis for the changes was continued acceptance of the current levels and deployment of Canadian forces in Europe. Some members of the Special Defence Committee of the House of Commons took issue on this matter, but this relatively new committee, even when in full agreement, did not have the political strength of the Armed Services Committees in the United States system. The Canadian military are said to be much more under the control of and less able to influence their civilian masters than Canadians think is the case in the United States.[39] But among themselves those military leaders who have been interested in NATO did not agree on the disposition of the Canadian contribution. Nevertheless, the strong current running in the direction of a more mobile role for a more special-

---

[39] See, for example, Charles Foulkes, "The Complications of Continental Defense," in *Neighbors Taken for Granted*, ed. Livingston T. Merchant (New York, Frederick A. Praeger, 1966), p. 115.

ized type of contribution eventually became the accepted policy.

With a parliamentary system, Canada's government is supposed to be freer than an American administration to make and carry out a particular policy, though subject to sharp questioning in the House of Commons on matters of concern to particular members. But how does the government make up its mind? Despite greater party responsibility in Canada, in recent years cabinet ministers have shown at least as much readiness to differ openly with each other on national security matters as do Americans. Prime Minister Trudeau has relied more than some predecessors on his own staff in the office of the Prime Minister to aid him in deciding issues; the government's position is *his* position rather than the cabinet's. However, members of the permanent civil service (which extends into higher brackets of the government than in the United States) have traditionally been extremely influential and are not so talkative as their American counterparts in subcabinet positions. Prime Minister Diefenbaker's estrangement from them in his last years in office (though not on the question of deployment of Canadian forces) had no policy impact in the longer run.

Prime Ministers and presidents come and go; the permanent civil service elites in Canada and the standing committees in the United States Congress help to form the climate in which specific policies are adopted. Not specific group pressures but the basic political system accounts for some calculated choices made by particular governments. In Canada there are two language groups, one strongly entrenched in the important province of Quebec; thus Canadian governments constantly strive toward a unifying, national policy against the centrifugal pulls of a federal system quite different from the American. Not only are the Canadian provinces more powerful than the American states with respect to the national government; they are making very strong economic demands on Ottawa that explicitly compete with the defense budget. That there are two minor parties somewhat limiting the two major parties has meant that for several years of the NATO period Canada has had minority governments which tended toward immobility.

The elements of the American governmental system as they relate to the American contribution to European security are too familiar to outline. Suffice it to say that limitations on the President's authority to commit forces are very hard to impose. Frustrations over the Vietnam war have sparked several senatorial efforts to reassert congressional authority over foreign and military policy, including the resolution on foreign commitments passed in June, 1969, in which President Nixon was forewarned not to promise future aid which would require the sending of American forces unless he had some kind of congressional approval. Additional efforts to curtail his actions in Southeast Asia have not drastically restrained the president's freedom of maneuver, at least through 1971. Furthermore, while a president cannot commit his successor (as Secretary Dulles pointed out to the European allies anxious for a long-term promise of United States troops in Europe when Germany was admitted to NATO), the next president is not free to start from scratch. He feels bound to consider the obligations incurred by his predecessor. Thus the governmental systems of the two countries impel the Canadian leaders to look inward while permitting the Americans to respond more readily to the demands of the international system. Even the Canadian pressure to deal sympathetically with France in NATO in the 1966 crisis has been interpreted as an expression of concern for the French-Canadian voter. De Gaulle's crude appeals to Quebec separatism in 1967 brought a dissident North Atlantic ally into the Canadian domestic arena; this did not arouse strong sentiments for the alliance whose organization he had attacked.

COMPETING PROBLEMS

Looking outward, however, the American executive branch has been distracted from European security problems by the Vietnamese engagement. Despite very different perspectives and preferences, such diverse leaders as Senators Jackson, Fulbright, and Stennis and Secretaries McNamara and Laird all admitted that there was a connection between the demands of the Vietnam war and NATO's need for American forces. Another diversion appeared with the growing troubles in the Middle East, although here attention, not troops, was demanded. A world power is bound to be continuously distracted by crises recurring all over the globe. In wrestling with another problem partly imposed from the outside, the adverse balance of payments, some American leaders, instead of tackling the deficiencies of the international monetary system at their roots, have tried to eliminate the symptoms, with special attention to American forces in Europe. "Rotating" (withdrawing forces to a dual base in the United States) is represented as "savings" in the balance of payments, but it would have the opposite effect on the defense budget. A budgetary competitor for any other type of defense expenditures is the space race, also partly imposed from outside.

On the other hand, the arms race, which is almost completely an input from the international system, has not greatly affected the particular question of American ground forces in Europe. The Rapacki Plan or variations on it leading to some kind of neutralization of Central Europe was rejected by the Western powers, all of whom could see that withdrawal of American forces would be highly destabilizing in view of the closeness of the Soviet Union and the lack of depth in the area available for Western defense. Pressure to accept this scheme was minimal in the United States. Since that time, arms control discussions have dealt more particularly with nuclear weapons. While they affect NATO, they have not been translated into demands for ground-force reductions. It was in NATO that proposals for mutual and balanced force reductions were initiated. Two years elapsed before the Warsaw powers began to respond. Their reasons for doing so were unclear, since the pressure from American proponents of unilateral withdrawals suggested that no price need be paid to gain the Russian objective. Those Americans who press for removing large numbers of American forces from Europe are not the same as those who work hard for disarmament. The former mainly aim to shift the locale of forces committed to NATO, although some would reduce the total.

Arms control finds a readier audience in Canada, as is usual among smaller states. With the more limited numbers of experts on national security available for policy analysis, the question can be a greater distraction from concern with the needs of NATO, whereas quite separate American groups become involved in support of either arms control *or* NATO (although the two are not antithetical). The Canadian government's more limited budgetary resources also cause it to look more closely at competing ways to spend its money abroad. The popularity of the UN and in recent years of aid to the Third World (especially the French-speaking countries) did diminish interest in continuing Canada's regular contribution to NATO's forces in Europe.

Canada has more reason to feel secure from external attack than practically any other country in the world. Thus Prime Minister Trudeau could say to students at Queen's University in 1968, "I am less worried about what is over the Berlin wall than about what might happen in Chicago or in New York or in our own great cities in Canada." [40] The menace of internal disorders to which he referred and which he found likely to arise because of hunger and because "large sections of our society do not find fulfillment in our society" is not so apparent in the demands of the poverty-stricken in Canada as in the autonomy-seeking Quebecois. Canada's contribution to NATO and the alliance's value to Canada are relatively unimportant issues to most articulate people in Quebec, but they do have some competing interests which the Canadian government is forced to consider. In all the provinces, political leaders are more concerned about constitutional reform and fiscal questions than about Canada's role in NATO, which seems unrelated to their major problems. A huge country with rich resources, a small population, and highly energetic entrepreneurs across the border requires the Canadian government to expend on development thought and energy that would otherwise be available for security problems. Whereas NATO once served both security interests and the internal political interest in producing a consensus between "continentalists" and Commonwealth-oriented leaders, the alliance now seems irrelevant to new domestic divisions.

Discontented Americans usually pit the high-priority domestic problems in the United States—the demands of militant Negroes and the interrelated urban blight—against the distraction of the Vietnam war: they do not blame domestic troubles on American

[40] Speech reported in *New York Times*, November 10, 1968.

commitments to NATO. Once the war in Southeast Asia dies down, would a similar revulsion to continued American contributions to European security occur? Although possible, numerous considerations argue against this. First, NATO forces are deterring war, not killing innocent people of another color in an apparently endless conflict. The costs of maintaining a successfully deterring force are not large compared to the billions spent on an unsuccessful fighting force. No one is dying as a result of the NATO commitment. Service in Germany is not regarded as unpleasant; poor morale there is almost all related to the racial unrest and social ferment to be found in military bases at home or to weaknesses produced by concentration on Vietnam. The forces have been maintained in Europe for twenty years, and Americans have been insensitive to their budgetary cost. Senatorial agitation could change this. Few except some traders, bankers, and government officials are strongly moved by the balance-of-payments problems. The twenty-year demand continues that the Europeans ought to do much more, not that the United States should do much less.

The rising resentment against "the Pentagon" which has become increasingly evident has been directed partly toward the continuing high defense expenditures. Since "general purpose forces" are a large part of that cost and do not have the local payoffs for some key congressmen which hardware projects provide, they are politically more vulnerable to cuts and easier to reduce. On the other hand, they are more closely related to foreign commitments. Anti-Pentagon resentment focuses on engagements like Vietnam rather than on habitual obligations bound by treaty, although a few even object to these because of the "inflexibility" they represent for American policy. Military problems other than the NATO contribution are so much more conspicuous and pressing that they may be sufficient by themselves to occupy the full attention of potentially critical congressmen for some time to come. Meanwhile legislative pressure compels the administration to try to avoid undiscriminating congressional cuts by seeking a leaner, more effective, if somewhat smaller, force in Europe.

These observations rest on the assumption that the social and economic evils attributable to the Vietnam war can be dealt with fairly quickly. If satisfactory readjustments do not occur and especially if inflation continues unchecked, a more general revulsion toward all foreign obligations including NATO is more likely than it appears in the early 1970s. Dissatisfaction over the draft did not arise because of objections to service in Europe. In any case, the American commitment to European security is much more a mutual problem, not so easily weakened unilaterally as American commitments elsewhere might be. Whatever the future developments in these other areas, *some* reduction in the size of American forces in Europe is likely. One task of the United States government is to ease the transition as much as possible through allied consultations, since any change will be unsettling and will usually appear "poorly timed" with related international negotiations. On balance, the signs do not point to radical withdrawals, and yet those who favor sharply reducing the military budget seldom completely lose sight of Europe and the cost of maintaining American forces in that affluent region.

NORTH AMERICAN ROLES
IN EUROPEAN SECURITY

What effect might domestic pressures in the two countries have on the future of European security? In the past the North American states have been vital to the existing system, both militariily and politically. But some possible "future Europes" exclude ipso facto further North American participation. A unified Europe excluding outsiders or a Gaullist *Europe des Patries* would be unaffected by North American withdrawal, and Alastair Buchan's regional groupings of members outlined in 1967 had no appropriate place for Canada.[41] Those European models which are posited on some continued contribution would naturally be affected if either the United States or Canada, but especially the former, were inhibited by other considerations from playing the desired part. Yet these pressures are hardly likely to be the determining factor in

[41] In "The Future of Europe," *International Conciliation,* November, 1967, pp. 34–35.

shaping the future Europe. Ample evidence is the lack of success of American leaders in promoting their conceptions of European unity, especially in the defense field, despite efforts made many times during the life of NATO.

Aside from this failure, what about American and Canadian willingness to try to shape a new European security system? American officials, in the administration and in Congress, talked throughout the 1960s about a long-term commitment to Europe so long as the Europeans wish it; they tended to stress that withdrawals must be mutual, to maintain a military balance, or at least that forces removed from Europe be ready in the United States for quick redeployment. The Canadians were much more cautious. They were only willing to commit themselves in the short run, apparently not having had much indication in the past that their presence would be missed.[42] Even the strongly put arguments of NATO leaders that projected long-term Canadian cuts would demoralize other lukewarm allies and were badly timed had little impact on the Canadian government. For internal political reasons, especially to demonstrate independence, the Canadian government had to take its step toward reduction of forces before an anticipated American move in the same direction.

Ever since the Canadians sponsored the inclusion of Article II in the North Atlantic Treaty they have stressed in one way or another the importance of consultation as a benefit from the alliance. Refusal to continue some kind of force desired by other allies would have prejudiced this advantage, as Prime Minister Trudeau has acknowledged. Canada was ready in the 1970s to provide special mobile support in Norway and to make its own territory available for the training and exercise of allied forces lacking room in their own countries, thus giving proof of a sustained interest in NATO. So long as Canada aspires to play a role on the world scene some means of influence seems necessary to provide the kind of leverage on which Lester Pearson could rely when making suggestions to

---

[42] Canadians have not held high command posts in SHAPE, and the Germans do not help to compensate for the expense of their forces (as is the case with the British and Americans), two signs that their contribution may be regarded as a token. The hole they have left in the front line was filled by a British brigade.

the American government about NATO matters during his time in power.

The Canadian government has long played an important role in arms control negotiations, and not all of its views have corresponded to those of the American government. American officials are more likely to listen to governments which put important contributions into joint defense. Leverage provided by either strategic territory or expertness in peacekeeping is likely to dwindle, while the special relationship with the United States and the excellent example Canada provides with its quality forces would seem to require a continued role, though perhaps not the same deployment of forces. Canadians who are seeking a nonprovocative function for their military forces while still participating in world politics may be trying to square the circle.

The NATO response to the occupation of Czechoslovakia was sufficiently cautious as to belie the claim of provocation. The Canadian government was among the most cautious; it simply promised in 1968 not to carry out its planned reductions immediately. Although the Americans did not *increase* their numbers, they did bring some dual-based forces back to Europe temporarily while looking to the European allies to bolster NATO's defenses. These differing responses suggest that the United States government could rely on an underlying mood among Americans of identification with and expectation of cooperation from the European allies; the Canadian interpretation seemed based on a more inward-looking detachment from Europe. In this respect Canada is clearly an aberrant member of NATO, for none of the others have such great leeway in opting out of collective defense without serious consequences for their own security. (The effects on Canada's political standing and the shape of the alliance are another matter.)

In determining their future roles in European security, the Canadians would seem to have greater choice than the Americans. A superpower cannot disengage from the essential rivalry with its competing superpower. A leading contribution through NATO represents for the United States a major value in the competition and a minor value in permitting Americans to play a large role in making Europe secure. The Canadians can take a greater risk that their withdrawal will not bring about the chain reaction their defense officials have feared in the past, while the Americans have been afraid to test whether or not the Europeans would satisfactorily fill in the gap left by their departure. The role of superpower minimizes the importance of domestic pressures in the United States regarding contributions to NATO, but Canada's role of middle-power neighbor to the United States and marginal contributor to NATO inhibits the United States from trying to alter a Canadian stand determined by domestic pressures in Canada.

/ *Annette Baker Fox*

nato and the american nuclear deterrent

One way to go from the known to the unknown in international politics is to examine the conditions surrounding particular policies of the United States government and to note whether and how changes in these conditions are likely to alter the effects of the policies in the future. This procedure may shed light on the consequences of different choices, point up the constraints on such choices as well as the constraints imposed by the choices, and suggest alternative models of the future.[1] Thus some hypotheses about the shape of European security in the 1970s and the American role in it may be formed by analyzing various policies that have been adopted by the United States or that might be adopted relative to NATO and the nuclear deterrent.

This discussion will focus on Western Europe, and "security" will refer to protection against threats from the Soviet Union, not against internal disruption, nor against a radically transformed Germany, nor against any Eastern European country. Eastern Europe's security is not threatened by the United States or Western Europe. Thus the Russian notion of a revanchist Germany, which is shared by some of Russia's allies, is here discounted as groundless, although the existence of the fantasy must be recognized.

---

[1] See Daniel Bell's introduction to Herman Kahn and Anthony J. Wiener and others, *The Year 2000* (New York, Macmillan, 1967), p. xxvi.

How Western European security may be affected or not by certain American courses of action is the subject here. This chapter does not deal directly with the global aspects of American nuclear strategy, American-Soviet strategic relations, or politics in European countries, but concentrates instead on United States nuclear policy in the context of NATO. The analysis deals primarily with intergovernmental relationships, not the effects certain policies might have on changing the character of these governments. (Effects of new technological possibilities not yet deployed—the ABM and MIRV—are dealt with in the companion volume.) In setting forth contingent courses of American action which concern the United States nuclear guarantee to the North Atlantic alliance, no explicit effort is made to relate them to the alternatives in global military policy and United States foreign commitments, which were the subject of a comprehensive study by the Nixon administration under the direction of Deputy Secretary of Defense David Packard during 1969.

The policies chosen for discussion include those pertaining to both the substance of decisions and ways of making decisions. Some of them are more remote from experience or likelihood than others, but they are included for logical symmetry and to stretch the imagination (no claim is made to logical completeness). In some cases the circumstances associated with particular policies may be only remotely construed as "factors," and changes in some "factors" may cancel out changes in others. Thus it is not necessarily true that if a particular policy is purposely maintained, the choice has to be accompanied by the conditions which have been in the past associated with that policy, or at least not all of them. Other factors could substitute for earlier conditions that are missing now or later. The contingent courses to be examined are not mutually exclusive; they are somewhat arbitrarily separated out to highlight their implications, but some of them could profitably be combined. There is no significance to the order in which they are presented.

With regard to the various policy contingencies, it should be noted that the context of national security policy has changed from 1949 to the present, from nuclear monopoly to nuclear balance between the two superpowers, to proliferation among three other powers, and to the spread of peaceful uses of atomic energy. Concurrent changes have been miniaturization (including the development of tactical nuclear weapons) and development of missiles and space satellites. Also noteworthy in the military field have been such changes as new kinds of submarines, aircraft, armor, air defense, and strategic concepts. Economic changes include the advent of European prosperity and shifts in international monetary conditions to the detriment of the dollar. The changes in the political milieu in the first decade included the Warsaw Pact, the rearming of two Germanies, and the Berlin Wall. Meanwhile the Cold War spread around the world, with dramatic confrontations outside Europe. Later came a more relaxed bipolarity, signing of the partial test-ban and nonproliferation treaties, the growing power of the People's Republic of China, and a rising interest in the needs and claims of the Third World. There were also important changes of government in the key countries. The reign of Charles de Gaulle profoundly affected all the contingencies to be discussed, and his departure from office has opened up some possibilities that he personally had closed off earlier.

Contingent Course 1: Maintain American Control over the Nuclear Deterrent. None of the changes just mentioned can be singled out as the determining factor in the different responses by European allies or Communist adversaries to unilateral United States control of the nuclear deterrent for NATO, responses which had implicit effects on European security. When the policy first applied to the Atlantic alliance, the allies acquiesced; they really had no alternative, since they were in all respects militarily dependent upon the United States (and upon Canada, especially for "mutual aid"). Only as Britain and France recovered economically as well as militarily did these two allies become so dissatisfied that they openly challenged the complete control by the United States. (The British had embarked on nuclear-weapon development prior to the establishment of NATO, the French a few years later.) Only in Britain's case did the United States modify the strictness of this control to enable that ally to pursue its policy of a national nuclear deterrent, and then with the understanding that the two countries' nuclear weapons would be coordinated in their targeting. Vain attempts were made by the United States to impede the French development, resulting in an increasingly unfriendly relationship between the two allies and no strong move to coordinate plans for the French deterrent with NATO planning, as in the case of the other two allies. In a kind of chain reaction, the question was raised (mostly by non-Germans) about the role of Germany in the nuclear-weapons field; although it was treaty-bound not to make such weapons, Germany was clearly as important to NATO as were France and Britain.

To meet the hypothetical demands of Germany, the United States tentatively put forward the MLF "concept," which would not have fundamentally changed the tight control of the United States over a jointly owned and jointly operated special surface fleet of nuclear-armed ships. (Nor was its relation to NATO ever entirely clear.) The move foundered, but a more satisfying consultative arrangement inside NATO, in which France did not participate, came into being. Ultimate control over the major nuclear deterrent of the alliance remained with the United States; only France had effectively escaped the nonproliferation net; none of the allies had become much less militarily dependent upon the United States for the ultimate deterrent; and Germany continued to be a loyal and active member of the alliance.[2]

Nevertheless, the changes listed in the introduction, especially those in the nuclear field, had alerted all the allies to the possibility that the American nuclear guarantee to Europe might fail them in time of need. Reiterated declarations made in the 1960s concerning the numbers and kinds of American nuclear weapons available for the protection of Europe and the explicit allocation of some Polaris submarines to NATO defense were not entirely reassuring. However, most of the allies have not expressed a desire for either a NATO deterrent separate from the American deterrent or

[2] In 1969, German and English experts from the NATO Nuclear Planning Group explored different criteria for the use of nuclear weapons, tactical and strategic, in case of a Soviet attack; as a result, the Nuclear Planning Group's suggested guidance on specifically when and specifically how tactical nuclear weapons should be used was accepted by the North Atlantic Council in December, 1969.

one of their own. Participation in the Nuclear Planning Group (NPG) in NATO has distracted them from their discontent over not being able to control their own destiny, a hopeless desire anyway. The practical limits to consultation on the use of nuclear weapons—though pushed outward by this device—still prevent a solution completely satisfying to all. Yet the NPG is a great improvement over earlier practice in clarifying nuclear problems. The very nature of unilateral control is a limitation on the guidelines set down by NATO in 1967 and elaborated by the NPG for tactical nuclear weapons in 1969.

The changes listed in the introduction have also altered the allies' fears that the United States either would rashly and unnecessarily use nuclear weapons (a fear current in the 1950s) or would not employ tactical nuclear weapons or would not use them soon enough (a fear current in the 1960s). Greater clarity on who can veto a proposed use of tactical nuclear weapons and under what conditions should result from the studies of the Nuclear Planning Group, begun in 1968.[3] In addition, the allies have lost their dread of imminent Soviet resort to nuclear violence, although they have often been reminded of the hundreds of MRBMs targeted on Western Europe. The United States–controlled nuclear deterrent had indeed protected European security, and most of the allies tacitly preferred the continuation of this condition to the conceivable alternatives.

This policy of the United States has meant that the constraints were on others, although with respect to tactical nuclear weapons the two-key arrangement suggests that a host country could prevent their use. Only one ally, France, strongly opposed the constraint imposed by the United States. (The "independence" of the British nuclear deterrent is more formal than substantial.) All the other allies were by the late 1960s more concerned about curbing the arms race than about "having a finger on the trigger," even if Germany and Italy had misgivings about the particular form of a particular effort at arms limitation, the nonproliferation treaty. On

---

[3] On the genesis and workings of the Nuclear Planning Group see Harlan Cleveland, *NATO: The Transatlantic Bargain* (New York, Harper & Row Publishers, 1970), chapt. 4, especially pp. 53–57.

the other hand, the continued cohesiveness of a NATO whose nuclear deterrent remained primarily under American control would seem to rest in part upon the wholehearted American implementation of the purposes of the Nuclear Planning Group. If the European allies continue to be satisfied with this method of sharing at an important working level in the planning for potential use of the nuclear deterrent, the NPG would provide a vital component in the securing of Europe through the commitment of nuclear weapons under American control. The "all azimuths" doctrine of France, announced in 1967, was a defiant gesture rather than an indication of military hostility. By 1969 even the French were coming around to American strategic views, although they did not participate in the NPG.

To offset a possible contradiction between stability produced by a balance of terror and European stability produced by an American nuclear guarantee, strong conventional forces would appear necessary to make the guarantee credible and to avoid the likelihood that it might need to be invoked.

Contingent Course 2: Promote Closely Integrated Defenses under NATO. NATO's defenses are only partly integrated. An international command composed of officers from various allied forces is responsible for planning for defense and for certain kinds of training. In case of war they would exercise command over those national forces committed to NATO to defend the area of Europe extending from the North Cape in Norway to the Mediterranean, but excluding England and Portugal. The one exception to peacetime national command is air defense, which is an integrated system for the area from northern Norway to eastern Turkey and is directly under SACEUR's command at all times. Until recently there was no permanently assigned naval force; what was created in 1968 is a small destroyer fleet comparable in purpose to the ACE mobile force for land defense. The strategic nuclear weapons committed to the defense of the NATO area have not been integrated, although their targeting has been "coordinated" by SACEUR and his staff at SHAPE. The same has applied to the tactical nuclear arms which the United States has provided to some of the forces committed to NATO, under a two-key arrangement. The question of integration of nuclear weapons is covered by implication under course 1 and course 4. The modest new development in the naval fleet—STANAVFORLANT or Standing Naval Force, Atlantic— suggests an adjustment to certain of the changes listed in the introduction, especially the lower expectation of strategic nuclear assault on the central front, and to fresh awareness of the chance of small-scale probes at the periphery of Western Europe. This move would seem to be an alliance repudiation of President de Gaulle's rejection of the usefulness of integrated forces.

Wherever integration has taken place has rested upon mutually agreeable allied cooperation. None could be forced, and the gaps in the integrated-force structure and the deficiencies in the quality of committed forces are all too visible proof of this. These gaps and deficiencies have persisted through the years, despite the urgings of many leaders in the European countries as well as American or NATO officials. Nevertheless, the cooperation which has taken place seems clearly to have induced great Soviet circumspection in intimidating any of the allies, regardless of how weak or exposed it might be. Russian efforts have all been symbolic, mostly verbal. Although the general strategy of the alliance has been directed by the giant partner, it has required consent by the others, which they gave at first because there was no alternative and later through persuasion and independent conviction, especially as the strategic planning became more multilateral. The Americans have relinquished control over specific tasks as well, including some in air defense, and are less prominent than earlier in manning the high command posts.

Readiness to implement or continue to maintain the integrated forces was impeded earlier by economic stringencies in the European countries, later by persuasion through American example that the strategic deterrent and massive retaliation strategy made conventional forces less important, and in recent years by disbelief in a continued Soviet threat, coupled with the distracting temptations of newly experienced prosperity. The continued American contribution, though made more and more grudgingly, in view of other American concerns, has enabled the integrated forces to present at least a facade of cooperative defense. The formal and informal mutual appraisals of each other's military contribution, which proceed in NATO annually and in recent years include a progressive five-year estimate of future forces, give substance to the idea of joint defense. Pre-positioned forces put the onus on the Soviet Union to move first militarily. Each time NATO's armed strength has appeared to lose credibility, the Soviet Union has done something outrageous which reminded the allies of why they had joined forces.

If the Soviet Union fails in the future to follow this pattern a main reason for any military integration will have disappeared. How can the allies safely judge that such a change has actually occurred? The interval between aggressive actions may be lengthy. It was six years prior to the invasion of Czechoslovakia that the Russians had last looked seriously threatening. One answer to the danger of miscalculating the possibility of another outrage could be that the danger will only have passed when the Russians are willing to accept the freely exercised self-determination of the peoples in Eastern Europe. When that occurs, the shape of the problem of European security will look very different from the way it appears today. Meanwhile, however, the willingness of the European allies (capacity is not in doubt) to continue integrated defense may be affected by how large an American contingent remains in Europe. A radical reduction would probably reinforce neutralist groups in the allied countries, especially those closest to possible Russian pressure. There would then be very little left to integrate. Genuine consultation will help to avoid misconceptions on both sides of the Atlantic regarding potential moves. However, the Americans' (and Canadians') knowledge that the Europeans could jointly do more for their own security than they yet have suggests that the European governments need to secure their own peoples' support for adequate contributions if they wish the North American contributions to remain sizable.[4]

Yet the mutuality of integration means that, as a result of the Vietnam war, the United States may have to earn over again the reputation for being a rational, humane, and trustworthy leader of

---

[4] In the words of the *London Daily Telegraph* (February 3, 1969), if Western Europe, with a population about the same as that of the Warsaw Pact countries and double their total production, and with only one frontier needing defense, does not make adequate contributions to NATO, this "is to admit Europe is not prepared to make even one-third of the effort to defend freedom that Russia makes to subvert it."

the alliance. A skillful and determined effort to extricate American forces from Vietnam should help to revive confidence in the United States among the other NATO allies. Yet the traumatic effects of this intervention may have the opposite effect on the American public. Europeans feared a mood of withdrawal from international responsibilities in general as the United States entered the seventies.

With imagination, the balance-of-payments problem presented by American and British forces in Germany can be alleviated through one or more economic measures.[5] More permanent answers await international monetary reforms and a broad view of the fungibility of allied resources, which may eventually be made comparable although they are unlike each other. Greater publicity about the various contributions of the allies to the common defense should help to mobilize support among the laggards. If the nihilistic thrust grows stronger among the more radically inclined youth, it will inevitably hinder European governments from continuing to fulfill some of their military commitments to NATO, especially in Germany. Such a trend would, in turn, greatly weaken the American willingness to bear a large share of the burden. On the other hand, the habit of cooperation some of the NATO members have acquired in the EEC may provide psychological support for working together in NATO.[6] In any case, there is a tendency for the larger members of a joint enterprise to bear a "disproportionate" share of its burden because they put a higher absolute value on the collective good it produces.[7]

Defense integration in NATO received a financial boost in De-

[5] Note Senator Charles Percy's proposal to the North Atlantic Assembly for a "clearing house" and "surplus" members' "payments" to those in deficit, *New York Times*, June 9, 1969. Other suggestions appear in John Newhouse with others, *U.S. Troops in Europe* (Washington, D.C., Brookings Institution, 1971), pp. 133–41. Not widely recognized was the NATO agreement to reimburse the United States if the French government refused to meet its claim for expenses incident to the forced removal of American installations in France (House of Representatives Committee on Foreign Affairs, Subcommittee on Europe, *Hearings, United States Relations with Europe in the Decade of the 1970's* [91st Cong., 2nd sess. (1970), p. 161]).

[6] Stanley Hoffman, *Gulliver's Troubles* (New York, McGraw-Hill Book Co., 1968), p. 376: "In Europe, the 'reconversion' of NATO into a diplomatic institution may well be the only way of preserving it as a military one."

[7] See Mancur Olson, Jr. and Richard Beckhauser, "An Economic Theory of Alliances," in *Economic Theories of International Politics* ed. Bruce Russett (Chicago, Markham Publishing Co., 1968), pp. 25–49.

cember, 1970, when the European members (all but France and Portugal) jointly promised to spend nearly one billion dollars over the next five years on improvements in NATO's infrastructure and their own forces. The following December they pledged the expenditure of an additional billion dollars for strengthening their forces in 1972, an unprecedented increase. The costs to the European allies of more effective joint defense would not necessarily be high if greater European specialization and cooperation in supply and logistics took place, as former British Defense Minister Healey among others has urged.[8] More joint arms-production programs would advance American interests in allied defense economies. It would still be necessary to prevent particular American groups from undermining such efforts by, for example, competitive arms sales. Considering the long record of below-standard implementation of NATO force goals, all those who provide forces will need to improve the forces' training, equipment, and mobility and to strengthen their reserves for local defense in Central Europe to compensate for inferiority in the numbers they are willing to contribute.

Contingent Course 3: Neglect NATO as a Political Instrument for Intra-Allied Negotiations. If the United States government should become convinced that its European allies have no real leverage because they are militarily unnecessary to American security, or if it no longer regards Europe as the area of highest security, or if it becomes almost totally immersed in domestic affairs, the readiness of the European allies to cooperate through NATO will vanish. For them, as for Canada, an important return on their military investment is that NATO offers an exceptional channel into American decision-making. From time to time suggestions are made about some special mechanism to bring NATO concerns right into the center of the American foreign-policy process.[9] Probably more ef-

[8] On the unexploited opportunities for coordinated supply and logistics, see Geoffrey Ashcroft, *Military Logistics Systems in NATO: The Goal of Integration, Part I: The Economic Aspects,* Adelphi Paper no. 62, and *Part II: Military Aspects,* Adelphi Paper no. 68 (London, Institute for Strategic Studies, 1970); also Cleveland, *Transatlantic Bargain,* p. 89.

[9] A *New York Times* editorial of February 25, 1969, for "the equivalent of a seat on the National Security Council."

fective than a formal arrangement is to have as presidential adviser on national security a person concerned for years about NATO and European security and as United States Ambassador to NATO a close associate of the president, as was the case in 1970. But such arrangements exist only intermittently.

At times the American government, under both Republicans and Democrats, has overlooked NATO in its bilateral dealings with friend and foe on matters related to European security. There is always an unfavorable reaction among the other allies when this is done, even though many of them, especially France, have done the same thing. In the late 1960s, within the alliance both the Europeans and the North Americans had publicly recognized that NATO could promote détente with the Soviet Union. Not only might a united military front induce the Russians to abandon efforts to intimidate some allies, but NATO could also provide a way to harmonize the efforts of individual allies in the "opening to the East." In the Harmel Exercise (a European initiative which was very welcome to the United States and which searched for suitable future tasks for NATO) the Americans had an example of European interest in continued political cooperation and a strong hint that the European allies wanted prior consultation before the United States undertook major discussions with the Soviet Union. This is not to suggest that America's allies object to United States–Soviet negotiations, which in fact they desire. The process by which NATO was engaged in the United States–Soviet negotiations about the nonproliferation treaty is often favorably compared by European friends of NATO to that by which the test-ban treaty was negotiated, even if some of the allies were not completely happy with the outcome. Since nonproliferation requires much cooperation from the allies, such a consultative process was clearly indicated.

It is usually difficult for American officials to believe that their allies have superior knowledge or judgment about international affairs. Yet they do need information on what their allies intend to do and they also need to have each ally informed of the others' intentions and in the presence of the others.[10] In 1970 Chancellor

[10] President Nixon told the North Atlantic Council on February 24, 1969, that he had come to Europe to listen. "One of the greatest values of having

Willy Brandt could carry on talks with members of the Warsaw Pact without rousing intense fears among United States officials, a situation unimaginable prior to the development of the consultative process in NATO. Using the North Atlantic Council as a political forum compels the other allies to take each other into account and to recognize how each member's actions affect the others, including the United States. This process, through which all look at problems together, creates an important addition to all the other kinds of intelligence available through NATO.[11] The Harmel Report, taken by itself, was less important than the exercise which preceded it, a process through which allies with very divergent views gradually came closer together on how to deal with the Soviet Union as well as on other aspects of NATO's future. The continuing analysis and appraisal of developments in the Warsaw Pact countries promotes a common appreciation of détente opportunities. In the Czechoslovak crisis the "nerve-steadying" function of NATO was very much in line with American preferences.[12] These benefits from using NATO as an intra-alliance political instrument are endangered not only by certain kinds of bilateral agreements but also by unilateral military measures that affect the alliance but are taken by the United States without consultation. (Such actions have usually reflected the greater weight of the Pentagon as compared to the Department of State, a relationship which could shift.)

---

an alliance is the chance it provides to share ideas, to broaden the horizons of our thinking, to multiply the resources of experience and perspective we can bring to our problems, not only in our own immediate areas but throughout the world. Surely one thing we have learned from these difficult years is that no one nation has a monopoly of wisdom."

[11] Writing of the Czechoslovak crisis, Harlan Cleveland said, "Because of the painstaking prior assessment, fifteen Foreign Ministers had a more or less common way of looking at and thinking about, and even talking about, an enormously complex situation" ("The United States and the Future of NATO," NATO's Fifteen Nations, February–March, 1969, p. 55). He expanded on the many-faceted process and virtues of, as well as obstacles to, political consultation in his NATO: The Transatlantic Bargain, pp. 13–33. The nuances of this process are frankly described by this former United States Permanent Representative to NATO.

[12] See John W. Holmes's phrase in "Fearful Symmetry: The Dilemmas of Consultation and Coordination in the North Atlantic Treaty Organization," International Organization, Autumn, 1968, p. 838.

The North Atlantic Council is one agency that can shape European security in the near future on an Atlantic rather than a purely European basis. If the European allies cannot stand up to diplomatic pressures from the Soviet Union individually in the absence of NATO, the United States also requires this political foundation when negotiating matters vital to Europe's future. A continued emphasis on the Atlantic tie does not rule out the usefulness of the "European caucus." This development has been welcomed by American officials as supportive of cooperation in NATO, as especially helpful in bringing British and Germans together and in stressing the need for a stronger European contribution to NATO forces. Such a caucus is a reminder that NATO includes three "second-tier" powers plus another (Italy) close to them in political importance.

Contingent Course 4: Pare Back the American Commitment to the Nuclear Guarantee. Course 4 is related to course 3 and is contrary to course 2. It would be in some ways a return to the situation prior to the establishment of NATO, when the North Atlantic Treaty essentially meant a nuclear guarantee to the European allies and did not include troops in Europe to complement the pledge. Some critics of the current troop commitment do not believe in the strategy of the flexible response, now official NATO doctrine, and see no further need for concerted preparations for conflict by conventionally armed forces. They think that a very small American contingent could be sufficient for hostage purposes. But how many Americans could go home without weakening United States control over the tactical nuclear weapons upon which rests, in their view, so much of the credibility of the United States guarantee?

Other critics believe that the weakness of NATO conventional forces already puts in doubt the plausibility of a real flexible response on the central front. But the changes in nuclear technology and other forms of warfare and in the strategic balance are making the nuclear guarantee less and less credible, standing by itself. Polaris and Minuteman missiles would not seem to be well adapted to preventing the forms of political or military pressure the European allies would most likely feel if the American forces committed to NATO were to languish or disappear. European security would probably become very fragile, subject to uncoordinated moves of allies for competitive reasons or to save a single country's skin, as well as more open to ambiguous Russian probes.

These effects are predicated on the assumption that without American forces in Europe as an important element in deterring the Soviet Union, the allies would reduce or cease their own cooperation in conventional forces.[13] The burden of proof rests on those who argue that European unity would be stimulated by a radical reduction in the American role, since the presence of the United States forces in Europe has coincided with unprecedented European integration. Why should such collaboration among the European allies *increase* with a sharp decrease in United States forces? Is it not more likely that at least some members would dissociate themselves in the manner of the neutrals of the 1930s, thus leaving them open to the kind of Soviet intimidation now discouraged by NATO? Leadership by the United States to counter such an eventuality would have lost its base.

One might conjecture the opposite course: to maintain all American obligations to European defense *except* the guarantee of initiating a nuclear blow if conventional forces proved inadequate to deter the Soviet Union from expanding an assault. The guarantee remaining would only be against nuclear blackmail. This somewhat unrealistic proposal might alter the Europeans' readiness to improve their conventional forces, but the possible effects are very unclear.

---

[13] Stanley Hoffmann summarized the adverse effects of withdrawing American forces from Europe along the following lines: As long as they were in Europe, Russia could only move at a great risk, whereas their withdrawal would give the Soviet Union the freedom of initiative even if they were later reintroduced. If the attack were large in scale, the airfields necessary for landing the American troops would no longer be available. A nuclear response would have to come much sooner than envisaged by the McNamara doctrine. If there were a small incident, an American decision to send troops back would make a large crisis out of a small one. And it would increase the uncertainties among the European allies regarding American protection (*Gulliver's Troubles*, p. 445). See Cleveland, *Transatlantic Bargain*, pp. 114–15, for a long list of arguments against withdrawal, and the balance sheet presented in Newhouse, *U. S. Troops in Europe*, pp. 145–63.

Contingent Course 5: Fail to Discourage a Separate European Nuclear Deterrent. Either course 4, or its opposite as touched on above, might result in new interest among Europeans for their own deterrent independent of the American deterrent. Some Americans who were concerned in the early 1960s about European desires to control the nuclear weapons upon which their security depended proposed from time to time that the United States deliberately aid such a step.[14] Usually they envisaged the European deterrent to be one controlled by NATO, but such an arrangement would not detach it from American decisions.

Whether or not the weapons were put under NATO, the development of a European deterrent would seem to require some American cooperation; this could run into strong domestic opposition, especially in the Joint Committee on Atomic Energy of Congress. (In the past, the administration had difficulty in securing those slight relaxations of the 1954 legislation on atomic energy that were made in 1958–59 and 1964 to enable the United States effectively to place its own nuclear weapons in Europe or in the hands of allied forces under the two-key system. By the late 1960s a somewhat more flexible attitude appeared among the leaders on the Joint Committee.) A critical issue in the negotiations with the Soviet Union over the nonproliferation treaty related to a separate European nuclear deterrent. To the Russians any such move would be "proliferation," and their undisguised fear was that it would make Germany a nuclear power.

In view of the same (latent) French fear and of the unfriendly Franco-American relations in the nuclear field, France's interest in such a "European" deterrent would depend upon whether or not it was in reality a French deterrent (the French say the NATO deterrent is American). One change brought about through the successful development of the *force de frappe* is that Franco-British coop-

[14] For example, the group associated with Robert Strauz-Hupé; Congressman Paul Findley; Joseph Kraft, *The Grand Design* (New York, Harper and Row, Publishers, 1962), p. 63; and in the early 1960s, Henry Kissinger, *The Necessity for Choice* (New York, Harper and Row, Publishers, 1961), pp. 121–28. Even in late 1968 it was not completely ruled out by the future head of ACDA (Gerard C. Smith, "The French Temptation," *Interplay*, February, 1969, p. 49).

eration in nuclear weaponry would no longer seem to run into the snag presented by American atomic-energy legislation, which had earlier prevented the British from legally sharing with a state lacking nuclear capacity. The high price France would exact from the British in detaching themselves from the United States is not likely to entice the British into such an arrangement unless the United States commits an even greater blunder than the Skybolt fiasco.

Some of the proponents of a separate European deterrent had in mind, among other things, that no invulnerable or mobile medium-range ballistic missiles existed in Europe that could counter the threat of Russian MRBMs. The development of the Polaris-armed nuclear submarine and the commitment of several such vessels to the defense of NATO helped to blunt this concern, especially since much apprehension was expressed over the dangers of positioning land-based medium-range missiles in Western Europe. In any case, the record of European cooperation in missile and space development and peaceful uses of atomic energy has been sufficiently discouraging to cast doubt on the success of a venture to provide a weapon independent of the American deterrent. All the arguments against "bee sting" national deterrents would still seem to apply to a European deterrent detached from the American deterrent, the more so since the Soviet Union has established a missile defense impressive enough when combined with a multi-headed missile capability to spur the United States to the same expensive development. Aside from the strategic arguments against the effectiveness of such a European deterrent, the electorates of the potential participants would seem even less favorable to such defense expenditures than they are to budgeting for conventional forces. Even President de Gaulle had to make drastic revisions in his plans for further nuclear development after the civil disruption of 1968 and the ensuing monetary crisis. Independence costs more money than most Europeans wish to pay.

In view of all these considerations, it seems unlikely that European security in the early 1970s would be based on a separate European nuclear deterrent. If the French and British were to come to an agreement on joining theirs, the problem of Germany's role would remain. Problems of control would seem to be at least as intractable as problems of shifting from a United States–controlled to a NATO-controlled nuclear deterrent. If and when the countries involved are united in a supranational community, these difficulties might be overcome. If the Europeans developed their own independent nuclear deterrent but did not closely coordinate its potential employment with NATO strategy, the alliance would be more likely to decay than if the American nuclear guarantee remained essentially under American control.

Contingent Course 6: Give NATO Complete Control of Some Tactical Nuclear Weapons. The discussion about course 5 concerned strategic weapons, but many of the arguments would seem to apply to tactical nuclear weapons as well, especially since the United States predominates in their development. (French tactical nuclear weapons are not expected to be available until at least 1973; the United States has deployed about 7,000 in Western Europe.) The fear of rapid and relatively uncontrollable escalation to a strategic exchange if tactical nuclear weapons ever were used has grown with the years except among certain Europeans. A few students of strategy have deplored the tendency to regard the firebreak between conventional and nuclear weapons as untraversable without holocaust, and NATO forces have depended heavily on the deterrent of tactical nuclear weapons to compensate for relative weakness in conventional forces. Nevertheless, the link between strategic and tactical nuclear weapons, regardless of the purpose of their use, is so close that course 6 might be ruled out by the nonproliferation treaty. The Russians, eyeing Germany, have made clear their view that a multilaterally owned nuclear deterrent is an additional one.

European members of NATO (especially the Germans) have been ambivalent about the use of tactical nuclear weapons, moving back and forth between a fear that they would not be used in time if completely under American domination (according to some interpretations of the McNamara strategy) to a fear that they *would* be used, with dreadful consequences to the homeland.[15] But they are

[15] A further complication is the West German reluctance to contemplate the use of tactical nuclear weapons in East Germany, because those who would suffer would also be German.

also afraid that too great a reluctance to make some use of these weapons will remove their power to deter a large Russian conventional assault. A separate European control would not free them from these fears. To some extent, disillusionment with the promise of tactical nuclear weapons has been induced by readier access to information about the possible effects of using them, information now provided in NATO. The consequences are likely to differ with the type of weapons, and there are many types, with purposes varying from battlefield use to destruction far behind the enemy front lines. A little knowledge may be a dangerous thing, but more complete knowledge, while helping to avoid catastrophe, can create a much greater sense of insecurity.

This sense of insecurity apparently had a constructive effect by 1970, as the European allies began to recognize that nuclear-armed and conventionally-armed forces are not interchangeable and that the latter have a role which the former cannot fill. The December, 1970, and December, 1971, joint agreements of ten European governments markedly to strengthen their defenses suggest not only a response to United States pressure but also a new understanding of the importance of conventional forces. They have observed the notable build-up of such forces on the other side. Perhaps more important, not only military but also political representatives of their governments have engaged in exercises to test NATO's ability to counter various imaginable crises. Facing such situations leads to considering at what point and with what effect tactical nuclear weapons should be employed. The capacity to recognize the nature of the threat also includes perceiving the dangers of undue dependence on such weapons.

Contingent Course 7: Develop a Separate Command and Control System for Tactical Nuclear Weapons Committed to NATO. As indicated earlier, the strategic nuclear deterrent is already under separate control, except for targeting coordination. From time to time there have been proposals for putting under a different allied command the forces committed to NATO that have been armed with nuclear weapons.[16] The main reasons adduced for separating

---

[16] Examples are to be found in F. W. Mulley, *The Politics of Western Defense* (New York, Frederick A. Praeger, 1962), pp. 112–17; and Alastair

nuclear-armed forces from conventional forces relate to control of the possibile stages of escalation and to the indissoluble link between tactical and strategic nuclear weapons.

One recognition of the extraordinary implications of battlefield nuclear weapons was the establishment of a special military Deputy for Nuclear Affairs to advise the Supreme Commander, an office which did not seem to have developed significantly and has now disappeared. The technical problems of dividing the forces according to whether or not they are equipped with nuclear weapons have seemed insuperable, thus dampening interest in the idea. Instead, during the McNamara era the United States itself put much stress on strengthening the conventionally armed forces to reduce the need for using tactical weapons.

Everyone concedes, however, that NATO's available conventional arms are insufficient by themselves to provide a reliable deterrent. At 1970 levels of conventional defense there is no clear way around the dilemma faced by allies unwilling to sacrifice more to reduce the risk of nuclear destruction. If never expected to be used first and if alternative conventional defenses do not exist, can tactical nuclear weapons deter? On the other hand, if they are relied upon for preemptive use in battle to compensate for conventional inferiority, what is to prevent the other side from anticipatory preemption?[17] Satisfying the European allies whose homelands might be attacked and simultaneously assuring that no ally could drag the alliance involuntarily into catastrophe depends upon confidence among the allies. Irrational as the mixture of nuclear and conventionally armed forces may be militarily, it does represent a remarkable degree of trust within NATO.

Development of the electronic "permissive action link" has mitigated the practical difficulty in controlling tactical nuclear weapons in Europe and has helped to ensure that the final decision re-

Buchan and Philip Windsor, *Arms and Stability in Europe* (New York, Frederick A. Praeger, 1963), p. 166.

[17] One conceivable answer is that, if used selectively on a small scale during an early phase in hostilities, they might deter, provided also that there is a large variety of nuclear weapons behind them in case the other side also employs nuclear force. This answer tends to overlook or deny the reality of a nuclear threshold.

mains with the president of the United States. Guidelines worked out by the Nuclear Planning Group in NATO for first-strike and second-strike contingencies provide some balance for this power. Thus the analysis returns to the basic question involved in course 1. Who do the individual allies trust more than the United States, if they are unable to defend themselves? This question also bears on the shape of European security in the 1970s if the United States is not to participate in it.

Contingent Course 8: Denuclearize Central Europe. This course is inconceivable except by agreement with the Soviet Union. Such agreement might not be difficult to secure, in view of the favorable Russian comment on repeated Polish pressure for the Rapacki Plan since it was set forth in 1957. Since nuclear weapons in Western Europe are under American control, they could conceivably be withdrawn by the United States, acting on its own. The adverse allied reaction might be so great, however, that a continuation of NATO in its present form would be out of the question; the move would completely undermine the confidence which underlies the alliance. In any case, the United States has the same reasons for opposing a denuclearized zone in Central Europe that it had when the allies turned down the idea in the 1950s. Under almost any kind of plan, the Soviet Union will remain at least in the wings because it is geographically a neighboring power; only the United States would truly be withdrawing, and the French and British nuclear forces would be no effective substitutes. So long as Americans feel this area to be important to the security of their world, and the allies consent to such forces, continuation of nuclear-armed forces somewhere in the region is likely. The United States would scarcely leave its forces in Europe unarmed with nuclear weapons.

An inspected reduction in such weapons within a narrow belt along the dividing line between East and West, long advocated by General Norstad, would not be ruled out by these considerations, so far as the United States and its NATO allies are concerned. It would offer greater protection from surprise attack, but how can the inspectors have accurate knowledge of the size of nuclear stockpiles and where they are located?

In the long discussions about a European security conference the agenda has always been hazy, but in any case a denuclearized zone is an unlikely item if and when such a conference occurs. Nothing seems to have come from the suggestion made in 1969 by the United Nations Association that the four occupying powers of Berlin establish a commission which would include among its tasks consideration of such a zone.[18] Perhaps this is partly due to the complexities of the question, among which are the status of the two Germanies and the relation of nuclear-armed to conventionally-armed forces stationed in the area.

Contingent Course 9: Empower NATO to Negotiate Directly with the Warsaw Treaty Organization. Some of the more independently inclined Communist states have been interested in having negotiations between the Eastern and Western alliance organizations on matters of European security; the Rumanians in particular have gone further, speaking of jointly ending the organizations. The Warsaw Treaty itself contains a provision for its abrogation if a system of European collective security is organized.[19] For several years, however, the Soviet Union's own suggestions on East-West talks did not refer to agreement with NATO but with its members, and usually only its European members. Since NATO's inception the Soviet Union has never ceased trying to destroy it. One reason for this attitude is that NATO legitimizes the presence of the United States in Europe. The Russians have derided the idea that through discussions in NATO some diminution in the Cold War confrontation could take place. Only in 1970 did they concede that the North American allies might properly participate in the discussion of European security.

When the Warsaw Treaty members, meeting in Budapest in March, 1969, reiterated their earlier suggestions that an all-European security conference be held, the North Atlantic Council picked up the idea very gingerly, shying away from an anticipated

[18] United Nations Association, *Toward the Reconciliation of Europe* (New York, 1969), p. 30.

[19] Prior to some new all-European security system, complete disintegration of the Warsaw Pact alliance would not necessarily serve European security any more than would the end of NATO.

260 / NATO and Nuclear Deterrence

propaganda circus. After some preliminary studies initiated early in the year, the December, 1969, meeting of the North Atlantic ministers issued a communiqué devoted almost entirely to questions related to such a conference. This response emphasized that measures which might be "explored with the Soviet Union and the other countries of Eastern Europe" should be concrete. It stressed verifiable, mutual, balanced reductions of forces and suggested particular steps that might be taken, such as advance notification of military movements, establishment of observation posts, and exchange of observers at military maneuvers. The ministers supported West German and other allies' approaches, bilateral and multilateral, in various fields of common interest that might reduce tension between East and West. As to the proposed European security conference (much desired by several of the allies), the official communiqué noted that an eventual meeting must be preceded by very careful preparation to discuss specific, well-defined subjects and that the North American members would be expected to participate.[20] That the American nuclear guarantee to Western Europe would hardly be included among negotiable items seems a reasonable assumption.

At the spring, 1970, ministerial meeting NATO members went somewhat further in endorsing exploratory talks which might eventuate in "multilateral contacts with all interested governments" looking towards a conference or series of conferences on European security. However, by the December meeting so little progress had been made in the Big Four discussions about Berlin that the allies declared that resolution of some aspects of this issue had priority over any European security conference. Within the next year the settlement of the Berlin problems had made such headway that at the December, 1971, meeting the North Atlantic Council spoke more positively about readiness to make multilateral preparation for a conference. The stress was still on individual NATO members talking separately to other European governments.

The European members of NATO have resented bilateral dealings between the United States and the Soviet Union without prior con-

[20] Communiqués from semiannual ministerial meetings of the North Atlantic Council are published in *NATO Letter*, now called *NATO Review*.

sultation with them; they are also unlikely to be willing to authorize NATO to speak in their joint behalf on particular arms control measures, even if the United States were so inclined. The days when the Americans could rely on their own views predominating in NATO are past, and insistence would disrupt, if not destroy, the alliance. France, which remains an important member of the North Atlantic Council, would surely object to using NATO as an agency; the French have constantly opposed bloc-to-bloc negotiations.

France did not join when the other members at the June, 1971, ministerial meeting agreed to appoint "a representative or representatives" to explore the possibilities of mutual and balanced force reductions with the Soviet Union and other interested governments. After they selected the recently retired Secretary General, Manlio Broslio, that autumn to make such soundings, he never received the anticipated invitation to Moscow. The December ministerial meeting to which he was to report came and went, and thus the first trial of a kind of NATO agent for arms control explorations had to be accounted a failure. In any case the Soviet Union has disapproved of direct negotiations between the two organizations.

No member of NATO is more immediately affected by negotiations on either the division of Europe or arms control than the Federal Republic of Germany. The allies' use of the North Atlantic Council not as an agency to negotiate with the Warsaw Treaty countries but for negotiating *within* the alliance has already proved useful in helping to loosen up the West German government's approach to Eastern Europe and the Soviet Union while continuing to satisfy the one ally with unfulfilled objectives, whose growing power might otherwise prove disturbing. The stronger West Germany grows economically, the less willing it is to submit to strategic or diplomatic moves not to its liking. Unfortunately for the West Germans, their economic power could not bring them a permanent seat on the governing board of the International Atomic Energy Agency, which has a prominent role in implementing the nonproliferation treaty, nor membership in the Nuclear Disarmament Committee even when it was enlarged from the original eighteen members. Thus NATO is especially important to the Federal Republic, not just for protection but also for gaining a hearing in Moscow. Willy Brandt has often acknowledged the indispensability of NATO in pursuing his *Ostpolitik*. The mutual need of the allies to have Germany in NATO and of Germany to be in it is constantly illustrated by the diplomatic support the North Atlantic Council has given to Germany.[21] Leonard Beaton's comment that NATO is in itself an effective arms control measure is nowhere better illustrated than by the way in which German armed strength is regulated in the interests of European security generally.

Ministerial sessions of the North Atlantic Council have stressed *harmonized* diplomatic moves (to prevent one ally from moving in a direction repugnant to others), but the members have not embraced the idea of a single diplomatic voice speaking for all. Former Secretary General Brosio himself underlined the inadvisability of such attempts. This does not prevent continuation of joint consultations on individual moves, each reinforcing the other. The long-established habit of bilateral as well as multilateral discussions between American officials and other allies, inside NATO's environs and in the national capitals, rather easily achieves effects which a joint agency for negotiating with the Communists might secure.

So long as the trend in NATO is away from greater integration on the military level, using NATO as a common diplomatic agent seems highly impractical. Nevertheless, the communiqués issuing from high-level meetings of the two alliances have revealed over the years a pattern of assertion and response which may be nothing more than a series of propaganda moves, but is certainly something different from individual government-to-government communication. In any case, NATO and the Warsaw Treaty Organization are quite unlike each other, especially because the governments of the lesser allies in each have diametrically opposed views on the

[21] Thus the December, 1969, communiqué commended the West German government for its proposals regarding a "modus vivendi between the two parts of Germany" and its other initiatives toward the Soviet Union and the Eastern European countries while it warned that a European security conference which served "to ratify the present division of Europe" (i.e., of Germany) would be unacceptable.

desirability of their respective superpower member remaining physically among them. Only the two halves of Germany are alike in this respect, since the government of the German Democratic Republic wants Russian forces to remain.

Contingent Course 10: Expand Functions of NATO into Non-military Fields. The declining sense of a military threat to the alliance, with the concomitant surfacing of divisive tendencies among the members, has impelled supporters of NATO to look for other values of the alliance. In fact, the North Atlantic Treaty's Article II, which contains among other provisions one for economic collaboration, was interpreted from the start to sanction and promote nonmilitary efforts. In 1956 NATO authorized a formal inquiry into the potentialities for promoting economic cooperation; the "Three Wise Men" concluded that NATO was unsuitable as a major agency for economic cooperation. Throughout the life of NATO, but especially in recent years, numerous though modest types of cooperation among some of the members have taken place, under the aegis of NATO, in areas only peripherally related to the military function. These include certain undertakings in the fields of science, technology, and communications. Worthy in themselves, both for substance and procedure, these programs have not contributed conspicuously to the strength of NATO, which remains a military organization with very important political overtones, intra-alliance as well as interalliance.

In any case, during the life of NATO a great many other organizations have been created for cooperation in nonmilitary fields, some of them on a Western European basis but at least one on an all-European basis, some within the United Nations or under United Nations auspices, some composed of countries within the industrialized world or the "North," and some global. There is scarcely any need for a specifically NATO agency. Nevertheless, its facilities and techniques can help to stimulate cooperation or at least mutual exchanges in new areas, such as the one suggested by President Nixon—the improvement of the environment in industrialized societies. Because this problem is widespread and not confined to NATO members, the North Atlantic Council has suggested that cooperation in the environmental field is especially suitable for eroding divisions between the East and the West. Joint pilot studies by different NATO countries are being conducted under the alliance's new Committee on the Challenge of Modern Society. In November, 1970, NATO sponsored an international conference on oil pollution of the sea which attracted publicity on this problem. With NATO's voice added to others, new environmental agencies have been established in several member governments. Whatever such extraneous activities, they would only indirectly affect European security, even as the other organizations, such as the EEC, have some indirect relation to peaceful ties among European countries.[22] For major powers, at least, military dangers are difficult to meet through economic, scientific, or other nonmilitary means, and the rivalry of the superpowers is inherently measured in military terms. This is one aspect of the world that is unlikely to change in the next five years.

Contingent Course 11: Encourage Regrouping of NATO. Alastair Buchan was one of those suggesting that the lack of vitality in NATO in the late 1960s might be related to lack of strong interest of some members in the security problems of others and that a possible solution would be to reapportion responsibilities to reflect regional (and in some cases continental and global) differences in concern.[23] Technological changes have rendered less vital the use of bases made available to American forces through the membership of Iceland and Portugal in NATO. The colonial conflicts of the latter country have been an increasing political embarassment to the United States (and to its other NATO allies). Greece and Turkey, who became members only because of United States pressure on the other original allies, have always been difficult for the alliance to assimilate because of their undemocratic aspects, need

---

[22] Consider Robert Osgood's suggestion that Europeans may have given up competition among themselves waged by military means and may compete instead in nonmilitary ways [*Alliances and American Foreign Policy* (Baltimore, Johns Hopkins Press, 1968), p. 72].

[23] "The Future of NATO," *International Conciliation*, November, 1967, p. 49; and Atlantic Institute, *Crisis Management*, The Atlantic Papers (Boulogne-sur-Seine, 1966), p. 32.

for military aid, internal political turmoil, and conflict with each other. They have somewhat less concern with the central security problem of Europe—Germany's division and lack of a peace settlement—than the modern, industrialized states of Western Europe. The other "outlyer" (Buchan's phrase) is Canada, whose contribution to the NATO forces since the time when Canadian mutual aid was no longer needed has probably less military than political significance for the security of Europe. (Canada makes NATO a transatlantic rather than merely an American-European alliance; it is a model for others in the high quality of its contribution; and its reduction or withdrawal of forces might signal further disintegration of the alliance.)

With the disappearance of the need for the United States as banker, groupings which do not depend upon American participation are conceivable. The obvious connection between defense and economics has led some to expect that the European Economic Community will eventually take on security functions. Whether or not this is logically necessary, it is unlikely to occur in the next few years. The Americans have gradually learned not to intrude into such European decisions as this. Yet they tend to see European developments in terms of the military security provided by NATO, as evidenced by the unhappiness of some United States officials when their allies sought to expel Greece from the Council of Europe.

Bilateral arrangements between the United States and any of the other NATO states may continue to promote stability in Europe, but some ask whether the whole alliance needs to get involved, if the conceivable threats to Europe are likely to be local and obscure, concerning some countries more directly than others.[24] It is hard to see how the United States could whittle back the nuclear guaranteee implicit in NATO by excluding some of the less important members. The pledge of the alliance that an attack on one is an attack on all is probably more meaningful for the United States than for any other member. If the peripheral members are not to

[24] A similar question was raised by Nils Ørvik, "NATO, NAFTA and the Smaller Allies," *ORBIS*, Summer, 1968. He was concerned, among other things, about the consolidation of the EEC to the exclusion of the interests of others in NATO.

fall by the wayside as NATO consolidates its strength, what considerations should the United States have in mind in working to maintain the integrity of the alliance?

The expectation of danger from the Soviet Union has shifted away from some grand assault on the central front, now reasonably well protected, to a fear of ambiguous military moves, particularly in soft but ill-defined border areas. Today a much greater sense exists in NATO that "defense is indivisible" than was true in earlier days. Trouble anywhere within the treaty area or near its borders, in Czechoslovakia, for example, sends shudders throughout the alliance, in the same way that the ruthless coup in Greece concerned all the other members. Sensitivity to such events is uneven within the alliance but is greatly enhanced by the elaborate methods of consultation currently used in the North Atlantic Council as well as by the physical proximity of political advisers from the various members at NATO headquarters.

Events in the Far East are a different matter, as the United States has taken a long time to learn. American efforts to expand the region of defense concern beyond that specified in the original treaty have always met almost universal opposition among the members of NATO. In a global context, NATO's protection against Russian expansion is definitely limited to a single region, but this one is so central to American interests that without its security there could be no real security elsewhere.

NATO has recognized the military need to meet local probes in Europe far from the central front by establishing the ACE Mobile Force. It also deployed special naval and air forces in the Mediterranean after the Soviet buildup in that ocean. Since NATO was first organized, there have been separate regional commands composed of forces of countries in the region plus the United States and one or more large powers. Only eight countries have forces on the central front. General Norstad often remarked that the meaning of NATO to the smaller exposed ally was that the whole alliance of fifteen states was behind it in its resistance when the Soviet Union tried to bully it, as the Russians have from time to time attempted. The other fourteen did not have to be on the spot for this support to be felt. The response represented by mobile forces is still inadequately supported for maximum effectiveness, and because of practical difficulties it will always be small. Yet, even without great allied military strength at the perimeters, the political cost to the Soviet Union of trying to nibble away at them would be great.

The argument of "all for one and one for all" does not mean that fewer governments than the total membership might not profitably consult and act (by agreement with all) in particular crises. The United States should welcome and support initiatives by allies who wish to collaborate with each other in defense of a particular region (such as Norway and Canada), so long as this takes place in some NATO framework. No sign has yet appeared that the smaller allies would be willing to relinquish their ultimate right to withhold their cooperation by accepting a big-power directorate for NATO, even as they acquiesce to or actively support such limited-member consultation on questions like Berlin. So long as the alliance lasts there are likely to be prior discussions among the allies most directly concerned; the closer these discussions are tied to the alliance framework, the more formidable they look to an adversary. If one by one the members decided that threats immediately affecting them were not sufficiently appreciated by the others to warrant continued membership, the United States might end up with only one ally in NATO: Germany.[25] This would hardly please anyone in either the West or the East.

The protection offered by the United States through NATO is too good a bargain to forego. Besides the security offered from possible Soviet intimidation, NATO provides a framework within which countries that used to arm against each other now pool much of their military resources to shield themselves from an external threat, thus making their own conflicts with each other far less dangerous. This is too valuable an asset for the United States to ignore through bypassing NATO mechanisms for keeping the peace in Europe.

Contingent Course 12: Make Agreements with the Soviet Union on Nuclear Arms Control. How would the various ways in which the

---

[25] Portugal comes closest to declaring that the allies are indifferent or hostile to its claims but apparently does not want to test its nonessentiality by seriously threatening to withdraw.

United States and the Soviet Union might come to agreement on arms control measures look to the NATO allies? All of them have been anxious for successful arms control agreements, with the possible exception of France under de Gaulle. (France did not participate in the eighteen-nation disarmament committee and withdrew from NATO but continued to participate in many alliance activities, including the deliberations of the North Atlantic Council.) Some allies are more eager than others, and some types of agreement are of more concern than others. By now, if not earlier (and partly because of discussions in the North Atlantic Council), the members recognize the need for balance between the two nuclear superpowers if their own security is to be protected. Ruled out are demands upon one to control its arms that are not also made on the other. The allies also see the relation to their own security of agreements which require inspection or some other reliable way to detect evasions.

Intensive studies of possible force reductions to be balanced between the two sides began in NATO during 1968. Such studies reflect, among other things, the concern of the European allies not to be passive onlookers while some kind of spheres-of-influence arrangement between the superpowers leaves Europe divided. For some of them, the proposed European security conference represents a way to express their interests that would balance SALT. Because of consultations within NATO, the United States could enter SALT strengthened by the mutual confidence the alliance discussions have generated.

Narrowly conceived, an ABM system might not concern the European allies (or even Canada) directly. But insofar as such a system could protect the strategic deterrent upon which their security ultimately depends, they are entitled to be consulted (but apparently were not consulted prior to Secretary McNamara's announcement of September, 1967, that the United States would build a "light" ABM system). The impact of such a development on the arms race is another reason for soliciting the allies' views. Furthermore, stress on this form of missile defense could give the appearance that *European* security as opposed to Atlantic security has lost its significance to the Americans. Proponents of the ABM had argued that Europeans would prefer it as a "defensive" system to a new program of "offensive" weapons. Whatever their unsolicited preferences, the strongly outspoken criticism has come from Americans and some Canadians rather than Europeans.

Some reduction in nuclear arsenals is likely to appeal to nonnuclear powers in Europe, as elsewhere, but especially to those who feel sensitive about their own nonnuclear status. For example, on more than one occasion in the past the French have claimed that a radical reduction in nuclear arms possessed by the superpowers would have prevented their own decision to go ahead with nuclear development. What particular weapons and how many were involved in an agreement would interest European allies. They are likely to be concerned about reductions in the tactical nuclear weapons forming part of the NATO defenses in Europe, which have long been relied on to compensate for larger Soviet conventional forces as well as to balance the Russians' tactical nuclear weapons. Inclusion of others, like the Russian MRBMs targeted on Western Europe, would be greatly desired by the NATO allies. Were a bargain to be struck leaving the level of armaments still relatively balanced but at a much lower level, the *raison d'être* of NATO would nevertheless remain.[26]

Because of their dependence on the tactical nuclear weapon deterrent, the allies are hardly likely to favor a no-first-use agreement, which in any case would have a dangerous tendency to lull the innocent. American opposition to early use of tactical nuclear weapons was one reason why France went its own nuclear way, since such an inhibition on strategy did not appeal to de Gaulle. The Germans, on the front line, would probably be particularly unenthusiastic. If such an agreement were to be consummated while the allies still held together in NATO, a necessary concomitant would have to be a major strengthening of conventional forces; the pledges made by the Eurogroup in 1970 and 1971 go only part of the way.

A comprehensive test ban might have less appeal than the lim-

[26] See Timothy W. Stanley and Darnell M. Whitt, *Detente Diplomacy: United States and European Security in the 1970's* (New York, Dunellen, 1970), pp. 63–66.

ited ban now in effect, since there is little danger of atmospheric pollution from further tests and since these might develop the kinds of tactical nuclear weapons which have interested several of the NATO allies for defense against what they misconstrue as the "hordes" available to the Communists. Peaceful uses of atomic energy that could be developed and tested under today's conditions might interest some allies. However, those who give high priority to arms control might welcome expansion of the test ban; from time to time this has included the British.

European attitudes on a denuclearized zone in Central Europe have already been discussed. In the technological stage already reached, however, most missiles do not have to be near their targets to be dangerous and would not have to be located anywhere near the sensitive area. Except for the argument that the chances for escalation would be reduced, the demand for a denuclearized Central Europe tends to boil down to a fear of nuclear weapons in German hands, a fear which is unlikely to disappear soon.

The close association of NATO with certain arms control arrangements can be seen in the belated West German signature of the nonproliferation treaty. A formal pledge of nonacquisition of nuclear weapons could be very dangerous to Germany by reducing its political weight if it afterwards lost the protection of the NATO deterrent. Therefore, the Bonn government stated that its signature was based on the understanding that the nuclear capacity of NATO would not be impaired, and the United States and Britain reaffirmed Germany's right to protection through NATO.[27]

What about agreements on removing conventional forces from this region, perhaps as one part of a mutual and balanced force reduction? Some Americans, including those senators who are eager to bring back troops from Europe, would move unilaterally regardless of what the Russians might do. Others, observing the qualitative asymmetry of the two sides' armed strength in Europe, cannot imagine a true balance being struck. One proposal that would ensure continued American engagement in Europe involves percentage reductions in stages, so that mutuality, stability, and confidence could be served while positive arms control steps were

[27] *New York Times*, November 29, 1969.

taken. Only since the summer of 1970 has the Soviet Union shown the slightest interest in mutual, balanced force reductions, which is hardly surprising since Senator Mansfield's resolution implied that no price need be paid for getting the Americans out of Europe. The Russians have been as diffident about the MBFR form of arms control as the Americans about the European security conference. However, after three or four years of obvious wariness each of the superpowers had by 1972 come closer to a serious consideration of the other's concern, and so had the two alliances.

Contingent Course 13: Withdraw into Fortress America. One alternative that has not yet been dealt with here occasionally arises in discussions so that it can be knocked down: total withdrawal from Europe. It was one of the "extreme" options among the kinds of commitment—or absence thereof—examined in the 1969 study of commitments and forces directed by Deputy Secretary of Defense Packard at the behest of the National Security Council. This course seems irrelevant, not for military reasons but for psychological ones. Europe has now been accepted as part of the security zone of Americans and cannot readily be cut off from considerations of American security. Even for those unmoved by such sentiments, the huge and extremely complicated defense arrangements which have grown up under NATO auspices look less costly to maintain than to remove; removal would be an expensive and almost too intricate task to contemplate. Consider the infrastructure which has been created for NATO: recently the United States has used more of these facilities than it is paying for.[28] Think also of the human connections which would have to be severed.

France's withdrawal from NATO is a poor example of the ease of such surgery, since a great deal of French collaboration continued despite General de Gaulle, and it increased further after his departure from office. The French experience does, however, show the great costs to all concerned, militarily, economically, and psychologically, when a major member tries to cut itself off from the others. There is no question that both European and Atlantic security have been weakened. The French action does indicate how

[28] Stanley and Whitt, *Detente Diplomacy*, p. 59.

some bases might be deactivated without disastrous loss, but even the French believed that the joint air-defense arrangements were likely to remain valuable into the foreseeable future.

For the United States to accept the fortress alternative would mean abandonment of its role of world leader, since one of the important attributes associated with such status is the capacity to gain the cooperation of strong and numerous allies.[29] Some Americans do not object to making the threat of withdrawal in order to get more burden-sharing by the Europeans, and some Europeans say they fear such withdrawal, as they try to justify their failure to do more for their own security. This has been true all through the life of NATO. And all that time the United States could probably have protected its own territory without European cooperation, but it did not choose to do so. Successful experience under NATO in preventing Soviet expansion has made the fortress alternative even less attractive than it was before NATO was created. To deter Soviet threats by unilateral military measures has become harder, while diplomatic maneuvers have increased in importance when compared to the military deterrent.

All arguments save that about world leadership apply also to a course which might be related to constructing the fortress—a massive buildup of all offensive weapons to achieve a first-strike capability. Such a course would not only seem hostile both to foe and friend, but would be strongly opposed by the American taxpayer and most members of Congress.

SUMMARY AND CONCLUSIONS

The contingent courses examined above that appear to meet best the tests of desirability, probability, and compatibility accord most closely with the European security model called Two-Spheres Europe (which, along with other model arrangements, is described in *American Arms and a Changing Europe*). Both superpowers are

[29] Stanley Hoffmann, *Gulliver's Troubles*, p. 73, indicates why the United States cannot choose isolationism, in view of the competitive aspects of world politics.

envisioned as still involved in Europe, with the United States an effective leader in Western Europe, especially through its nuclear guarantee and its physical presence. The allies are still not taking a free ride, since they make important nonnuclear contributions to their collective security. Nor are their separate defense policies under the control of the United States, but only coordinated to the extent that consultation can foster. In the global balance of power, NATO is playing its part in Western Europe and is, as Alastair Buchan has said, "neither transitory nor transcendental." [30]

The least objectionable of the several alternatives involving control of the NATO nuclear deterrent would seem to be, if European security is the objective, a continuation of the present policy, i.e., ultimate decision left in the hands of the United States. Russian opposition to proliferation would suggest that such a course would also be preferred by the Soviet Union. Now that France is out of the North Atlantic alliance's organization, probably the only member that might feel some symbolic discrimination is Germany. With expanded information and consultation, now well under way, and with suitable recognition of Germany's power in economic fields as well as in providing the largest conventional forces in the integrated command, this problem may be overcome. Such recognition of Germany would thus be part of the development of a "multi-hierarchical system," noted by Stanley Hoffmann and others.

Regarding integration, there is no sign yet that pre-positioned forces, trained together in peacetime to operate according to plans multilaterally worked out through NATO, will not continue to serve Western European security for some time to come, particularly in the central region. There is likely, nevertheless, to be constant political controversy over how much, who pays, where the forces shall be deployed, and what military task they should perform. To make continuation of these policies (unilateral control of the nuclear deterrent and continued integration) palatable, there will be greater need than ever before for using NATO as a political forum and instrument, as the tasks of ensuring European security grow more complicated. The weight of the North Atlantic

[30] "The Purpose of NATO and Its Future Development," *NATO's Fifteen Nations*, February-March, 1969, p. 50.

Council will continue to depend on the will to use it and on some significant military underpinning. As Robert Osgood has pointed out, the intra-alliance function of NATO is very important and not always recognized.[31]

It would seem a serious error for the United States to pare back its treaty function to the nuclear guarantee, even though this guarantee is likely to serve as a fundamental factor in maintaining European stability and thus security. The guarantee needs to be associated with the elaborate NATO activities in the conventional field to be credible and to keep the allies working together to ensure their own security. In view of the lack of prospects for a useful function, the practical obstacles, and the difficulties of mobilizing American support, conditions for development of a separate European strategic deterrent seem unfavorable, at least in the next few years. The same holds for tactical nuclear weapons developed by the Europeans.

As for separating the nuclear from the conventional forces in the military organization of NATO, this is an idea no longer likely to be pressed on the United States. Trust continues to be the basic question here, and American actions elsewhere as well as in Europe are watched by Europeans to judge whether the Americans have the proper qualifications of judiciousness, intelligence, and courage to bear their nuclear responsibilities for NATO. The United States is likely to have to earn this trust continuously and tangibly, however much its leaders may deplore the constant European importuning and the need for perpetual reassurances of commitment.

Among the courses which do not seem profitable to pursue are isolated efforts at a denuclearized Central Europe, in view of more promising alternatives; use of NATO as a negotiating instrument with the Warsaw Treaty Organization, especially as decentralization in the Atlantic alliance proceeds; and reliance on expansion of NATO functions into nonmilitary fields to solidify the alliance, since NATO is essentially a security organization. Some kinds of regrouping of members for particular areas of defense seem not only possible within the NATO framework but also likely to take

[31] Osgood, *Alliances*, p. 57.

place as the alliance becomes more decentralized; the United States should probably not try to inhibit but rather should encourage these tendencies so long as they do not seriously erode the common defense of Western Europe.

Regarding arms control agreements with the Soviet Union, most of the European members are eager for some of them, and all the allies desire to economize on defense. The smaller members are especially anxious for such agreements, since they look more to arms control than to military measures for security. To enjoy the confidence of its allies, the United States should continue to follow President Nixon's promise to the North Atlantic Council of February 24, 1969, to consult with NATO members before, during, and after negotiations with the Soviet Union. Contrary to the opinion of some critics of NATO, arms control and the alliance are not incompatible but in fact can support each other as long as a balance between the Eastern alliance and the Western alliance is maintained.

Especially in view of the professed desires of the NATO allies, there is currently no clear sign on the horizon that the United States will not be wanted in Europe for at least the next few years. Nor is there any strong movement in the United States to reject the commitment, although some senators press for reduced troop deployments in Europe (not reduced commitments). Western European security has grown to be part of America's own security, not in word only but in twenty years of joint activity.

The kind of Europe that might be projected from the courses outlined above probably comes closest to one envisioned by Robert Osgood: the two superpowers will still, by their preponderant military power, maintain the nuclear balance. America's allies, becoming more independent of earlier domination by the United States, will present the need for the United States to try to orchestrate its particular relationships with each and accommodate "their divergent political positions in a reasonably harmonious coalition." This will mean, he believed, a less intensive involvement and less exclusive responsibility for the United States.[32] Yet even Osgood regarded this situation as a historical anomaly, while others specu-

[32] Ibid., pp. 158–60.

lating on the future are more impatient for a united Europe responsible for its own security. For the near future, however, most of them continue to accept a view expressed in 1967, that NATO is

an essential element of political and military stability and a basis for formal or tacit arms control . . . ; the most important instrument the West Europeans possess to influence American policy and strategy; . . . the international framework within which both the policy and the defence of the Federal Republic can be adapted without having to turn to a purely national policy.[33]

Rather than interfering with the development of a European security system, NATO would seem to facilitate its ultimate creation. When the Europeans are ready to accept the risks of a different system, the United States should try to ensure that the pieces of the framework of European security provided by NATO are not removed until the substitutes show that the edifice can still carry the weight, and the last piece to go is likely to be the American nuclear guarantee. Can it not be said that without NATO there would be no American nuclear guarantee, and without that guarantee there would be no NATO?

[33] Curt Gasteyger, *Europe in the Seventies*, Adelphi Paper no. 37 (London, Institute for Strategic Studies, 1967), p. 15.